Biblical counselors, self-styled, see their trade as one-on-one churchly service to the troubled, the perplexed, and the hurting. Lambert writes to equip counselors with the biblical truths and wisdom that they need to do their job. He does this most effectively, and his book makes an excellent training manual.

J. I. Packer, Regent College

Having dealt with the sufficiency of the Scriptures in some depth, Dr. Lambert courses through the corpus of Systematic Theology, briefly sketching the meaning of each topic together with instances of how it worked out in changing the lives of various sorts of counselees. For those unfamiliar with the idea of using biblical truth, systematically understood, in counseling, this book will become a useful eye-opener; for those already familiar with the approach, it will prove a welcome refresher. Pastor, counselor, you will want to have a copy.

Jay E. Adams, author of *Competent to Counsel* and a member of the Academy of ACBC

Heath Lambert has updated Adams's work in *A Theology of Biblical Counseling*, showing that biblical doctrine is sufficient to address the problems of human life and therefore is the foundation for godly and effective counseling. He has done this job well, and I hope many readers will take advantage of this excellent book.

John M. Frame, Professor of Systematic Theology and Philosophy, Reformed Theological Seminary

Lambert's depth of research, critical engagement, and accessible style have provided the church with a helpful tool the likes of which we have not seen since Adams's *A Theology of Christian Counseling*. This book should prove to be a helpful tool in navigating the oft misunderstood disciplines of Systematic Theology and Biblical Counseling. I heartily recommend it to anyone desiring to know the why behind the how of biblical counseling.

Elyse Fitzpatrick, author of *Counsel from the Cross*

I wholeheartedly recommend this volume by my friend Heath Lambert. He provides a great basic theology for the field of Biblical Counseling that is sorely needed. . . . His well-thought-out arguments and addressing of controversial issues give much for the seasoned biblical counselor or academic (or even critic of Biblical Counseling) to consider. In short, I believe any Christian committed to or interested in counseling will benefit from reading this book.

John Babler, Professor of Counseling,
Southwestern Baptist Theological Seminary

A Theology of Biblical Counseling is an outstanding contribution to the entire evangelical community. Heath demonstrates with real-life examples that theology is important not only for counseling but for living an authentic Christian life. Anyone, counselor or not, who wants to help a fellow believer along the way will profit greatly from this book.

Jerry Bridges, author of *Trusting God Even When Life Hurts*

Heath Lambert demonstrates the vital connection between the message of the Bible, its relevance to life in a broken world, and its significance in the practice of counseling. Building on the foundation of Jay Adams, he summarizes key theological doctrines and imbeds them deeply into the counseling practice using compelling case studies throughout each chapter . . . every counselor's counselees and practice will benefit from reading this book.

Kevin Carson, Professor of Biblical Counseling,
Baptist Bible College and Theological Seminary

Counseling cannot be considered biblical without a proper orientation to God and his Word. Heath Lambert brings clarity and help to the counselor as he tackles often misunderstood issues like sufficiency, common grace, and general revelation. I would recommend this book to any student of the Bible but particularly those who call themselves biblical counselors.

Garrett Higbee, Executive Director of the
Biblical Counseling Coalition

After reading this volume I am convinced that Christian counselors and teachers of counseling will find it one of the best and most helpful counseling manuals presently available. I will certainly use this book as a required-reading assignment for my students.

Dr. Wayne Mack, Professor of Biblical Counseling, Director of Strengthening Ministries Training Institute, ACBC Africa; Pastor/elder, Lynnwood Baptist Church

If you are a counselor your counsel has no authority if it is not built upon a solid biblical theology. In *A Theology of Biblical Counseling*, Dr. Heath Lambert has made a significant contribution to biblical counseling by demonstrating how good theology must inform both the theory and the practice of Christian counseling. Every sincere Christian counselor should read and digest this book!

Dr. John D. Street, Chair, MABC Graduate Program, The Master's College and Seminary; President, Association of Certified Biblical Counselors (ACBC)

There is no other book like this. . . . Dr. Lambert does a wonderful job of using case studies to connect biblical counseling to each area of theology in very practical way. . . . This book makes me excited about the future of biblical counseling (and I don't excite easily).

Jim Newheiser, Executive Director of the Institute for Biblical Counseling and Discipleship

A Theology of Biblical Counseling is a delight to read. Heath Lambert shows us with great wisdom and skill that evangelical theology and practical ministry go together beautifully! If you are looking for a readable, bite-sized volume that relates powerful biblical truth to the everyday challenges of Christian living, this book is for you.

Lance Quinn, Senior Pastor, Thousand Oaks Bible Church

Due to its maturity and depth, *A Theology of Biblical Counseling* is sure to become a text used by friends and foes alike. Get it. Read it. Ponder it. Discuss it. Give it away. May it be used to advance the cause of Biblical Counseling and the Kingdom of the risen, reigning King of Kings.

George C. Scipione, Director of the Biblical
Counseling Institute of the Reformed
Presbyterian Theological Seminary

A Theology of Biblical Counseling is an invaluable book for biblical soul care within the church. Theologian John Frame has written that true theology is application. Lambert's book is certainly an example of this truth in how it applies theology to real-life discipleship counseling scenarios. In his work, he clearly shows us just how the Scriptures can be sufficient for counseling issues of the heart and life.

Dr. Stuart W. Scott, Professor of Biblical
Counseling, The Master's College

One of the most important books written on biblical counseling in this generation. Heath Lambert does an excellent job of addressing crucial biblical truths in a practical and understandable way. This book will be helpful for everyone from the beginning counselor to the seasoned practitioner or professor. . . . I wholeheartedly commend it to you.

Dr. Stephen Viars, Senior Pastor, Faith Church

A THEOLOGY

OF BIBLICAL

COUNSELING

Also by Heath Lambert

Finally Free: Fighting for Purity with the Power of Grace

A THEOLOGY

OF BIBLICAL

COUNSELING

The Doctrinal Foundations
of Counseling Ministry

Heath Lambert

ZONDERVAN ACADEMIC

A Theology of Biblical Counseling
Copyright © 2016 by Heath Lambert

ISBN 978-0-310-51817-4 (ebook)

Requests for information should be addressed to:
Zondervan, 3900 Sparks Dr. SE, Grand Rapids, Michigan 49546

Library of Congress Cataloging-in-Publication Data

Names: Lambert, Heath, 1979-
Title: A theology of biblical counseling : the doctrinal foundations of counseling ministry /
    Heath Lambert.
Description: Grand Rapids : Zondervan, 2016.
Identifiers: LCCN 2015039601 | ISBN 9780310518167 (hardcover, printed)
Subjects: LCSH: Counseling—Religious aspects—Christianity. | Theology.
Classification: LCC BR115.C69 L36 2016 | DDC 253.5—dc23 LC record available at http://lccn
    .loc.gov/2015039601

Art direction: Chris Tobias, Outerwear for Books
Interior design: Kait Lamphere

Printed in the United States of America

20 21 22 23 24 25 26 27 28 29 /LSC/ 20 19 18 17 16 15 14 13 12 11 10 9 8 7

To Lauren—

The best wife ever

CONTENTS

ACKNOWLEDGMENTS

The fact that my name appears on the front of this book could lead to the appearance that I did not have any help in writing it. That is not true. In fact, I have had so much help in writing that I scarcely know where to begin to say "thank you," but I shall start with the big picture of my theological influences.

The people most instrumental in my thinking about theology are Bruce Ware, Wayne Grudem, Jay Adams, John Frame, R. C. Sproul, and Bill Barclay. I am privileged to know Drs. Ware, Adams, and Barclay but have only met Drs. Grudem, Frame, and Sproul. I have been influenced by the teaching of each one in their writing and speaking. I have read the works of many theologians, but these have been the most influential in my thinking. I owe a debt to each of these men who have so influenced me. The deficiencies in this book flow from my failures to measure up to their high standards.

Apart from these theological influences, I am also incredibly thankful for the efforts of people who helped more directly with the writing of this book. I am grateful to Al Mohler, Randy Stinson, and the board of The Southern Baptist Theological Seminary. They graciously gave me a sabbatical so I could work on this book.

I am also grateful to the board of the Association of Certified Biblical Counselors (ACBC). I am accountable to these incredible men as the executive director of that organization, and I am glad they encouraged me to work on books like this one. I am grateful to the staff of ACBC, a wonderful group of Christian servants who have greatly encouraged my work on this project. In particular, my assistant, Rebecca Maketansky, has diligently labored to make room in my schedule to complete this project. I also must thank my Introduction to Biblical Counseling class in the fall semester of 2015. Their support on this book was meaningful and immeasurable.

I am also thankful to Zondervan. I am so appreciative of the entire team there who make it a privilege to be in ministry partnership together. In particular, I am grateful for my editor, Ryan Pazdur. Ryan and I have been working together for years now, and he has become a friend. He is a godly man who loves Jesus, has a keen editorial eye, and approaches his projects in a pastoral way that I have never seen from anyone else.

Many people worked to review this manuscript and provide helpful comments. I am so grateful to Wayne Johnston, Lance Quinn, and Stuart Scott, whose comments greatly improved this project. I am also thankful for Renee Jarrett, the office administrator at ACBC, who has a great eye for grammar and bailed me out of trouble before anyone else saw problems. In particular, I am so thankful for the work of Coty Hoskins. He spent hours working on the notes for each chapter and making other helpful comments. I don't think I could have finished this book without his help.

When I come to the end of a book, I am always amazed at how much it is a product not just of my labor but of my wife, Lauren's, as well. I simply could not write without my wife's kindness to me in her encouragement, care for me, and care of our children. She is my very favorite person in the world, and I am so glad she is my wife. There is no person who has ever been more helpful to me, except for Jesus himself.

Which leads me to the most important person there is to thank. As I have been working on this book, the reality that impressed itself upon me most significantly is the amazing grace of Jesus Christ, who has saved me from sin and revealed such precious truth to his church in the pages of his Word. I am so thankful for a Savior who does not just promise a seat in heaven, but who gives power to live life on earth. Oh, how I desire the readers of this book to know that there is nothing good in me, or in the pages that follow, that did not first come from him.

CHAPTER 1

COUNSELING AND THEOLOGY: A CRUCIAL INTRODUCTION

✝

C ounseling is a theological discipline.
    There.

If you have continued to read beyond that first sentence, you have already completed the most controversial part of this book. That very first sentence should be the most debated statement in this entire work. *A Theology of Biblical Counseling* will do what theology often does—inspire questions and debate. But the most controversial statement I know to make in this context is to assert that counseling is, by definition, theological.

Most people do not assume the theological nature of counseling. Most believe that theology is what future ministers of the gospel study in seminary in order to be qualified to lead a church and preach sermons or go on the mission field. They do not understand that theology has a serious role to play in helping people with their counseling problems. They believe instead that counseling happens in the realm of psychology. Most believe that theology is to ministers what psychology is to counselors, and the two do not really have much to do with each other.[1]

---

1. David G. Myers, "A Levels-of-Explanation View," in Eric L. Johnson, ed., *Psychology & Christianity: Five Views* (Downers Grove, IL: InterVarsity, 2010), 49–78.

Christians have never believed, however, that theology serves so limited a role. They have insisted that theology informs all of life. Surveying the evidence for such a biblical position will demand more of this book than it should be expected to bear. Before we can proceed, however, it is essential to demonstrate, at the very least, that theology informs counseling. We will understand this when we see what theology is, what counseling is, and what counseling requires.

The Nature of Theology

We will not be ready to understand the theological import of counseling until we first understand what theology is. The definition of systematic theology provided by Wayne Grudem and John Frame is the definition I will use for theology in this book. These men say that theology is "what the whole Bible teaches us today about any given topic."[2] Three obvious elements of this definition stand out.

First, systematic theology is about the teachings of the entire Bible. It is not uncommon to hear some people express disapproval of theology in favor of biblical interpretation. They are concerned that our theological systems will exert a controlling and distorting effect on texts of Scripture. This concern is a possibility, but when it happens, it is bad theology, not good theology. Good theology is concerned with doing careful interpretation of all of the relevant texts in Scripture about a topic and then doing the hard work of discerning how to place those texts together. Good theology is not at odds with careful biblical interpretation, but stands on faithful interpretation of individual texts that seeks to understand these texts together in the context of the entire Bible.

A second element of this definition of theology is that it concerns what the whole Bible teaches us *today*. Good theology must be contemporary theology. Contemporary theology does not mean that we develop

---

2. Wayne A. Grudem, *Systematic Theology: An Introduction to Biblical Doctrine* (Grand Rapids, MI: Zondervan, 1994), 21. In his systematic theology, Grudem provides this definition in the form of a question. He says that systematic theology asks, "What does the whole Bible teach us today?" He also makes clear that he learned this definition from John Frame, who has profoundly influenced him in his theology.

new truth in each age. Instead, it means that we seek to understand how the old truths in God's Word apply to our contemporary setting. Many textbooks on Christian theology have been written during the history of the church. You might wonder why Christian authors continue to produce new works of theology when there are so many from the past. One reason is that the church continually confronts new threats to the truth of God's Word. When this happens, Christians must take the ancient text of Scripture and apply it in ways that are freshly relevant. Good theology is not just a recitation of what the church has believed, though that is important. It also includes what the church must believe today in the midst of contemporary threats.

Finally, the definition of theology emphasizes that theology is concerned with establishing what the Bible teaches today about any given topic. The work of theology is to understand what God thinks about any topic. When we pay careful attention to every relevant passage in the Bible on a topic, we should know what God has revealed to us about that topic. In this book we are concerned with establishing what God has revealed about counseling. But first, we must understand what counseling is.

The Nature of Counseling

What is counseling? It is important to supply a definition of counseling at the very beginning so we know what we are talking about. This is the definition I use in this book: *Counseling is a conversation where one party with questions, problems, and trouble seeks assistance from someone they believe has answers, solutions, and help.*

This definition is an intentionally inclusive one. Many people with many different counseling commitments could map all manner of conceptual and practical assumptions onto this definition, but I believe it covers the counseling that all of us are doing, whether it is at the lay or professional level or done with religious or secular commitments. Let me make two observations about this definition.

First, according to this definition, people are counseling all the time. *You* are counseling all of the time. Counseling is what happens when a woman with a diagnosis of seasonal affective disorder talks in the office of a man with degrees from Yale who is licensed by his state, charges a fee for their conversation, and bills her insurance company for it. Counseling is also what happens when a pastor talks with a woman who is considering leaving her husband and seeks advice from him about her options. Counseling is what happens when a boss calls an employee into the office to discuss a problem with job performance. Counseling happens when a fourth grader talks with his parents about kids being mean to him at school. It is what happens when a man calls his friend to ask for advice on taking a promotion at work.

Counseling, as all of these examples indicate, might be formal or informal, highly relational or more professional, religious or secular. Counseling happens whenever a person with questions, problems, and trouble seeks to talk with someone they believe has answers and solutions and can offer help. All of us do it all the time. There is no person or group of people who can lay claim to the exclusive right or prerogative to be a counseling practitioner.

Second, this definition has two sides. On the one hand, counseling requires one party in the conversation to have questions, problems, and trouble. One member of the counseling conversation must have a dilemma.[3] The potential dilemmas are legion. The questions, problems, and trouble that consume counseling conversations are a lengthy list that defies enumeration. The list includes decisions about whom to marry, where to go to school, which job to take. It involves counseling those who are suicidal, in abusive marriages, addicted to drugs, hearing strange voices. Counseling conversations comprise doubts about whether someone should trust in Jesus Christ, what permissions the

---

3. It is worth noting that this person must usually have an awareness of his dilemma if counseling is to continue for very long. Obviously persons can have all manner of difficulties that do not seem to them to be problems. They might be in a toxic relationship that they rather enjoy. They may fume with sinful anger while insisting that they are being reasonable. They may be lost as can be and hate God. Such people have serious trouble but do not know it. If we cannot persuade them of their trouble, then counseling will not happen for very long. From the perspective of biblical counseling, we would say such a person is not a counselee.

Bible grants about divorce and remarriage, whether the Holy Spirit is a vibrant part of one's daily life. All of these and gazillions more are the kinds of things that hurting people put on the table when they seek assistance in conversations that we so often call counseling.

On the other hand, counseling requires another party in the conversation to have answers, solutions, and help. That means one party in the discussion must offer assistance for the dilemma being experienced by the struggling person. From the perspective of this book, and the larger biblical counseling movement, counseling is not mere commiseration. It is more than just hanging out. In order for counseling to occur, one participant in the conversation must move toward the struggling person with answers, solutions, and help.

For our purposes, we will refer to the person with questions, problems, and trouble as the counselee. We will consider the person with answers, solutions, and help to be the counselor. Counseling is a conversation that a counselee has with a person they believe to be a counselor.

What Counseling *Requires*

Now that we have a definition of what counseling is, I want to state what counseling *requires*. However, it will be most helpful to discuss first what it does *not* require.

Counseling does not require any of the trappings of professionalism. Though we often picture counseling as a very professional activity, it is not required that you be an expert in order to do it. Indeed, if what I stated above is true, most of the people doing counseling (i.e., teachers, parents, coworkers, friends, church members, etc.) lack any formal expertise to do it. As much as we often cherish the trappings of professionalism, like formal offices, distinguished degrees, and state licenses, none of that is required to do counseling—or even to do it well.[4]

---

4. I want to be clear here that this is not a statement of preference but of fact. I certainly value a commitment to do counseling well and believe that honing skill will often require things like quality training and certifications. I am simply pointing out the fact that most of the people who do counseling have no formal qualifications to do it.

I should also make another, potentially awkward, admission right out of the gate. In counseling there is no requirement that the person providing the counsel have *correct* answers, *faithful* solutions, or *effective* help. Do not misunderstand. We should *want* people doing counseling to offer sound answers, assistance, and help. Unfortunately, many people do not. Today, as you read this book, counselors all over the world—whether professional or unprofessional, trained or untrained, experienced or inexperienced—will offer counsel that is absolutely dreadful. A mother will tell her daughter to divorce her husband when she should not. A college student will tell his friend not to stress out about an overwhelming problem, which will be the very thing in his friend's mind when he takes his own life. Right now counselors are telling men who hate being sexually attracted to other men that it is okay to be gay. This afternoon counselors will be harsh when they should be kind. Others will be flippant when they should be firm. Sometime today some counselor will send a woman with a black eye back into the house where her abusive husband lives. Unfortunately, there is no requirement that a person who practices counseling be any good at it.

So what is required to do counseling? If you do not need degrees or skill—things most would assume are a must—then what do you need? To do counseling, the one thing the counselor must do is articulate some vision of reality that understands the dilemma of the counselee and offers a response to that dilemma.

Everyone has commitments to a certain way of seeing life. Some people call this a worldview.[5] Whatever the label, it is a vision about life, what it is, and how it works. This vision of life may be wise or foolish. People may or may not be self-conscious about their vision of life. But everyone possesses such a vision.

---

5. Ronald H. Nash, *Worldviews in Conflict: Choosing Christianity in a World of Ideas* (Grand Rapids, MI: Zondervan, 1992), 16: "In its simplest terms, a worldview is a set of beliefs about the most important issues in life. . . . These beliefs must cohere in some way and form a system. A fancy term that can be useful here is *conceptual scheme*, by which I mean a pattern or arrangement of concepts (ideas). A worldview, then, is a conceptual scheme by which we consciously or unconsciously place or fit everything we believe and by which we interpret and judge reality."

Anyone engaging in counseling will have a vision of life that includes who we are, what is wrong with us, what should be right with us, and what it would take to fix the problem. When someone is having a conversation about a problem they are having, that other person in the conversation is articulating an understanding of what it means to be human and experiencing life. He is explaining his understanding of why this person's life does not appear to be working for them. He is providing his understanding of what is the normative standard for the person's life—that is, the standard the person departed from that brought on the problem. Finally, he has some sense of how to help the person move from the dilemma to a solution.

Counseling Is Theological

Understanding that counseling requires some vision of life is crucial to understanding the theological nature of counseling. The reason is that such a vision of reality is *always* theological. God defines what it is to be a human being, and he describes that in his Word. God knows what is wrong with us and diagnoses the problem in the Bible. God prescribes a solution to our problems—faith in Christ—and reveals him to us in the Scriptures. God authorizes a process of transformation and shows us what it looks like in the pages of the Old and New Testaments.

God has spoken about these realities because he created them, forming them out of nothing. They are not subject to debate. We are who God says we are. What is wrong with us is what God says is wrong with us. There is no solution to our problem and no process of change other than the one God has provided. There is no other option available but to have a theological vision of reality. Every vision of reality about counseling will be theological. The only question is whether a counselor adopts a theological vision of reality that God believes is faithful—or unfaithful. We cannot choose to have a vision of reality that is *not* theological.

[handwritten margin note: IF GOD PRESENTS A PROBLEM THEN HE HAS THE SOLUTION]

Theology and Secular Counseling

The twentieth century witnessed the ascendancy of a theological vision of reality characterized by a disavowal of the authority of God in counseling. This approach to counseling was marked by a nearly complete rejection of the Godward nature of counseling practice. This was a distinct change from the preceding centuries, which had been characterized by religious dominance regarding counseling.[6] By the 1900s, Christians had been largely excluded from counseling work and were on the defensive about that task.[7] Secular counseling practitioners failed to appreciate that they were engaging in theological work and did not appreciate that efforts at instructing people about how to live in God's world are eminently theological. The problem is that they were engaging in faithless, God-disavowing theology that hurts rather than helps people.

The work of secular counseling practitioners is not neutral and is not scientific.[8] Secular counseling is a conversational intervention where an unbelieving man or woman seeks to provide secular answers, solutions, and help to a person with questions, problems, and trouble. Such counsel bubbles up out of the overflow of a commitment to a secular view of life. Examples of this reality are many. To demonstrate the point, I want to examine just two instances.

Secularists and Counseling Failure

Peter Kramer is a leading psychiatrist committed to a secular vision of reality. In one of his books, *Moments of Engagement*, he describes numerous counseling interactions. One such interaction is with a young couple he calls Rick and Wendy. They had been married for several years when Wendy went to see Dr. Kramer. She was very sad, even desperate, and Kramer thought there was some risk of suicide.

---

6. E. Brooks Holifield, *A History of Pastoral Care in America: From Salvation to Self-Realization* (Nashville: Abingdon, 1983).

7. See Heath Lambert, *The Biblical Counseling Movement after Adams* (Wheaton, IL: Crossway, 2011), 21–48.

8. There can be science involved in counseling in ways which will be discussed later, but counseling is not scientific work in the way that biology and meteorology are.

Wendy's problem was despair over her marriage. Married life used to be fun, adventurous, and mutual. She and Rick had fallen in love and had enjoyed a vibrant sexual relationship. Several years into marriage, that was all different. Now Wendy stayed at home with their twin daughters, and Rick was disinterested in her. Rick would spend time with other people, including women. He earned money illegally and would use the proceeds to take trips to Las Vegas, gamble away the money, and do other things that nobody else knew about.

Kramer was able to get the couple to come to counseling together. He explained to them that their troubles were very serious. In fact, he said they were so serious that he did not know if they could be helped. He told them they would have to take aggressive action. His counsel to them was that Wendy must have access to Rick's private books of illegal money. She must discover how much money he usually lost when he went to Vegas, and then she must travel with him on the next trip and commit to losing more money than he normally lost.

Kramer explains that the intervention was calculated to explode in a number of directions. One goal was to provide Wendy a peek at Rick's private books so she could have some idea of how much extra money he had in case of a divorce. Another goal was to pry Wendy away from her kids and help her to be adventurous again. Still another goal was to increase Rick's desire for Wendy by seeing her cavorting around Las Vegas, gambling away money.

Kramer summarizes his work on the case this way:

> Most of the cure lay in our one crafted instruction: go to Vegas and lose money.
>
> If anything, our intervention was too effective. Wendy flourished so dramatically that I began to fear for the marriage.
>
> Over a year after treatment stopped, Rick called me complaining that Wendy wanted to leave him. He sounded paranoid and clinically depressed. He was now even more involved with drugs than in the past. He showed up once or twice, but he never

really turned into a patient, and my last impression of the couple was that they were about to divorce.

Whether this outcome is desirable in a couples treatment of this sort is hard to say. In individual therapy we congratulate ourselves when a masochistic wife manages to leave a neglectful husband. In family therapy we tend more to wonder whether the marriage couldn't have worked after all.[9]

Kramer presents this case as a success ("our intervention was too effective"), but most Christians reading Kramer's case study are likely to be concerned about his involvement in the marriage of this couple. That concern is well founded. The questions for us to consider are, Why? What is wrong with Kramer's counseling?

The answer is that Kramer's theological vision of reality is incorrect. When Kramer looks at Rick and Wendy, he does not see two human beings who are accountable to the God who made them in his image. He does not see this because he does not believe in God. He suppresses the truth in unrighteousness (Rom. 1:18). Because he does not see God, or Rick and Wendy as accountable to God, he does not see the sin issues present in their marriage. Rick is sinning against his wife, and Wendy is suffering because of his sin. Because Kramer does not see the issues of sin against the living God, he cannot call Rick to repentance and help him know how to change in Christ. Nor can he call Wendy to find her comfort and strength in a Redeemer who loves her. Because Kramer cannot see God, it never occurs to him to look in God's Word to find a standard for the marriage of Rick and Wendy. This lack of a standard is why Kramer is confused about how to evaluate the details of the counseling results. He does not know because he has no authoritative benchmark. He has no authoritative benchmark because he does not know where to find one beyond his own ponderings.

The point here is that Kramer's counseling failure is due to a prior theological error. Because Kramer has theological commitments that

---

9. Peter D. Kramer, *Moments of Engagement: Intimate Psychotherapy in a Technological Age* (New York: Penguin, 1994), 134.

place him at odds with the living God, he never had a shot at actually being able to help Rick and Wendy. This should not surprise us. In fact, it is exactly what Christians should expect from the counsel of unbelievers.

Secularists and Counseling "Success"

But counselors with a secular vision of reality do not always fail so obviously. In fact, they often have many counseling successes to report. Let us look at another example. In his huge best seller *Feeling Good*, David Burns talks about a very popular counseling technique known as "cognitive behavioral therapy."

For Burns and other therapists like him, our negative emotions are the result of improper and unhelpful thinking. Burns is critical of a Freudian vision of reality, that therapists must accept the self-assessment of counselees.[10] Burns has a competing theological vision of counseling problems. His vision of counseling leads him to conclude that the negative conceptions people have of themselves should be challenged, not embraced. He insists on a "triple-column technique" where people keep a record of their thoughts, describing their automatic thoughts when stress comes, what is wrong with these thoughts, and a response that makes more sense. He describes this process, using his counseling with a woman named Gail.

> Start by writing down your automatic thoughts and rational responses for fifteen minutes every day for two weeks and see the effect this has on your mood. . . . You may be surprised to note the beginning of a period of personal growth and healthy change in your self-image. This was the experience of Gail, a young secretary whose sense of self-esteem was so low that she felt in constant danger of being criticized by friends. She was so sensitive to her roommate's request to help clean up their apartment after a party that she felt rejected and worthless. She was initially so pessimistic about her chances for feeling better that I could barely persuade

---

10. David D. Burns, *Feeling Good: The New Mood Therapy* (New York: Harper, 2008), 55–59.

her to give the triple-column technique a try. When she reluctantly decided to try it, she was surprised to see how her self-esteem and mood began to undergo a rapid transformation. She reported that *writing down* the many negative thoughts that flowed through her mind during the day helped her gain objectivity. She stopped taking these thoughts so seriously. As a result of Gail's daily written exercises, she began to feel better, and her interpersonal relationships improved by a quantum leap.[11]

Burns's vision of counseling is a collage of faithful and unfaithful theological commitments. He has unwittingly embraced some counseling realities that God reveals in the Bible. He has rejected many others.

For example, Burns is on to something with his triple-column technique. The basic idea behind it is to create intentionality in the thinking of a counselee. Christians should object to Burns's notion that our initial thoughts are always wrong, just as we object to the Freudian vision that they are always right.[12] We would instead assert that all thoughts should be tested according to Scripture and deemed valid or invalid, based on what is revealed there.

Still, Burns's larger point is correct. It is a bad idea to let spontaneous thoughts have free rein in our self-evaluations. This is very close to the biblical idea of taking our thoughts captive to Christ (2 Cor. 10:5–6) and being transformed by the renewal of our minds (Rom. 12:1–2; Eph. 4:22–24; Col. 3:10). Because we find this idea in Scripture, biblical counselors would agree with Burns—not because it is just some good idea, but because it is *biblical*. It is a theologically appropriate counseling intervention that God thought of long before any cognitive behavioral therapist did and which he revealed in his Word. David Burns has embraced this biblical concept, though he does not know how to be thankful to the God who brought this reality into existence.

However, Burns's counseling has plenty of theological error in it

---

11. Burns, *Feeling Good*, 67, emphasis in original.
12. See Sigmund Freud, *Collected Papers*, trans. Joan Riviere, vol IV, 1917, *Mourning and Melancholia* (London: Hogarth, 1952), 155–56.

too. The most central error is the most significant: God is nowhere in sight. In case that sounds a bit clichéd, let us consider all of the bad things that flow into Burns's counsel because God is not even on the periphery of his vision of reality.

Because Burns does not have a vision of reality that includes God, he cannot see Gail as a woman made in the image of God with a body and spirit that will live forever. This leads Burns to reduce Gail down to something fairly small—namely, a collection of thoughts. That turns counseling into something relatively mechanical—like tweaking the thoughts that run through her head when she feels stressed. Because Burns does not see Gail as an ensouled woman with thoughts and feelings for which she is accountable to the living God, counseling becomes a bit more like solving an equation than engaging a unique image bearer.

Because Burns does not have a vision of reality that includes God, he has no standard by which to evaluate the helpfulness or unhelpfulness of Gail's thinking. For example, Burns reported that Gail felt rejected and worthless after her roommate asked for some help cleaning up. Who is to say that it is wrong to feel rejected and worthless after such a request? As Christians, we might agree that she should not feel that way, but we would think that because the Bible tells us so. If her roommate was unkind in her request, Christians would point to the need to speak graciously to avoid causing others pain (Col. 4:6). If her roommate was kind, but Gail interpreted it as rudeness, we would point to the need to believe the best of others and to eagerly serve (1 Cor. 13:7; Phil. 2:4). In any event, we would want people like Gail to know that our self-assessment should always be based on God's verdict of us and not, primarily, on that of others. Christians know these things because we have access to information that Burns rejects. Who is to say what the standard is without such an authority?[13]

Because Burns does not have a vision of reality that includes God, he cannot offer Gail a powerful path to change. I am grateful for the

---

13. Jay Adams, "Change Them? . . . Into What?," *Journal of Biblical Counseling* 13, no. 2 (Winter 1995): 13–16. It was this issue of the absence of a standard that Jay Adams focused on in an address to psychiatrists in Europe.

very practical counseling intervention that Burns offers Gail to lay hold of her wild and reckless thoughts. As I have pointed out, this strategy is very close to something offered in the pages of Scripture. When the apostle Paul talks about it in the Bible, however, he does it in a very different context. Take Paul's instructions in Colossians as an example.

In Colossians 3:10, Paul urges Christians to "put on the new self, which is being renewed in knowledge after the image of its creator." Paul exhorts Christians to exert effort in putting on the new self, indicating that this new self is established as our knowledge is renewed. How Christians think is crucial. All by itself that sounds a lot like David Burns until you realize that there are two and a half chapters of instruction in Colossians before you get to that exhortation. In the instruction that comes before Colossians 3:10, Paul talks about the existence and centrality of Christ, how he made the world, how he holds it together, and how he is the firstborn of creation (Col. 1:15–20). Paul instructs that the central problem people have is their sin, and their greatest need is to be reconciled to God through Christ (Col. 1:9–14, 21–23). He makes clear that it is possible for those who have thus trusted in Christ to live in new ways (Col. 2:6–7; 3:1–4). By the time the apostle Paul gets to a person's mastery of thinking, it is not *mere* thought modification. Colossians 3:10 is something that Christians do by the power of the resurrected Christ because of their new life in Jesus that gives glory to Christ, who made and sustains them.

Thought mastery in the Bible is Christ-centered, done by Jesus' power and for his glory. In Burns's triple-column technique, thought mastery is man-centered and done with the power of paper and pen. You do not need to have any counseling experience to understand how important this distinction is. You only need to be aware of the persistent nature of our negative self-reflections. These reflections are stubbornly resistant to change. Thinking in new ways requires massive amounts of power. The only power David Burns has to offer is the triple-column technique. It does not take a doctoral degree to recognize that this is simply not enough for a person to change in a way that honors Christ.

Unbeknownst to Burns, he has mingled theological error with theological accuracy. Unfortunately, in the grand scheme of things, the theological commitments he has chosen to reject are more important than the ones he has chosen to accept. In his counseling with Gail, Burns has just enough correct to provide the appearance of success. Even though there is the appearance of success, true success—counseling success that honors Christ, is based in the Word, and leads to qualitative and lasting change in the heart of a person—has eluded both counselor and counselee. Real change comes in the theological commitments rejected by Burns and not shared with Gail. Although partial commitment to an accurate theological vision of reality can lead to partial change and the appearance of success, real change that honors Christ requires total commitment to a fully orbed theological vision of reality.

Burns's counseling, though it appears to have worked, was unsuccessful. His counsel made Gail a more successful worshiper of herself. He was able to help her live life without Christ while feeling the pain of his absence less acutely. Even though Gail felt better, this was a counseling failure. The failure is due to theological error.

Theology and Christian Counseling

The twentieth century was marked not only by the incursion of secular practitioners into counseling ministry, it was also marked by the embrace of secular counseling principles by conservative Christians. Christians who rely—to one degree or another—on the counseling insights of secular people have been called integrationists, Christian counselors, and Christian psychologists—among other things.[14] I have detailed elsewhere how this Christian embrace of secular counseling happened.[15] I have also detailed my concerns with it.[16] I shall not

---

14. This is a broad group of thinkers who are united in their belief that the Bible is necessary for counseling but not sufficient for it. I shall refer to this broad group as Christian counselors.

15. Lambert, *Biblical Counseling Movement after Adams*, ch. 1.

16. Stuart Scott and Heath Lambert, *Counseling the Hard Cases: True Stories Illustrating the Sufficiency of God's Resources in Scripture* (Nashville: B&H, 2012), ch. 1.

repeat that work here. Instead, I want to show how the decision to be a Christian counselor is a theological decision. In order to do that, I will describe areas where biblical counselors agree with our brothers and sisters in Christian counseling, as well as some areas where we disagree.

Areas Where Biblical and Christian Counselors Agree

Biblical counselors and Christian counselors have had their fair share of disagreements over the years. Because that is true, it is easy to lose sight of all the areas of agreement that exist between biblical and Christian counselors. I have noticed five areas of agreement.

First, biblical counselors and Christian counselors have, for the most part, been located in Christian circles marked by conservatism. More often than not, we have agreed on the theological realities most central to Christianity, such as the creation of the world by God, the inspiration of the Scriptures, the virgin birth of Christ, his sinless life, his payment for sins through his death and resurrection, and the indwelling nature of the Holy Spirit. Such agreement is not insignificant. Biblical counselors and Christian counselors have the most important things in common—we are brothers and sisters in Christ.

Second, biblical and Christian counselors care for hurting people in need of help. We all want to offer the best care possible. When we as counselors debate our positions, we are not doing what comes most naturally to us (perhaps that is the reason we often have done it so poorly!). Every counselor I know—regardless of their theoretical commitments—has been motivated into counseling by heartbreak over the pain people experience in this fallen world. Our disagreements, while often strong, have sprung from the same desire to offer help.

Third, biblical and Christian counselors agree that psychologists make true observations that are often helpful. This really is an area of agreement. Few have doubted that Christian counselors embrace this view. Many have doubted that biblical counselors agree with it. Those doubts notwithstanding, a belief in the helpful nature of psychological observations goes back as far as the foundational ministry of Jay Adams. The vast majority of biblical counselors today accept that the modern biblical counseling movement began with the ministry of Jay Adams, particularly in the publication of *Competent to Counsel*. In the very first pages of that book Adams wrote,

> I do not wish to disregard science, but rather I welcome it as a useful adjunct for the purposes of illustrating, filling in generalizations with specifics, and challenging wrong human interpretations of Scripture, thereby forcing the student to restudy the Scriptures. However, in the area of psychiatry, science largely has given way to humanistic philosophy and gross speculation.[17]

Adams does two things here: He affirms the use of science in areas like psychiatry. He also states the nature of any objections he might have whenever they arise. He goes on to say that, essentially, he does not like *bad* science. When one's secular vision of life (i.e., humanistic philosophies and gross speculation) crowds out actual scientific observation, Adams grows concerned. I think this is essentially the view all biblical counselors have about science in general and psychology and psychiatry in particular.

In spite of all the accusations in this regard, I am aware of no biblical counselor who outright rejects the findings of psychology. This is an area of agreement between our two camps.

Fourth, biblical and Christian counselors agree that secular psychology gets things wrong. This point is on the other end of the continuum from the previous one. Few have doubted that biblical counselors embrace this belief. Many, I think, would be surprised to discover that Christian counselors embrace it as well, but they do.

---

17. Jay E. Adams, *Competent to Counsel: Introduction to Nouthetic Counseling* (Grand Rapids, MI: Zondervan, 1986), xxi. In another early book, *What about Nouthetic Counseling?: A Question-and-Answer Book with History, Help, and Hope for the Christian Counselor* (Grand Rapids, MI: Baker, 1977), Jay Adams talks about how he has learned much from psychology.

This "destructive" mode of functioning is vital, in many ways, for Christians today. There are times when the best response of the Christian is to "demolish arguments and every pretension that sets itself up against the knowledge of God" (2 Cor. 10:5). But we contend that the appropriate time for such apologetic efforts is when the views actually are raised up against God. In other words, when the views of romantic humanist Carl Rogers, for instance, are presented *as ultimately satisfying answers to the major questions of life*, the right Christian response is to point out critical flaws in the approach and to reject his views.[18]

Our brothers and sisters in Christ, like Stanton Jones and Richard Butman, are not wholly given over to secularism as some have slanderously charged. They have a strong desire to think carefully and biblically about how to filter out secular visions of life. We might have disagreements about how best to do this, but we should admit that we all are trying to place the Bible in authority over psychology.[19] Whenever biblical counselors have not been honest about this, we should repent.

The final area of agreement between biblical and Christian counselors that I shall mention is that we all agree that not all problems are counseling problems. We all agree that the presence of a problem does not mean that the solution for that problem is necessarily counseling. To say it a bit differently, both biblical and Christian counselors believe that people have physical problems that require medical treatment. Any faithful Christian will confess that it is important to minister to the souls of people enduring medical difficulties. This is different from denying the presence of physical problems and the necessity of treating them with medical care.

---

18. Stanton L. Jones and Richard E. Butman, *Modern Psychotherapies: A Comprehensive Christian Appraisal* (Downers Grove, IL: InterVarsity, 1991), 41, emphasis in the original. One point here that will bleed into disagreement is at what point secular answers present themselves against God. Christian counselors are certain to have a different answer for this than biblical counselors will. These answers will be based on commitments to issues I shall discuss in due course.

19. I will address this issue very carefully in chapter 3 on the doctrine of common grace.

This observation is important. Some believe that asserting the profound relevancy of Scripture for solving problems rules out legitimate medical care. Both biblical and Christian counselors advocate for the necessity of proper medical care to treat physical disorders.[20]

Areas Where Biblical and Christian Counselors Disagree

All of that agreement still leaves more than enough room for disparity when it comes to our positions regarding counseling. In the face of many areas of agreement between biblical and Christian counselors, there are two central areas of disagreement.

Biblical and Christian counselors continue to disagree on the question of whether it is *necessary* to use secular counseling techniques to help people in the counseling relationship. In spite of our agreement on the ability of psychologists to make true observations, our two movements continue to disagree on whether it is necessary to augment the Scriptures with secular counseling practices.

The position of Christian counselors on this matter is clear. Just one example is the work of Mark McMinn in *Integrative Psychotherapy: Toward a Comprehensive Christian Approach*. He says,

> By way of analogy, consider the temperature system in an automobile. On one end of the continuum is hot air and on the other end is cool air. Often a person selects a temperature in the middle, mixing the hot and cool air for the desired effect. The climate is more desirable and adaptable by combining both sources of air than it could be if only one source of air were available. . . . In this analogy we are considering two sources of information: psychology and Christian faith. To what extent do we let the "air" from both systems mix in order to achieve an optimal balance? Or should we trust only one source of information and not the other? Reciprocal

---

20. Heath Lambert, *The Gospel and Mental Illness* (Louisville, KY: Association of Certified Biblical Counselors, 2014). See appendix A on mental disorders.

interaction involves the assumption that caring for people's souls is best done by bringing together truth from both sources.[21]

McMinn is one of the leading Christian counselors today. He bases his integrative approach on the assumption that it is necessary to add secular counseling techniques to biblical ones in order to provide the best help for struggling people.

Then there is the argument of someone like David Powlison, one of the leading biblical counselors today. Powlison has a very different position from the one advocated by McMinn:

> Do secular disciplines have anything to offer to the methodology of biblical counseling? The answer is a flat no. Scripture provides the system for biblical counseling. Other disciplines—history, anthropology, literature, sociology, psychology, biology, business, political science—may be useful in a variety of secondary ways to the pastor and the biblical counselor, but such disciplines can never provide a system for understanding and counseling people.[22]

Whereas McMinn believes it is required to add secular counseling techniques to Scripture in order to be maximally effective, Powlison responds to this suggestion with a "flat no." As of the publication of this book, I see no evidence that biblical and Christian counselors are any closer together on this issue than they have ever been.

The foundational reason for this dispute is due to the second area of fundamental disagreement between biblical and Christian counselors: the question of whether the Bible is a *sufficient* counseling resource. Christian counselors believe that secular counseling strategies are a necessary adjunct to the Bible. They do not believe that the Scriptures are a sufficient counseling resource. This is the argument of Stan Jones in an important article he wrote:

---

21. Mark R. McMinn and Clark D. Campbell, *Integrative Psychotherapy: Toward a Comprehensive Christian Approach* (Downers Grove, IL: InterVarsity, 2007), 23.

22. David Powlison, in *Introduction to Biblical Counseling*, eds. John MacArthur and Wayne Mack (Nashville: Nelson, 1994), 363.

There are many topics to which Scripture does not speak—how neurons work, how the brain synthesizes mathematical or emotional information, the types of memory, or the best way to conceptualize personality traits.[23]

Because Scripture and the accumulated wisdom of the church in theology leave many areas of uncertainty in understanding and helping humanity, we approach psychology expecting that we can learn and grow through our engagement with it.[24]

Jones's logic is apparent. Because the Bible lacks information Christian counselors believe to be pertinent to counseling, they move toward psychology, expecting it to fill in the gaps.

A Theological Debate

I will have more to say in the chapters ahead by way of response to these issues, particularly the areas of disagreement. My point is to highlight the issues and show that the terms of debate between biblical and Christian counselors are inherently theological.

When Christian counselors and biblical counselors agree, the basis of that agreement is theological. When we agree that the discipline of psychology makes true observations, that agreement is based on a theological commitment that God has given grace to all people (believers and unbelievers alike) to understand true things. When we agree that the discipline of psychology gets many things wrong, that agreement is based on a theological commitment that sin has so stained the thinking of human beings, we cannot see many crucial realities without the enabling of divine grace. When we agree that not all problems are counseling problems, that agreement is based on a theological conviction that people are physical and spiritual beings and can be afflicted with problems in both aspects of their nature.

When biblical counselors and Christian counselors disagree, the

---

23. Stanton L. Jones, "An Integration View," in Eric L. Johnson, ed., *Psychology & Christianity: Five Views* (Downers Grove, IL: InterVarsity, 2010), 116.

24. Jones, "Integration View," in *Psychology & Christianity*, 125.

basis of that conflict is also inherently theological. Biblical and Christian counselors debate the necessity of secular counseling resources and the sufficiency of biblical resources because of different theological commitments about the contents of Scripture. When biblical and Christian counselors advocate their competing positions, they are making a statement about the contents of Scripture. This is a theological claim requiring theological knowledge, demanding a theological investigation, and resulting in clear articulation of a theological position.

The point of all this is to show that counseling is necessarily theological. Engaging in counseling practice is a theological engagement. Evaluating and debating with various counseling practitioners, whether secular, Christian, or biblical, is a theological enterprise. You are simply not ready to think about counseling—let alone practice it—until you have thought long and hard about theology. That is the reason for this book.

On the Shoulders of Giants

I am not the first person to think of this link between counseling and theology. I have already mentioned that the founder of the biblical counseling movement in the twentieth century was a man named Jay Adams. The publication of his first book on counseling was a significant milestone in the Christian conversations about how to understand counseling in relationship to the Scriptures. His first book was followed by many others, including a book on counseling and theology entitled *A Theology of Christian Counseling.*[25] In that book, published the year I was born, Adams said this:

---

25. The language here can be confusing. Many today refer to integrative counseling as "Christian counseling," as I have been doing here. This is not what is intended by Jay Adams's title. Adams often referred to his brand of counseling as nouthetic counseling. He wrote assuming that people would understand his commitments in this regard. In 1979 he could not have been sensitive to language that is common today. When Adams wrote his theology book, he was simply trying to describe the kind of counseling that is uniquely Christian.

All counseling, by its very nature (as it tries to explain and direct human beings in their living before God and before other human beings in a fallen world) implies theological commitments by the counselor. He simply cannot become involved in the attempt to change beliefs, values, attitudes, relationship and behavior without wading neck deep in theological waters.[26]

Adams began the work of rediscovering a theological vision for counseling. But he did not complete it.

In that same book on counseling and theology, Adams appealed for others committed to biblical counseling to follow his initial work:

Truly, the situation is complex (I almost wrote "horrendous"). You can understand, then, why I am begging for volumes to be written, and why I make no claims about doing more than making a beginning at discussing the many matters of anthropology that confront the Christian counselor who wants to be thoroughly biblical. It is hard enough to know where to begin my sketch, let alone attempt anything more ambitious.[27]

The biblical counseling movement has grown and developed in the years since Jay Adams first wrote those words in 1979. Biblical counselors have written a great deal about many diverse issues in counseling. Yet beyond a few attempts over the last three decades, they have not followed Adams's admonition to write volumes that systematically develop the theology of the movement. My prayer is that this book will build on Adams's good work in helpful ways.

Though I hope to develop much of the theology that Adams initiated in that early book, I am aware that I face many of the same limitations. It is impossible for me to engage in anything like a comprehensive treatment of theology and its relationship to counseling.

---

26. Jay E. Adams, *More Than Redemption: A Theology of Christian Counseling* (Grand Rapids, MI: Baker, 1980), 14.

27. Adams, *More Than Redemption*, 97.

Instead I shall constrain myself to issues that, as they appear to me, are absolutely impossible to overlook in a theology of biblical counseling. Doubtless, I will choose some things others would have overlooked and will ignore things that would have consumed others. Such is the nature of things. Perhaps my limitations will encourage others in the years to come to continue this work of developing a theology of counseling.

In the meantime I invite you to consider my effort in this book, *A Theology of Biblical Counseling.*

CHAPTER 2

BIBLICAL COUNSELING

and a

THEOLOGY OF SCRIPTURE

Friendships blossom regularly in the kind of candid conversations that happen between counselors and counselees. One of the greatest joys of my ministry is that many of my dearest friends are people I first met in counseling. One of my favorite counselees is a girl named Trenyan. Over time I came to know her as a delightful, committed Christian woman. When I first met her, though, she was a teenager in utter turmoil.

She came to our first meeting with her pastor's wife. Trenyan had been a very involved member in the church's youth group for years. She was pretty, active, funny, and artistic. People were naturally drawn to her warm personality, her genuine care for people, and her amazing ability to play classical piano flawlessly.

While Trenyan had always been somewhat introverted, she had become withdrawn and distant over the last year. She was a genuinely caring young woman, but lately she seemed cool toward people and often edgy. For months people in the church tried to crack through the tough exterior, but Trenyan never let anyone in. Her parents went to a different church in town and were not interested in entertaining questions about their daughter's behavior. So, though her friends at church were concerned, they had no idea what was going on. Then one day their questions were answered.

Trenyan's best friend was her pastor's daughter, Rebecca. One afternoon Trenyan was changing clothes at Rebecca's house when Rebecca accidentally walked in on her. She was only in the room for a second, blurted an apology, and left. But it was enough time for Rebecca to see bloody lines all over Trenyan's thighs. Trenyan asked her not to tell, but Rebecca told her mom what she had seen.

Rebecca's mom knew immediately what the marks on Trenyan's legs were because she had experimented with cutting when she was much younger. She reached out to Trenyan and was able to persuade her that she needed to talk to a counselor and get some help. I had helped several of their church's members in the past, so they came to see me.

Trenyan's story directly engages the debate I mentioned in the last chapter: whether the Bible has anything to say, or *enough* to say, to address problems like this. Cutting is a serious and dangerous problem, and one that many Christians believe falls outside the material addressed in Scripture. In this chapter I want to look at the Christian doctrine of Scripture and show that the Bible is relevant and useful in addressing the kinds of difficult counseling issues that Trenyan's story exemplifies.

The Doctrine of Scripture

When Christian theologians teach the doctrine of Scripture, they often discuss the four characteristics of Scripture. One characteristic of Scripture is *authority*. The authority of the Bible means that the Bible is our supreme standard for what we should believe and how we should behave because it comes from God, who cannot lie.[1] Another character-

---

1. The inerrancy of Scripture is often discussed under the authority of the Bible. The inerrancy of Scripture means that the Bible is completely free from any error, since it was given by God, who always tells the truth. The inerrancy of Scripture does not mean that there are no passages in the Bible that are difficult to interpret or challenging to reconcile with other passages. The inerrancy of Scripture also does not deny that later editors and copyists added things to the Bible. The inerrancy of Scripture means, instead, that when the human authors wrote the original documents of Scripture (called autographs), they were carried along by God in their work so that they were protected from error.

istic is *clarity*. The clarity of Scripture means that the Holy Spirit makes the Bible understandable to all who read it seeking to be submissive to what it says.[2] The third characteristic is the *necessity* of Scripture. The necessity of Scripture means that it is impossible to live the Christian life without the Bible. Finally, the fourth characteristic, the *sufficiency* of Scripture, means that the Bible contains all that we need to know God's will and live a life pleasing to him.

Each of these characteristics is of crucial importance and could be meaningfully unpacked in constructing a theology of biblical counseling. In this section, however, I will primarily focus on further developing our understanding of only Scripture's sufficiency. This aspect of Scripture has been the most debated in the recent history of the biblical counseling movement. It is also the doctrine on which the biblical counseling movement will succeed or fail. The sufficiency of Scripture for counseling determines, to a large degree, whether Christians have meaningful help from the Scriptures to offer Trenyan.

The Sufficiency of Scripture

The sufficiency of Scripture is important for a very practical reason. In counseling, when people share their most serious and secret problems, counselors need to have something to say. We need guidance about how to respond to such information. Trenyan is a great example. I sat in my office listening to her that day as she shared some very painful information with me. She told me of deep heartache in her life and how she came to begin cutting her legs with a small knife she bought at a craft store. After Trenyan shared her story with me, she quit talking. It was my turn to speak.

That moment when the counselor must respond to the pain that has been revealed by a broken person is one of the most sacred occasions

---

2. The clarity of Scripture does not mean there are no passages that are hard to understand in Scripture (2 Peter 3:15–16), that Christians are protected from any error of interpretation when reading the Bible, or that faithful Christians will not disagree about the teachings of the Bible. This doctrine means that you do not have to possess intensive and technical training to be able to understand the plain meaning of Scripture.

in all of life. Another human being has just revealed something intimate, profound, and difficult about her life, and now she is waiting for a response. Those moments make me powerfully aware of my responsibility as a counselor to offer wisdom and care.

Those moments are very telling because what we say in them reveals where our trust is. Whatever we say demonstrates a reliance on some source of authority. There is no flight from this reality. In those times, like the one I experienced with Trenyan, the words that fill the silence show what counseling resources you believe to be the most informative, helpful, and trustworthy. The "wisdom" that comes out of your mouth demonstrates where your trust is—whether it is the "wisdom" of the world, the "wisdom" of secular psychology, your own personal brand of "wisdom," or the wisdom of God in the Bible.

Whenever you speak, you do it out of a commitment to some kind of wisdom. The doctrine of the sufficiency of Scripture is a promise that God himself will give you something from him to say in those sacred moments. It is a great comfort to me to know that I do not have to make up my own "wisdom" and I do not have to rip off the "wisdom" of secular therapy. I can go to Scripture and find something to say to people like Trenyan that will be God's sufficient word for them.

Some people do not agree with this statement. In fact, many Christian intellectuals who teach and write about counseling disagree profoundly with the doctrine of sufficiency that the biblical counseling movement advocates. They believe good things about Scripture. They believe the Bible is inspired, inerrant, and authoritative. They often think that the Bible is *necessary* for people who need counseling, but even then do not believe the Bible is *enough*. They think the Bible is a book about how to get saved and walk with Jesus but is not focused on offering insight to the most serious counseling topics. They believe the biblical counseling movement has distorted the classic understanding of the doctrine of the sufficiency of Scripture. They assert that when biblical counselors talk about sufficiency, they do so in a way that is foreign to the way Christian theologians have understood the concept.

Eric Johnson has offered a critique of the biblical counseling view of

Scripture that is more academically robust and theologically astute than most other critiques available. Johnson identifies himself as a Christian psychologist who does not believe that the Bible is sufficient for the work of counseling. He argues that the Bible is sufficient only for salvation and doctrine. He believes that the view of sufficiency advocated by the biblical counseling movement constitutes an "egregious misunderstanding of . . . the form of the Bible."[3] His point is that it is a serious error to argue that Scripture provides sufficient resources for the work that counselors do.

Johnson believes that the brand of biblical sufficiency advocated by those in biblical counseling is inappropriate. He bases this on his understanding of the history of Protestant theology. Johnson traces the sufficiency of Scripture back to the Protestant Reformation. He points out that the roots of the doctrine actually have to do with debates between the Reformers and Catholics.[4] One of the major debates of the Reformation had to do with the sources of authority that Christians were to use. Rome believed that authoritative pronouncements from the teaching office of the Catholic Church, known as the Magisterium, were essential in explaining the meaning and application of the biblical text. The Reformers believed this was untrue and argued that no teaching office was required for Christians to understand the Scriptures. They believed that Scripture itself was sufficient to interpret the Scriptures.

Johnson points out that when biblical counselors ground their counseling work in the sufficiency of Scripture, they are talking about the doctrine in categories that are different from the ones Protestants have used. Johnson tries to show that the issue of sufficiency had nothing to do with counseling for most Protestant theologians. Instead, Protestant Christian theologians have argued for Scripture's sufficiency only in the categories of salvation and doctrine. Johnson refers to this as salvific doctrinal sufficiency.[5]

---

3. Eric L. Johnson, *Foundations for Soul Care: A Christian Psychology Proposal* (Downers Grove, IL: InterVarsity, 2007), 119.
4. Johnson, *Foundations for Soul Care*, 178–79.
5. Johnson, *Foundations for Soul Care*, 182.

Johnson's critique goes to the heart of the biblical counseling movement. The faithfulness—even the existence—of the movement is at stake in a critique like this. An authentic counseling movement grounded in the Scriptures requires a view of the Bible that is consistent with classic Christian theology. It also requires an understanding of and respect for the form of Scripture that God has given us. I want to respond to Johnson's challenge by examining the nature of systematic theology and by reviewing a few historical statements concerning the sufficiency of Scripture.

Sufficiency and the Nature of Systematic Theology

Johnson is correct when he says that the biblical counseling movement has talked about the sufficiency of Scripture in ways that are different from the beliefs of other theologians since the time of the Reformation. There is a reason for this. The Reformation debates were primarily about the sufficiency of Scripture in relation to the doctrinal debates with Catholics. Today the counseling debates about the sufficiency of Scripture relate to whether it is appropriate or necessary to use secular systems of thought in counseling. Obviously this is fresh territory, but the fact that the discussion is new—a matter for contemporary theological reflection—does not mean that it is unfounded or wrong.

First, we need to remember what theology is. Our definition from the last chapter is that theology is what the whole Bible teaches us today about any given topic. Our goal is to discern what the whole Bible says about the sufficiency of Scripture for counseling in our contemporary context. The sufficiency debates of the past were important. I am thankful for those who faithfully taught the Scriptures and interacted with the doctrinal questions of their time. The divisions of the Reformation are now historical theology. They relate to what the church believed and taught in the past. This does not negate the need for a fresh engagement with systematic theology that demonstrates a concern with what the Bible teaches *today*.

Threats against God's truth did not end at the Reformation. New threats confront every generation and affect our understanding of almost every doctrine. That is certainly true with regard to the sufficiency of Scripture today. It was the job of John Calvin, Martin Luther, Ulrich Zwingli, and others to defend the sufficiency of Scripture against attack from Roman Catholics. The greatest threat today to the doctrine of the sufficiency of Scripture is one that the church has never faced before. Today, it has become the task of the biblical counseling movement to defend the sufficiency of Scripture from attack by those who believe the Bible is not a sufficient resource to help when life's challenges confront a person. My point is simply this: doing good theology requires us to talk about the sufficiency of Scripture in ways that are different from the Reformation because now, half a millennium later, the church confronts different threats. We will be like the Reformers, not merely by repeating their arguments but by applying their biblical convictions to threats they never faced.

Sufficiency and Church History

At the same time, I'm not ready to concede the point that the church has never been concerned about the kind of sufficiency related to what we know today as counseling. To limit the church's view of sufficiency to the Reformation debate would be to ignore much of what the church has had to say about this doctrine. A survey of noteworthy confessional statements from church history reveals that the church has often described two strands of sufficiency in its articulations of the faith. These statements speak to the sufficiency of Scripture for *doctrine*, but they also address the sufficiency of Scripture for *living the Christian life*.

We shall look at two examples, but many more could be addressed.[6]

---

6. "The Second London Confession" affirms the sufficiency of Scripture in nearly identical terms as "The Westminster Confession." "The New Hampshire Confession" applies the sufficiency of Scripture to all conduct and opinions, as does "The Baptist Faith and Message." "The Abstract of Principles" of The Southern Baptist Theological Seminary says that the Scriptures are the only "sufficient, certain and authoritative rule of all saving knowledge, faith and obedience."

The Second Helvetic Confession and The Westminster Confession of Faith both include helpful statements on the issue of sufficiency. The first of these two confessions says this of Scripture:

> SCRIPTURE TEACHES FULLY ALL GODLINESS. We judge, therefore, that from these Scriptures are to be derived true wisdom and godliness, the reformation and government of churches; as also instruction in all duties of piety; and, to be short, the confirmation of doctrines, and the rejection of all errors, moreover, all exhortations.[7]

This statement teaches the sufficiency of Scripture for doctrine with such expressions as "the confirmation of doctrines" and "the rejection of all errors." But notice that the statement also focuses on issues that pertain to life and godliness with references to wisdom, godliness, and instruction in all duties of piety. The authors of this confession, which summarizes the core doctrinal beliefs held at that time, believed that Scripture was sufficient not merely for what we believe but also for how we live life in the face of difficulties.

The second example is The Westminster Confession of Faith. Concerning the sufficiency of Scripture, the Westminster divines wrote,

> The whole counsel of God concerning all things necessary for His own glory, man's salvation, faith and life, is either expressly set down in Scripture, or by good and necessary consequence may be deduced from Scripture.[8]

This profoundly influential confession emphasizes faith and life in its understanding of sufficiency. Again, the church leaders saw no reason to limit the sufficiency of Scripture to matters of doctrine. They believed that it was equally sufficient for the matters of life, which would include the types of issues addressed in counseling today. We could look

---

7. "The Second Helvetic Confession," ch. I, https://www.ccel.org/creeds/helvetic.htm.
8. "The Westminster Confession of Faith," ch. I, sec. VI, http://www.reformed.org/documents/wcf_with_proofs/.

at others, but these two confessions demonstrate that it is historically consistent to see the Scriptures as sufficient for doctrine and life.

The point of all this is that we need doctrine to live the Christian life. It would be impossible to live a faithful and happy life without knowing the truths we must confess. We also need to know how to respond to the issues and problems that plague us as we walk through life in a fallen world. The Bible has as much instruction about these matters as it does about the truths we must confess. Both are crucial and, in fact, they are inseparably related to one another.

Counseling is concerned with addressing the questions, problems, and troubles we face in our life. Those who articulated the confessions of faith we cherish today did not live in a time when the language of "counseling" was popularly used. Yet when they wrote confessions, they affirmed the sufficiency of Scripture for the same issues that we address today in counseling. Prior to the eighteenth century, if you were a Christian and you had problems in your life and had to talk to someone, you would look to a pastor or other religious leader. There was hardly anywhere else to go. All that began to change in the late 1800s and early 1900s.[9] Since that time, a culturally credible alternative to Scripture has arisen as the source of wisdom to help people respond to their problems in living. That alternative is the counseling interventions offered by secular therapy.

As we saw in the previous chapter, secular therapists offer counseling solutions that are at odds with the solutions offered by God in his Word. This means that secular therapists are a threat to Christian ministry, which is concerned with offering God's solutions to people in pain. To this extent, secular therapies offer solutions that are at odds with true help. The biblical counseling movement has identified this threat and sought to address it by advancing the understanding of the sufficiency of Scripture in evangelicalism today, articulating it anew in response to these threats and challenges. While biblical counselors have added fresh perspective in their approach to this topic, they have

---

9. See chapter 1, notes 6 and 7.

not been recklessly innovative. Instead, they have helped to direct the church toward greater faithfulness on the doctrine of sufficiency.

Four Categories of Sufficiency

Doing good theology requires applying ancient truth to fresh problems. To make the case that the doctrine of the sufficiency of Scripture extends to the discipline of counseling, I want to first state that the sufficiency of Scripture is not a simplistic doctrine. In the discussion that follows, I highlight four different categories of sufficiency: progressive sufficiency, completed sufficiency, formal sufficiency, and material sufficiency.

Progressive Sufficiency

Progressive sufficiency means that the amount of revelation that God's covenant people have at any point in redemptive history is sufficient for them at that particular time.[10] The Bible was written in stages over long periods of time, and different people have had different access to it at various points in redemptive history.

For example, when Abraham left Ur, the revelation of God sufficient for him at that point was God's audible words to leave his country and go to a new land to be a blessing to all the world (Gen. 12:1–3). The Israelites entering Canaan had many more words of God than this. Indeed, they had the written words of God in Genesis, Exodus, Leviticus, Numbers, and Deuteronomy. These books would have contained God's sufficient revelation to them so that they would know how to live a life honoring to God at that time in history. The entirety of the Hebrew Scriptures would have been sufficient revelation for God's people at the dawn of the millennium before the birth of Jesus. These Hebrew Scriptures were the ones Timothy would have had access to and which he learned

---

10. See John M. Frame, *The Doctrine of the Word of God* (Phillipsburg, NJ: P&R, 2010), 225–28. Frame discusses this concept of progressive sufficiency using the language of "general sufficiency." I use the term *progressive* because it seems to me to be a bit more descriptive of what we are talking about. It is also the same language used in influential resources like "The Chicago Statement on Biblical Inerrancy."

from his mother and grandmother (2 Tim. 3:14–17). For us today, the entire Christian Scriptures, from Genesis to Revelation, are our sufficient Word from God about how to live our lives.

The doctrine of progressive sufficiency teaches us that God's people in the days of Moses were not held accountable for what the apostle Paul would later teach in 1 Corinthians. God's Word for us is enough regardless of when he caused us to be born and what revelation he provided to us. This doctrine also helps Christians today to be thankful, since we exist in a time of such extensive revelation. The doctrine of progressive sufficiency reminds us that we have a treasure trove of sixty-six books where we can learn how to honor God. This is more than any other of God's covenant people had at any other point in redemptive history.

Completed Sufficiency

Completed sufficiency means that the completion of God's work of redemption leads to the closing of the Christian canon and the completion of revelation.[11] For thousands of years, God was progressively adding to the revelation his people could access. The culmination of this revelation was the life and ministry of Jesus Christ. The New Testament records this ministry in the Gospels and unpacks it in the Epistles. The New Testament teaches that the Bible is complete now that this foundational work of description and explanation is complete (Eph. 2:20; Rev. 22:18–19). One such place where we discover this is Hebrews 1:1–4:

> Long ago, at many times and in many ways, God spoke to our fathers by the prophets, but in these last days he has spoken to us by his Son, whom he appointed the heir of all things, through whom also he created the world. He is the radiance of the glory of God and the exact imprint of his nature, and he upholds the

---

11. See Frame, *Doctrine of the Word*, 225–28. I am using the language of completed sufficiency, where Frame uses the language of particular sufficiency, because, as noted above, I think it is a bit more intuitive. Others have talked about this issue as they described the issue of a "closed canon." See also Wayne A. Grudem, *Systematic Theology: An Introduction to Biblical Doctrine* (Grand Rapids, MI: Zondervan, 1994), 129–30.

universe by the word of his power. After making purification for sins, he sat down at the right hand of the Majesty on high, having become as much superior to angels as the name he has inherited is more excellent than theirs.

This passage does not say explicitly that no more books will be added to the Bible. It actually says more than that. It indicates that Christians have received the culmination of revelation in Jesus Christ. We have no more need of revelation now that we have the description and explanation of the gospel that even the angels have longed to see (1 Peter 1:12).

Completed sufficiency teaches us that though God was adding to the Bible over millennia, the text of Scripture that we now recognize is completely sufficient. We are not waiting for any more additions to the canon to have a sufficient text. This doctrine is also embraced by continuationists who, though they believe in the ongoing gift of prophecy, argue that the prophecy today is of a different variety than the authoritative type that we have in the Old Testament.[12] Completed sufficiency is, therefore, a doctrine that is widely embraced by Christians and encour-

---

12. Wayne Grudem is the best example of a continuationist who holds to completed sufficiency [Grudem, *Systematic Theology: An Introduction to Biblical Doctrine* (Grand Rapids, MI: Zondervan, 1994), 131–33], but who nevertheless embraces an ongoing gift of prophecy [Wayne A. Grudem, *The Gift of Prophecy in the New Testament and Today* (Westchester, IL: Crossway, 1988]. I should point out that I am a cessationist and find Grudem's argument for ongoing prophecy rather problematic. This issue is beyond the scope of this book. I do, however, want to point out a very important issue about sufficiency, continuationism, and the biblical counseling movement. Some in the biblical counseling movement have expressed great concern about continuationists. They say that they cannot be committed to biblical counseling because their belief in the ongoing nature of prophecy undermines the sufficiency of Scripture. I respond to this important concern in two ways. First, continuationists who are committed to biblical counseling do not believe their view undermines the sufficiency of Scripture for counseling. Like many, I find this assertion debatable, but the beliefs of continuationists have some merit since they do make a distinction between the kind of authoritative revelation in the Bible and the qualified nature of prophecy they embrace. We may choose to disagree with their belief and practice, but they are being intellectually consistent. As long as they uphold this intellectual consistency in their actual practice, we should not be concerned that their beliefs undermine the biblical counseling commitment to sufficiency. A second response is to say that the nuanced categories of sufficiency that I am supplying here provide some help to us. I will argue below that material sufficiency (which refers to the actual subject matter of Scripture) is the center of the sufficiency debate for counseling. That means that Christians could disagree about the doctrine of completed sufficiency and still agree on the material sufficiency of Scripture for counseling. For both of these reasons I see no reason, in principle, why continuationists and cessationists cannot participate in common cause when it comes to biblical counseling.

ages us to trust in and be thankful for the completed Bible that we have. It encourages our confidence in this Bible, as we do not need to wait for any more authoritative words from God about how to live our lives.

Formal Sufficiency

Formal sufficiency means that Scripture contains everything essential for its own interpretation. This aspect of sufficiency was the central issue in the debates between Catholics and Protestants during the Reformation, as I noted above. The issue in this debate concerns what role church tradition plays in the interpretation of Scripture. Though the Reformation debate concerned the teaching office of the Roman Catholic Church, this issue continues to separate Protestants and Catholics today. Christians still face contemporary threats to this category of formal sufficiency.

One way to understand this idea of formal sufficiency is to ask the question: What resources should Christians point to in order to justify a particular belief or practice? The Protestant position has been that we must appeal to Scripture as that which fully and finally interprets Scripture. Though it might sound circular, the formal sufficiency of Scripture is thus grounded in the authority of Scripture. This is true for any ultimate authority, since appealing to a higher authority would undercut its claim of authority. Christians have always appealed to Scripture when interpreting Scripture since appealing to another source for authority would make *that* source the authority.

Formal sufficiency does not mean that Christians should never consult other sources of information. If that were the case, you should stop reading this book since it is not Scripture. There are many reasons why it is helpful for Christians to appeal to outside sources when interpreting Scripture. We may want to know what other people have believed about a particular issue and would need to examine other resources to determine that. We also would look to outside resources because they are produced by Christians who know more about an issue than we do, and we want them to instruct us in the Scriptures on that topic. Viewed from this perspective, the creation and study of outside sources is justified by the spiritual gift of teaching (Rom. 12:7; 1 Cor. 12:28; Eph. 4:11). So we dare not avoid outside sources of instruction. The point of the formal sufficiency of Scripture is to affirm the authority of Scripture and ensure that all use of outside sources points back to the authority of Scripture. In counseling this means, very practically, that we must always ground our instruction in Scripture and be open and candid when we are not doing that.

Material Sufficiency

The material sufficiency of Scripture refers to the actual contents of Scripture and means that the Bible tells us everything we need to know from God about any topic.[13] This category of sufficiency concerns the extent to which various subjects are addressed in Scripture. Of the four categories of sufficiency, this one is where biblical and Christian counselors have disagreed. It is the category that is the most controversial, and so in the section that follows, we will spend some additional time unpacking it.

The Extent of Material Sufficiency

When we say that the Bible is sufficient for counseling, we are referring to all four aspects of sufficiency, but in particular, we mean that the *material* sufficiency of Scripture extends to the subject matter of counseling. John Frame, in his book *The Doctrine of the Word of God*, provides a framework for us in appreciating how the Scriptures can sufficiently address the subject matter of counseling. In a lengthy section on the sufficiency of Scripture, he writes,

---

13. Timothy Ward, *Words of Life: Scripture As the Living and Active Word of God* (Downers Grove, IL: IVP Academic, 2009), 108. See also Timothy Ward, *Word and Supplement: Speech Acts, Biblical Texts, and the Sufficiency of Scripture* (Oxford: Oxford University Press, 2002), 38–51.

Christians sometimes say that Scripture is sufficient for religion, or preaching, or theology, but not for such things as auto repairs, plumbing, animal husbandry, and dentistry. And of course, many argue that it is not sufficient for science, philosophy, or even ethics. That is to miss an important point. Certainly, Scripture contains more specific information relevant to theology than to dentistry. But sufficiency in the present context is not sufficiency of specific information but sufficiency of divine words. Scripture contains divine words sufficient for all of life. It has all the divine words that the plumber needs, and all the divine words that the theologian needs. So it is just as sufficient for plumbing as it is for theology. And in that sense it is sufficient for science and ethics as well.[14]

What is Frame saying here?

First, Frame discusses what I shall call material sufficiency in the *particular* sense. He does this when he observes that "Scripture contains more specific information relevant to theology than to dentistry." He is pointing out that the subject matter of Scripture is more about some particular kinds of information than it is about others.

Second, Frame describes what I shall call material sufficiency in the *general* sense. He does this when he states that "Scripture contains divine words sufficient for all of life. It has all the divine words that the plumber needs, and all the divine words that the theologian needs." God has given enough of his words to us to know how to honor him in every discipline. Both of these senses of material sufficiency are needed for us to see how the Bible is sufficient for the task of counseling. We will look at each one, beginning with this general sense of material sufficiency.

Material Sufficiency in the General Sense

In a very real sense, we can say that the Bible is sufficient for everything. Frame describes this by talking about the sufficiency of divine words for all of life. God has given us all the divine words we need for

---

14. Frame, *Doctrine of the Word*, 221.

anything. When Frame says that the Scripture is sufficient for plumbing, he means that God has given to plumbers a sufficient amount of revelation to know how to do their work in a way that honors him. This does not mean that the Bible is a guide for all information about plumbing, because it is not. There is, indeed, very little specific information about plumbing, but a great deal of specific information about plumbing in the world.

This is the kind of general scriptural sufficiency that John Piper describes when he says,

> The sufficiency of Scripture means we don't need any more special revelation. We don't need any more inspired, inerrant words. In the Bible God has given us, we have the perfect standard for judging all other knowledge. All other knowledge stands under the judgment of the Bible.[15]

Material sufficiency in the general sense means that God has told us everything we need to know about his perspective on every single topic we could consider.

Material Sufficiency in the Particular Sense

The material sufficiency of Scripture is not limited to this general sense. The Bible not only includes broad information relevant to all topics in general, it has some very specific instruction about a number of particular things. There are some subjects for which God intends Scripture to provide very detailed information. Some of these subjects are obvious. The doctrine of God is a relatively self-evident example. All Christians believe that the Bible is sufficient to inform our view of who God is. When Christians confess the sufficiency of the Bible about God, they do not mean it in the general sense just discussed. They mean

---

15. John Piper, "Thoughts on the Sufficiency of Scripture: What It Does and Doesn't Mean," last modified February 9, 2005, http://www.desiringgod.org/articles/thoughts-on-the-sufficiency-of-scripture.

that the Bible is sufficient to give us enough precise information for us to actually know God as he wants to be known. We can say that the material sufficiency of Scripture extends to the doctrine of God in a very particular sense.

That is an easy example. What about a harder one? What about issues of sexuality and gender? What about the days of creation? What about counseling? Each one of these examples has inspired great debate about whether Scripture provides enough information to be considered sufficient in a particular sense. Determining whether the Scriptures are sufficient for a topic is a complicated task that must be undertaken with great care. The Scriptures are not sufficient for everything in this particular way. To determine whether the material sufficiency of Scripture extends to a given topic in a particular sense, we must undertake a two-fold investigation.

The first part of the investigation is to understand the nature of the issue we are considering. Before we can understand whether Scripture sufficiently and particularly addresses a certain topic, we must be sure that we understand that topic. The second part of the investigation is to understand all that the Bible has to say about that topic. We are not ready to say that the Bible does not address a topic in that sufficient, particular way until we understand all that the Bible says about that issue. Determining the extent of material sufficiency in a particular sense requires us to know the issue under consideration and know the contents of Scripture on that issue.

The Extent of Material Sufficiency to Counseling

Before we can embrace or reject a belief in the sufficiency of Scripture for counseling, we must first investigate the nature of the discipline of counseling and then the contents of Scripture regarding that discipline. In the previous chapter, I looked at the nature of counseling, showing that counseling is a conversation where one party with questions, problems, and trouble seeks assistance from someone they believe has answers, solutions, and help. Counseling is an exchange of wisdom in relationship. This wisdom might be correct or incorrect, and the relationship might be formal or informal, but regardless of these variations, the essential task of counseling is unchanged.

Next we must investigate whether the Bible includes enough information about counseling to be considered materially sufficient in the particular sense that we are looking at. To decide this, we must discern whether God, in Scripture, supplies wisdom to inform the answers, solutions, and help that counselors provide to a person with questions, problems, and trouble. I would argue that the Bible is, rather self-evidently, about the problems we face and God's solutions to those problems. People come to counseling when they are confused and need wisdom and when their relationships are broken and in need of restoration. They come to counseling when they are afraid and need courage, when they are sad and need joy, when they are weak and need strength, when they are angry and need peace, when they are overwhelmed and need help. For millennia Christians have believed that God supplies all of these things to his people and that he reveals how he supplies them in the Bible. The issue at stake in the sufficiency of Scripture for counseling concerns whether God has words to say to people who are in trouble, and whether he has shared those words with us.

Historically, the only Christians who have seriously doubted whether this was true are those in the last century who advocated the alternatives to God's solutions offered by secular therapy. In our contemporary culture, many Christians deny the sufficiency of Scripture for counseling and thus are drawn to the resources of secular therapy rather than to God's resources. Christian practitioners of counseling who deny the sufficiency of Scripture for their work have tended to do so for two central reasons: One is the apparent richness of resources outside of Scripture. The other has to do with the apparent limitations of resources within Scripture. Let us look at each one.

Rich Resources Outside Scripture

Some believe that embrace of the sufficiency of Scripture for counseling necessarily entails rejection of true information outside of the Bible. This is a fairly common objection to the kind of biblical sufficiency that I am discussing here. Counseling approaches to the theological left of biblical counseling have been concerned that an embrace of biblical sufficiency will lead counselors to dismiss or ignore the extra-biblical information available to Christians.[16]

The problem with this objection is that it is hypothetical. It is a *potential* critique, but not an *actual* one. I can say this because there is nothing about an embrace of the sufficiency of Scripture for counseling that *requires* someone to reject the presence of other sources of knowledge outside the Bible. While some may choose to embrace the sufficiency of Scripture and reject extra-biblical information, it is not necessary to do this. In fact, I am aware of no biblical counselor who has made this error.

From the very beginning of the biblical counseling movement, leaders have made clear their belief in the legitimacy of sources of information outside of Scripture.[17] Biblical counselors do not ignore or outright reject extra-biblical sources or counseling insights. In fact, I would argue that biblical counselors have demonstrated a high level of theological sophistication about the use of extra-biblical data, often greater than our brothers to the theological left. The biblical counseling position is that there is much true information that exists outside the

---

16. See Johnson, *Foundations for Soul Care*, 113; Stanton L. Jones and Richard E. Butman, *Modern Psychotherapies: A Comprehensive Christian Appraisal* (Downers Grove, IL: InterVarsity, 1991), 27–59; Eric L. Johnson, ed., *Psychology & Christianity: Five Views* (Downers Grove, IL: InterVarsity, 2010), 274–75.

Stanton L. Jones, *Psychology and the Christian Faith: An Introductory Reader* (Grand Rapids, MI: Baker, 1986), 279–80.

17. Jay E. Adams, *What about Nouthetic Counseling: A Question and Answer Book with History, Help and Hope for the Christian Counselor* (Grand Rapids, MI: Baker, 1977), 31; Wayne Mack, *Totally Sufficient: The Bible and Christian Counseling*, eds. Ed Hindson and Howard Eyrich (Fearn, Scotland: Christian Focus, 2004), 51; David Powlison, in Mark R. McMinn and Timothy R. Phillips, *Care for the Soul: Exploring the Intersection of Psychology and Theology*, eds. (Downers Grove, IL: InterVarsity, 2001), 14–15.

Bible—that found in the sciences, for example. Any objections from biblical counselors to data outside Scripture have been objections about the *relevance* of that information to biblical counseling, the *accuracy* of that information, and the degree to which that information encroaches on territory that rightly belongs to the realm of Christian ministry.[18] To be clear, biblical counseling does not reject sources outside the Scriptures. We simply believe that these sources need to be examined critically in the light of what the Bible teaches. These are deep waters, and I shall have more to say about them in chapter 3 on common grace. For now, however, we must affirm that the sufficiency of Scripture does not require the rejection of true information outside the Bible. Biblical counselors have often been accused of being "anti-science" to one degree or another.[19] There is simply no evidence that this charge is true.

Limited Resources within Scripture

Another objection to the kind of sufficiency I am advocating here is to say that the Bible does not include enough resources to do counseling well. Some believe that biblical resources are missing key information necessary to care for counselees, so we must rely on the rich resources outside Scripture to fill in the gaps. Our friends committed to other counseling approaches advance this tactic in two ways.

One way is by pointing out highly technical information that is not included in Scripture. Johnson provides one example of this:

---

18. See Jay E. Adams, *Competent to Counsel: Introduction to Nouthetic Counseling* (Grand Rapids, MI: Zondervan, 1986), xxi. Adams made clear that there was much to learn from psychology as a science. He was adamant, however, that psychology stopped being scientific when it veered into humanistic philosophy and "gross speculation." For Adams, psychology is a competitor to Christianity and dangerous when it emphasizes such philosophy which overflows in counsel given to troubled people. Adams is not threatened by and is never critical of the science of psychology.

19. Myers issues this charge very charitably to Powlison [Eric L. Johnson, ed., *Psychology & Christianity: Five Views* (Downers Grove, IL: InterVarsity, 2010), 274–75]. James issued the charge to Powlison much more maliciously [James Beck, "Psychology and Christianity: Four Views," vol. 4 (January 2001), http://www.denverseminary.edu/article/psychology-and-christianity-four-views/].

The Bible gives us many *general* soul-care principles, goals and means. But it does not contain, on the one hand, higher-order *theoretical statements* regarding, for example, cognitive, emotional and volitional aspects of the soul, the structure of the personality or psychospiritual abnormality, or, on the other hand, lower-order detailed, step-wise treatment strategies for applying the gospel and remediating sin and biological and psychosocial damage. Such higher- and lower-order discourse is the fruit of scientific reflection and research.

For example, the Scripture says that sin comes out of the heart (Matt. 15:19), but it nowhere describes the components that make up the heart, how the heart is related to the memory, emotion and reasoning subsystems, how original sin develops into specific sins, or how genetics and social experiences influence these processes. The Bible also tells us to cast our anxiety on Christ (1 Pet. 5:7), but it does not spell out the precise cognitive, emotional and volitional steps for how to take anxiety to him from within our hearts and leave it with him. While the Bible is sufficient for salvation, doctrine and morality, the phenomena of Scripture itself forces upon us the conclusion that it was not God's design to have the Bible answer *directly* all the concerns of psychologists or counselors for all places in all times, containing everything that would be of value to soul care in the future.[20]

---

20. Johnson, *Foundations for Soul Care*, 184–85, emphasis in original. This passage has a number of problems. First, Johnson asserts that the Bible nowhere describes the components of the heart or how original sin develops into specific sins, yet he suggests that science does address these topics. It would be an astounding claim to say that science can speak with any authority about the biblical components of the heart or the concept of original sin. Second, Johnson addresses Peter's command to cast our anxiety on the Lord, and he seems to be saying that God has commanded us to do something that he has not told us how to do. Yet Johnson has overlooked that the very information about how to cast our anxieties onto God, which he claims is not shared with us, is taught in the verse prior to the one he has cited. Finally, Johnson states that the Bible does not give us strategies for applying the gospel and remediating sin. This is an alarming statement. If true, it would undermine everything the church has ever believed about the Bible. I raise these concerns because they illustrate the danger of trying to prop up the science of psychology by minimizing the teaching of Scripture. We must never make it sound as if God does not teach us how to trust him with our anxieties, or that God places us in the morally impossible position of commanding us to do things without explaining how they are to be done. Such statements are irresponsible when souls are at stake.

Stan Jones provides another example:

> There are many topics to which Scripture does not speak—how neurons work, how the brain synthesizes mathematical or emotional information, the types of memory, or the best way to conceptualize personality traits.[21]

These two examples are very instructive for us. We agree that the information referenced here is not included in the Bible. I am aware of no place in Scripture where we are treated to descriptions of the structure of the personality, psycho-spiritual abnormality, how neurons work, or how to conceptualize personality traits. However, I would argue that this information is beside the point when it comes to actual counseling. I have counseled hundreds of men, women, and couples and have never once had a counseling conversation where the counselee needed information of this variety in order to respond well to their personal problems. The question is not whether such information is in the Bible (it is not) or whether scientists have information on these subjects (they do). The issue is that these authors—and others like them—have made a wrong conclusion about the sufficiency of the Bible because they have misunderstood the subject matter of counseling.

To determine the extent of material sufficiency for a given issue, we must first rightly understand the nature of that issue. With respect to the examples above, I would say that, for example, counseling is not primarily about an exchange of highly technical information developed by neuroscientists. It is an exchange of wisdom about life's problems. Counselors who deny sufficiency on the grounds noted above have done so based on a faulty understanding of the kind of information that is required in counseling.

There is a second way to advance the view that the resources in Scripture are limited concerning counseling. This tactic involves pointing to very difficult and complicated counseling problems and attempting to

---

21. Johnson, *Psychology & Christianity*, 116.

show that these problems involve a level of complexity that is not covered in the Bible. Difficult problems are presented using secular, sometimes technical, language to describe the counseling problem. Because the Bible does not replicate that type of language, this makes it appear that the Bible is not concerned with the kinds of problems being discussed.

One book-length example of this, edited by Stephen Greggo and Timothy Sisemore, is entitled *Counseling and Christianity: Five Approaches*. The book relates the story of a man named Jake who has a set of very complex counseling and medical problems. Jake comes from a very troubled background, has a history of traumatic brain injury, is plagued with troubling nightmares in the aftermath of difficult service in the military, has a child out of wedlock, regularly uses illegal drugs, abuses alcohol, and recently pressured a woman to use drugs and have sex with him. The goal of the book is to observe how five different Christian contributors each implement their unique approach to counseling to help Jake. The book reveals a great deal about the resources available in Scripture and secular therapy and the commitments of the book's contributors to those resources.

The five approaches in the book are levels of explanation, integration, Christian psychology, transformational psychology, and biblical counseling. There is far more to say about the distinctions in these approaches than I can cover here.[22] However, I would note that the only approach that believes in the sufficiency of Scripture for counseling is the biblical counseling approach. The other four argue against this kind of sufficiency and, in one way or another, refuse to ground their counseling in the Bible.[23]

When these other counseling approaches avoid using the Bible, they make a statement about the ability or the appropriateness of the Bible to address Jake's counseling issues. What statement do they make? They are saying that the Bible is less relevant in addressing Jake and his

---

22. See Johnson, *Psychology & Christianity*.
23. See Stephen P. Greggo and Timothy A. Sisemore, eds., *Counseling and Christianity: Five Approaches* (Downers Grove, IL: IVP Academic, 2012), Plante, 61; McMinn, 87; Langberg, 118; Moon, 141.

problems than the techniques of secular therapy. There is a significant problem with this.

A careful survey of the interventions of each of the counseling practitioners reveals that they each spent time addressing four of the same issues. Each approach wanted to engage Jake in a meaningful relationship, make sure his medical and physical needs were addressed, engage in crisis care to ensure he did not harm himself, and address the complex elements in his past. Though each approach desired to deal with the same core issues, they went about this work in different ways. The levels of explanation, integration, Christian psychology, and transformational psychology approaches engaged Jake using secular therapeutic interventions. Conversely, the biblical counseling approach engaged Jake using biblical interventions. Stuart Scott, who articulated the biblical approach to counseling Jake, made this observation about using the Bible and other sources of information.

> Most vital to every practitioner is that his or her counseling flow directly out of the Scriptures and into practical life application. There is an operative conviction that God's Word is relevant to all of life and can be practically applied to every heart and every circumstance of difficulty. While this does not imply that Scripture is the only source of information in the counseling process, biblical counselors are consistent in their detailed biblical analysis of information and in their overwhelming focus on special revelation—the Bible—which alone is infallible and authoritative truth.[24]

Scott argues that it is crucial to use the Bible to address the issues that he and his fellow contributors agree are essential in counseling Jake. He is clear that this does not mean the Bible is the only source of information possible in the counseling process. He nevertheless finds more than enough information in the Scriptures to provide God's perspective on Jake's problems.

---

24. Stuart Scott, in Greggo and Sisemore, *Counseling and Christianity*, 158.

The five different approaches agree on the *issues* that need to be addressed in Jake's counseling. The disagreement among the approaches concerns which resources need to be used in responding to these issues, whether biblical or secular. Scott's biblical counsel demonstrates that the important issue is not whether the Bible has sufficient resources to help Jake. He shows that it does. The issue is whether counseling practitioners are willing to mine Scripture for resources relevant to Jake's problems and share God's Word with him or are unwilling to do this in favor of embracing other resources.

These case studies of actual counseling end up being compelling evidence for the sufficiency of Scripture. When biblical counselors use the Scriptures to understand specific problems of particular counselees and to chart a course toward change, this confirms the sufficiency of Scripture. Scott used the Bible in this case not to argue for sufficiency in general terms but to show the sufficiency of Scripture in Jake's life. When biblical counselors can demonstrate how Scripture comes to life to change the difficulties of real counselees, they establish that the material sufficiency of Scripture extends to the work of counseling.

The Sufficiency of Scripture for Trenyan

It is in that spirit that we return to Trenyan. I got to know this young woman over a period of months in the context of counseling. We met every week and talked about her troubles and what God says about them. As I listened to her situation, I came to understand why Trenyan would cut her legs the way she had been doing. As it turned out, she had been having a great deal of trouble with her parents. Her mom had committed adultery with someone in the church her parents attended, a friend of Trenyan's dad. The news of this affair had sent shock waves through their church and home.

Trenyan began to witness a level of hostility and anger in her home that she had never experienced before. Her parents would scream at one another and yell obscenities back and forth. Sometimes these arguments would turn violent. It created a horribly toxic atmosphere. This situation was particularly painful for Trenyan because her family had always been very stable. This awful situation was made worse because Trenyan's parents would each appeal to her to take their side. Trenyan's dad would try to get her to agree that her mom was an immoral woman and an awful wife. Trenyan's mom would plead with her to understand that she did not really know her father and that he had been emotionally distant for years.

The pressure was crushing. Trenyan would retreat to her room, but it did not work. She could hear her parents arguing through the closed door. At times they would try to catch her to bring her into the dispute. Trenyan needed a break from the pressure and wanted help but was too humiliated to talk to anyone at her church.

Then Trenyan discovered a way to get a break. Whenever Trenyan saw blood, she had a physical reaction and would pass out. One night, Trenyan was so overwhelmed with sorrow that she made a small cut on her leg and steeled her resolve to look down at the wound and watch the blood come out. When she did she, predictably, passed out. It seemed to work. Losing consciousness provided a break from her misery, and when she awoke she was preoccupied with cleaning up the mess and covering her tracks. Over time and with increasing frequency, Trenyan sought relief from the pressures by cutting herself.

However, her attempt to find a break from her pain in this way only *seemed* to work. Cutting brought new trouble into her life. She was experiencing shame over her behavior that was creating distance in her relationship with the Lord. Keeping her secret was also creating even more separation in her relationship with her parents and was damaging her friendships. She was also experiencing increasing pain as the cuts on her legs multiplied. On a few occasions, cuts became infected and were even more painful. Trenyan began to fear that she would need medical treatment, which only increased her personal shame and distance in her relationships.

Trenyan's method of dealing with her pain made a certain kind of twisted sense. It had an immediate payoff. But she was beginning to understand that the cost of her behavior was not worth any benefit. By the time she realized this, she did not know how to break the cycle. She continued to keep her secret and to suffer silently.

Trenyan and I had dozens of conversations about all manner of issues. The most important element of our conversations together came to be Psalm 55. Trenyan would tell you that this passage of Scripture was the most important one in giving her hope and changing her situation.

Psalm 55 Captures Trenyan's Experience of Pain

In Psalm 55, David is in great personal anguish. God did not inspire him to describe the details of the situation he was facing. Instead, God inspired him to relate his response to the pressure in a prayer to God. A portion of David's cry to God in Psalm 55:4–8, 12–14 says,

> My heart is in anguish within me; the terrors of death have fallen upon me. Fear and trembling come upon me, and horror over-whelms me. And I say, "Oh, that I had wings like a dove! I would fly away and be at rest; yes, I would wander far away; I would lodge in the wilderness; I would hurry to find a shelter from the raging wind and tempest." . . . For it is not an enemy who taunts me—then I could bear it; it is not an adversary who deals insolently with me—then I could hide from him. But it is you, a man, my equal, my companion, my familiar friend. We used to take sweet counsel together; within God's house we walked in the throng.

As Trenyan and I looked at this passage, we found much that Trenyan could identify with.

In the first place, David is honest about his overwhelming pain: "My heart is in anguish within me." There is no attempt on David's part to hide his pain from God. He comes before God and deals honestly with his difficulties. Second, the source of David's pain is someone very close to him: "It is not an enemy who taunts me . . . it is not an adversary who deals insolently with me. . . . But it is you, a man, my equal, my companion, my familiar friend." David is not just in pain but is experiencing the same kind of pain as Trenyan—the painful taunts of someone close. Finally, David wants to escape: "Oh, that I had wings like a dove! I would fly away and be at rest." David shares a desire for escape that Trenyan understands very deeply. Though David wrote this psalm, and though his situation was undoubtedly different from Trenyan's, he uttered words in response to his pain that Trenyan could have composed word for word.

Trenyan and I camped on this idea for a while together. It was so encouraging for her to know that there were words in the Bible that gave expression to her sorrow. It was comforting to know that her desire to escape from her pain was not freakish. Instead she dealt with the same pressures and temptations as other people of faith—even authors of Scripture!

Psalm 55 Points Trenyan to a Better Path

Psalm 55 does more than identify with Trenyan's pain. There is the description of a different and better path forward. Even as David describes similar pain as that which Trenyan is experiencing, he does something that she does not do. David begins the psalm with these words: "Give ear to my prayer, O God, and hide not yourself from my plea for mercy! Attend to me, and answer me; I am restless in my complaint and I moan" (Ps. 55:1–2). He continues a bit later, "But I call to God, and the LORD will save me. . . . Cast your burden on the LORD, and he will sustain you; he will never permit the righteous to be moved" (Ps. 55:16, 22).

David expresses pain and a desire to flee, but the crucial difference between Trenyan and David is that the psalmist turns his pain into an occasion to pour his heart out to God. My counselee turned her pain into an occasion to retreat into her own heart and bring physical pain into her life. After identifying with David, Trenyan needed to learn from him. Through David, God taught Trenyan how to reach out to him in her moments of pain: "Give ear to my prayer, O God." Trenyan learned that through the immediacy and dynamism of prayer, it was possible to cast her burden on the Lord. Trenyan learned that even when challenging circumstances remain unchanged, she could reach out to God and he would help her—in the moment and in person—not hiding himself from her plea for mercy.

Part of my counseling with Trenyan involved attempts to change her circumstances. We looked at biblical methods of approaching her parents with resolution, love, and respect to try to resolve conflicts. Unfortunately, Trenyan's parents never heeded any counsel. They continued to fight, and their marriage eventually came to a bitter end. Counseling with Trenyan was a success, though. Years later I presided over her marriage to a wonderful and godly Christian man. I watched at the wedding as her parents, still embittered toward one another, had come to see their daughter as a source of strength in each of their own conflicted lives. Trenyan learned that trials do not require a retreat inward. They can, instead, become an occasion to grow in God's grace and be a conduit of that grace to others who need it.

The source of the changes in Trenyan is none other than God himself. His actions of love and grace, as expressed in his Word and applied to Trenyan, resulted in change. God exposed motives through his active use of the Scriptures (Heb. 4:12–13). He also answered many of Trenyan's and my own prayers because of his love (Ps. 62:8). God's own kind work of upholding and strengthening his child, Trenyan, through his mercy and grace caused vital change in her time of need (Heb. 4:14–16).

The Evidence of Sufficiency:
The Relevance of the Entire Bible to Problems

All that positive change grew out of just one passage of Scripture, Psalm 55. There were many other passages that we examined together, but the principle passage God used to transform Trenyan was one psalm. Consider and be amazed that an entire life can be transformed from just one passage of Scripture. When I ponder this, I am astounded that anyone would say the Bible is not sufficient for someone like Trenyan.

It has been common for biblical counselors to defend the sufficiency of Scripture by turning to a few classic passages. Psalm 19, 2 Timothy 3:10–17, and 2 Peter 1:3–4 have all been used with great regularity and to profound effect. I am thankful for the attention these passages have received and have even gotten mileage out of them myself.[25] Trenyan's story reminds us that these passages are not the only ones that bear on the sufficiency of Scripture. As we see when we look at Trenyan's life, Psalm 55 is a passage that proves sufficiency as much as 2 Timothy and 2 Peter. The application of Psalm 55 to Trenyan's life demonstrates that any passage we use to understand the difficulties of counselees and to aid their move toward change becomes an indispensable text in the argument for the sufficiency of Scripture for counseling. We need not rely on only a handful of passages to prove the sufficiency of Scripture because we have an entire Bible that God has given us to change our lives and demonstrate the sufficiency of Scripture for counseling.

---

25. Stuart Scott and Heath Lambert, eds., *Counseling the Hard Cases: True Stories Illustrating the Sufficiency of God's Resources in Scripture* (Nashville: B&H Academic, 2012), ch. 1.

CHAPTER 3

BIBLICAL COUNSELING

and a

THEOLOGY OF COMMON GRACE

When committed Christians have adopted counseling approaches to the left of biblical counseling, they typically have done so for two reasons. First, they have rejected the notion that Scripture is sufficient for counseling. I addressed this issue most directly in chapter 2 on a theology of Scripture. I have also labored to have this entire book be an argument for the counseling sufficiency of the theological themes that Scripture describes. All of God's resources in Scripture— his teaching about who he is, the nature of Christ's person and work, the operations of the Holy Spirit, the biblical categories of sin and suffering, everything—come together to create a sufficient resource for counseling.

A second reason some Christians have embraced counseling approaches other than biblical counseling is because they do not want to be guilty of rejecting helpful counseling interventions found in secular psychology that exist outside the Bible. Stated positively, they want to use every helpful resource and counseling intervention that is available in God's world. They do not want to disregard something helpful simply because it is not included in the pages of the Bible. Stanton Jones, in his book *Psychology: A Student's Guide*, wrote,

> Psychological approaches can help people who are depressed, anxious, experiencing relational conflict, and the like, and in the absence of a strong justification for withholding the kind of help that tangible, empirically validated approaches offer to such persons, Christian compassion should incline us toward helping them.[1]

This quote from Jones grounds the use of extra-biblical resources in Christian compassion and a desire to offer help. The implication is that if one chooses not to use such "tangible" and "empirically validated" resources which offer help, then that person is not compassionate or is needlessly withholding the maximum amount of care from a person experiencing trouble.

This book will introduce you to numerous people. Their names and other identifying information have been changed to protect their privacy, but their stories are real. You have already met Trenyan, Rick, Wendy, and Gail. Later you will meet Jenny, Scott, Drew, Amber, Sean, and Sarah. These people sought counseling help for problems that threatened to ruin their lives. When we talk about what resources we use in counseling, we are talking about those people. This is not merely an academic debate. It is an issue that tests our personal commitment to offer the best available care to actual people with serious problems. Our desire to demonstrate the love of Christ to people God sends to us should lead us to a commitment to offer the best care available to our counselees.

The call to be compassionate counselors requires that a thoroughgoing theology of biblical counseling must not only address the sufficient resources for counseling within Scripture but must also address the relevance of resources that exist outside of Scripture. This is an issue that has the highest practical and personal implications for counselors. We must consider this matter very carefully if we are to be compassionate.

---

1. Stanton L. Jones, *Psychology: A Student's Guide* (Wheaton IL: Crossway, 2014), 89.

Considering the matter in this way requires that we understand the doctrine of common grace.

Common Grace

Common grace is the good kindness of God that he shows to all people regardless of whether they have experienced the salvation that comes through Jesus Christ alone. It is called common because it comes to all people—believers and unbelievers alike. It is referred to as grace because this kindness of God is undeserved. People are born in sin and so do not deserve any blessing from God, only judgment. That God would allow people to live and to experience many blessings of life is a great kindness.

One place in Scripture where we see common grace is in 1 Timothy 4:10: "For to this end we toil and strive, because we have our hope set on the living God, who is the Savior of all people, especially of those who believe." Paul says that God is the Savior of all people, and yet Paul does not believe that everyone will be saved. God is especially the Savior of those who believe in Jesus Christ, but that does not exclude the possibility of him being the Savior of all people in some other, lesser sense. Every person, whether a believer or an unbeliever who has been ill, injured, or in trouble and has recovered, been restored, or rescued, has been saved by God in some temporal sense if not in the ultimate eternal sense. In this chapter we discuss three different categories of God's common grace to believers and unbelievers.

Divine Moral Provision

In chapter 8, I note the corruption of mankind and describe the human race as totally depraved. I am clear that this total depravity means that sin has affected every aspect of mankind. It does not mean that people are as sinful as it is possible for them to be. Such an exhaustive level of depravity would make the world miserable and unlivable. We have been spared such a horrendous existence because of God's common grace.

The Bible teaches that, in his kindness, God works to restrain the evil that human beings commit. He restricts people from harming Cain with a mark and promise of retribution (Gen. 4:15). God disrupts the sinfulness of the people at Babel by throwing their language into confusion (Gen. 11:6–9). He keeps Abimelech from committing adultery with Sarah (Gen. 20:6). He restrains the man of lawlessness (2 Thess. 2:7). These are just a few examples.

The point is that God restrains the sinful nature of mankind so that we do not do all the bad things it is possible to do. The remarkable grace of God spares us in this way from ourselves. When we discover this teaching in the Bible, we should be thankful to God for his common grace to all people, providing moral restraint on those who are inclined toward evil.

Divine Physical Provision

Not only does God provide for us morally by restraining our sin, he also provides for our physical needs in his common grace. One of the clearest places we see this in the Bible is in Matthew 5:43–45:

> "You have heard that it was said, 'You shall love your neighbor and hate your enemy.' But I say to you, love your enemies and pray for those who persecute you, so that you may be sons of your Father who is in heaven. For he makes his sun rise on the evil and on the good, and sends rain on the just and on the unjust."

Jesus urges his hearers to be like God in being kind to people who hate them. The point he makes is that God is kind to all by sending the sun and the rain to all people, believers and unbelievers alike. You do not have to be saved to enjoy the sun at the beach or to have your crops watered. God sends those blessings to everyone. When Jesus commands his people to be kind to their enemies, he grounds that exhortation in God's common grace.

Divine Intellectual Provision

God's common grace also makes provision for our intellectual life. Saved and unsaved people are able to know correct information. Many unbelievers have access to more accurate information about the world than Christians often do. In 1 Corinthians 1 and 2, Paul makes a distinction between the wisdom of the world and the wisdom of God. Paul's point is clearly to show that God, through the cross of Christ, wants to make a mockery of the so-called wisdom of the world. God does not want people to trust in their own wisdom, so he destroys it through his own wisdom, the wisdom of the cross. However, Paul mentions that there are blessings from this worldly wisdom. Although worldly wisdom does not lead to salvation, good things come from it, like the production of useful information and wealth (1 Cor. 1:26). These are blessings we receive even when trusting in them leads to our destruction.

The knowledge that believers and unbelievers possess about the world is real knowledge that comes from Jesus Christ. John calls Jesus "the true light, which gives light to everyone" (John 1:9). Jesus Christ is the living Word who illumines all the thoughts of everyone in his world.[2] The minds of people work properly—even the minds of unbelievers— because Jesus Christ gives common grace that allows them to function.

When you understand the biblical teaching on common grace, you understand how much we need and use the benefits of this grace every single day. Consider all of the common grace that is necessary for you to be reading these words right now. I learned how to read and write from numerous people—believers and unbelievers alike—who experienced the grace of God in knowing things I needed to learn. I am writing these words on a laptop that requires materials produced by all sorts of people with incredible intellectual abilities to know how to translate my keystrokes into words that appear on the screen. As I write this, I am quite ill. Last night my wife went to the pharmacy on roads paved by people who did not need to be Christians to do their work with

---

2. D. A. Carson, *The Gospel According to John* (Leicester, England: InterVarsity, 1991), 123–24.

excellence. A pharmacist gave medicine to my wife, and it is working to make me feel better, whether or not the people involved in its sale and production know Christ. The publisher, Zondervan, has contracted with countless people to proofread my words, to print them on paper, and to deliver copies all over the world. This book was delivered to you because someone figured out the best way to get it in your hands. Some skilled person made the chair you are likely sitting on as you read it.

You get the point. You could not live your life—or even read the book you are holding—if God did not provide common grace to the world. God's common grace requires gratitude from Christians because this is one of the main ways God is kind to his people. As an overflow of our gratitude for God's kindness to Christians, we must use and be grateful for the good gifts produced by unbelievers through God's common grace. It is sinful for Christians, who know the God who distributes the grace, to fail to be thankful for the display of that grace.

When we speak about common grace in the area of counseling, the most important issue is God's intellectual provision to all people. God enables the minds of unbelievers to operate and to be able to know true things. Secular psychologists are able to make discoveries that are often true and helpful. Christian theology requires biblical counselors to be grateful for this true information. But our response to secular psychology must include more than appreciation grounded in common grace. As Christians we must balance our appreciation with caution, because the doctrine of common grace is held in check by another theological reality—the doctrine of the noetic effects of sin.

Common Grace and the Noetic Effects of Sin

In the chapter on sin, I will explain that the noetic effects refer to the impact of sin on our thinking. Because we are sinners, our minds do not operate as they should. In Ephesians 4:18 Paul says, "They are darkened in their understanding, alienated from the life of God because of the ignorance that is in them, due to their hardness of heart." The Bible teaches that our hard hearts darken our understanding and render us ignorant. As sinners we cannot think properly.

Because of God's common grace, unbelievers are able to know true things, but common grace does not guarantee that everything an unbeliever says is correct. Because of the injurious impact of sin on the mind, our thinking is damaged most significantly on the issues of maximum importance in our life.[3]

Romans 1:18–23 teaches that God has plainly revealed himself to humanity in the things that he has made, but human beings in their sin suppress that truth. Unbelievers are dishonest about issues that relate to God and his authoritative rule in the world. God does not use common grace to overcome the sinful suppressing of creation's testimony to its Divine Author. Common grace makes it possible for unbelievers to know facts, but the noetic effects of sin make it impossible for them to embrace the most important facts. The closer unbelievers get in counseling to issues having to do with God, the ultimate meaning of life, and the problems that plague humanity, the greater will be the impact of the noetic effects of sin on their thinking and the more cautious Christians must be in accepting the information they produce.

Abraham Kuyper grasped this quite well in his work. Describing the created order as a building made of stone, wood, paint, and metal, he says,

> We can certainly acquire correct knowledge about stone and wood and paint and metal, but we can no longer arrive at a correct view of the style, the fundamental idea, the theme, and the goal of this building called creation. Surely science does not consist simply in examining wood and stone and metal, but an investigation most properly and essentially becomes science when it succeeds in

---

3. Some Christian counselors have confused the doctrine of common grace with the doctrine of general revelation. This is an important mistake because general revelation is authoritative, whereas common grace is held in check by the noetic effects of sin. For a longer discussion of this matter, see appendix B.

capturing a mirror image of the whole. Precisely for that reason the darkening of sin obstructs the acquisition not of the knowledge of the details but knowledge in its more exalted and nobler sense.

As long as you look at creation while excluding human beings and discounting God, science still conjures up wonders by its precise dissecting of things and tracing the laws governing their motion. But no sooner do you take humans into account than you arrive at spiritual questions that bring you into contact with the center of all spiritual life, namely, with God. At this moment, all certainty vanishes, as one school of scientific opinion stands alongside another, as one paradigm opposes another, until at last pervasive despair overcomes the researchers. Their knowledge advances, of course, as long as they are studying the human body and can observe anything of the human psyche that comes to physical expression, but the moment they enter the characteristically *spiritual* arena, the outcome is speculation and assumption, with one theory displacing another theory, leading finally to doubt and skepticism.[4]

Kuyper says that science does not merely engage in observation about the building that is creation; it also seeks to understand and provide interpretations for those observations. Kuyper refers to the interpretations of these observations as "knowledge in its more exalted and nobler sense." He says that sin most darkens our thinking at this exalted place where we consider the center of human life—people and their relationship to God.

---

4. Abraham Kuyper, *Wisdom and Wonder: Common Grace in Science and Art* (Grand Rapids, MI: Christian's Library, 2011), 56, emphasis in original. On page 79, Kuyper develops the point further: "To the extent that results are governed by factual observation, obtained by weighing and measuring and counting, all scientific researchers are equal. As soon as people move above this lower kind of science, however, to higher forms of science, at that point the personal subject makes a contribution, in terms of which the difference between the 'natural' man and the 'spiritual' man comes into play. This phenomenon is definitely not restricted to the science of theology, but is present in every spiritual science, including the philosophical framework for the natural sciences." Kuyper here helps us to make a distinction between the observations of scientists (lower kind of science) and the interpretations of those observations where they seek to understand and interpret what they saw (higher forms of science). Kuyper states that as you move from the lower form of science in observation to the higher form in interpretation, it becomes important whether one is an unbelieving natural man or a believing spiritual man.

As far as this truth relates to counseling, we can say that the doctrine of common grace teaches that the findings of secular psychology will often be accurate. But that assertion must be balanced with a Christian understanding of the doctrine of the noetic effects of sin: that our thinking is corrupted—and is corrupted most seriously—on the issues of human existence that secular therapy seeks to address. This requires Christians to evaluate secular psychology very carefully. As with all unbelievers in any discipline, God's common grace allows them to know true things. And yet secular therapy, unlike meteorology, for example, addresses matters uniquely related to the center of human existence (who we are, what is wrong with us, what needs to happen in order to change) where the noetic effects of sin are most prominent.

The biblical counseling movement has tried to balance each of these theological themes in its evaluation of secular psychology. Some have accused the biblical counseling movement of rejecting the possibility of there being accurate information outside of Scripture. They point to biblical counselors not utilizing the interventions of secular therapy, constructing instead a uniquely biblical approach to counseling. It is true that the biblical counseling movement has refused to include secular interventions in its counseling model. Yet this refusal does not mean a denial of the doctrine of common grace. In the rest of this chapter I will evaluate secular psychology in a way that is theologically consistent with the truths of common grace and the noetic effects of sin we have been examining. I will argue in theological terms that it is unnecessary to include the findings of secular psychology in a faithful and relevant counseling approach that is uniquely biblical.

A Theological Evaluation of Secular Psychology

In spite of attempts to carefully balance a belief in common grace with the noetic effects of sin, some have argued that the biblical counseling movement has rejected science. One such objection is from David

Murray. Murray pushes back against an "extreme sufficiency" position, saying, "The sufficiency of Scripture does not mean that we should shun every nonbiblical source of knowledge."[5] A bit later, Murray elaborates:

> In some areas we need to use our Bible as spectacles to read and learn from the knowledge God has distributed and deposited in the world. If we refuse to do this, if we say that we must separate ourselves from all knowledge outside the Bible, there is the risk of inadvertently undermining the sufficiency of Scripture. It is effectively saying that the Bible is not sufficient to help us read this world and learn from it, so we must separate ourselves from it. I believe the Bible is sufficient to enable us to read science and separate the wheat from the chaff, to separate valid observations and conclusions from the false, and so make use of the knowledge that God, in His "common grace" or "providence," has made known in His creation.[6]

Murray is making the same point I have been making in this chapter. God has given good gifts to his people in the world, and we must use the Bible to tell the difference between those things that result from common grace and those that result from the noetic effects of sin.

The problem is that Murray believes he has articulated a theological position at odds with the biblical counseling movement.[7] Murray

---

5. David P. Murray, *Christians Get Depressed Too: Hope and Help for Depressed People* (Grand Rapids, MI: Reformation Heritage, 2010), 107. Murray places "extreme sufficiency" in quotes, using the language from Eric Johnson's critique of the biblical counseling movement. It is clear that he has the biblical counseling movement in mind when he makes this observation. See Eric L. Johnson, *Foundations for Soul Care: A Christian Psychology Proposal* (Downers Grove, IL: InterVarsity, 2007), 121.

6. Murray, *Christians Get Depressed*, 110.

7. Murray specifically links this concern with the biblical counseling movement in a blog he wrote entitled *Where Is Biblical Counseling's Ken Ham?* Murray says, "I'd like to see the biblical counseling movement mature and develop, and it could do so by taking a leaf out of Ken Ham's book. When compared with biblical counselors, Ham and his creationist colleagues seem to be much more informed about the science they are interacting with and much more capable and courageous in entering the scientists' world, taking the scientists' facts and findings, and re-framing them within the biblical worldview. I don't see so much evidence of that in biblical counseling, a field I read a lot in, teach in, and do almost daily as well. What is much more common is disinterest in, hostility towards, or even outright rejection of the whole

is not alone in expressing this concern.[8] The criticism of the biblical counseling movement seems to be that there is a confessional belief that common grace allows unbelievers to know the truth, but the information they produce is of no real use. The critics' point is that if biblical counselors really believe in common grace, they must demonstrate their belief by actually utilizing the findings and therapies of secular psychologists.

This objection is a concern because it overlooks the overwhelming evidence that biblical counselors have been engaged with scientific information that exists outside the Bible.[9] It also does not properly articulate the essential balance between common grace and the noetic effects of sin.

Critics accuse those who are skeptical of using the interventions

---

field of psychology and pharmacology IN PRACTICE." David P. Murray, "Where Is Biblical Counseling's Ken Ham?," February 7, 2014, accessed April 23, 2015, http://headhearthand.org/blog/2014/02/07/where-is-biblical-counselings-ken-ham/.

8. Johnson, *Foundations for Soul Care*, 111–25.

9. From the beginning of the movement, biblical counselors have been characterized by robust engagement with the world of secular psychology. As a brief summary, see some of the following examples: Jay E. Adams, *Competent to Counsel* (Grand Rapids, MI: Zondervan, 1986), 1–19. Adams interacts with the work of Freud and Rogers, who were the dominant figures at the time and who still exert influence today. Jay E. Adams, *What about Nouthetic Counseling: A Question and Answer Book with History, Help, and Hope for the Christian Counselor* (Grand Rapids, MI: Baker, 1977), 31. Adams appropriates the language of secular behavior therapy in his use of dehabituation and rehabituation. Jay E. Adams, *The Christian Counselor's Manual* (Grand Rapids, MI: Baker, 1973), 191–216. To be clear, I object to using such language as I believe it imports unhelpful concepts into the biblical framework. At the very least, this is evidence of the founder of the biblical counseling movement interacting with and utilizing the findings of secular people. See Robert D. Smith, *The Christian Counselor's Medical Desk Reference*; Edward T. Welch, *Blame It on the Brain?: Distinguishing Chemical Imbalances, Brain Disorders, and Disobedience*; Dr. Jim Halla, *Depression through a Biblical Lens: A Whole-Person Approach*; Dr. Laura Hendrickson, *Finding Your Child's Way on the Autism Spectrum: Discovering Unique Strengths, Mastering Behavior Challenges*; Dr. Laura Hendrickson with Elyse M. Fitzpatrick, *Will Medicine Stop the Pain?: Finding God's Healing for Depression, Anxiety, and Other Troubling Emotions*; Dr. Charles D. Hodges, *Good Mood, Bad Mood: Help and Hope for Depression and Bipolar Disorder*; Stuart Scott and Heath Lambert, eds., *Counseling the Hard Cases*, see especially 60–66, 90–92, 204–7; Marshall Asher and Mary Asher, *The Christian's Guide to Psychological Terms*. There are far too many references to mention from the *Journal of Pastoral Practice* (the name of the *Journal of Biblical Counseling* when Jay Adams was the editor). A few examples are Joseph R. Vander Veer Jr., "Pastoral Psychopharmacology," *Journal of Pastoral Practice*, vol. III, no. 2 (1979): 65–73; James E. Alpaugh, "Indicators of Learning Disability," *Journal of Pastoral Practice*, vol. II, no. 1 (1978): 30–41; Gary G. Plumlee, "Adlerian Theory and Pastoral Counseling," *Journal of Pastoral Practice*, vol. III, no. 4 (1979): 32–36; Richard A. Heckman, "The Tennessee Self-Concept Scale As Applied to Three High School Students," *Journal of Pastoral Practice*, vol. VIII, no. 4 (1987): 32–41; Edward Welch, "Sin or Sickness? Biblical Counseling and the Medical Model," *Journal of Pastoral Practice*, vol X, no. 2 (1990): 28–39.

of secular psychology of rejecting common grace. These critics do not appreciate the doctrine of the noetic effects of sin. They also are relying on a deficient evaluation of the different levels of knowledge available in psychology. Below I examine three such levels in order to help us rightly balance common grace with the noetic effects of sin.

Secular Psychology: Three Levels of Analysis

A simplistic assessment of psychology would be one that either completely rejects the information in the discipline or completely accepts it. Christians who believe in common grace *and* the noetic effects of sin must reject these extremes. It is most helpful to understand the information available in psychology as existing on three levels: observations, interpretations, and interventions.

The *observations* of psychologists consist of the information they come to know through their careful work. Observations are the information all people come to know through God's common grace. We can be glad that believers and unbelievers alike know all kinds of things, including information about weather patterns, how anesthesia works, how fertilizer makes flowers grow, and innumerable other things. Secular psychologists have access to all kinds of observations in their own field, including how human behavior often works, much empirical research, the diagnosis of mental illness, and a massive body of brain research—to name just a few. These observations may be closely related to counseling or tangential to it, they may be right or wrong, or they may be debated. These are the discoveries psychologists consistently compile over the years as they grow our information, correct our presuppositions, are themselves proven false, or their discoveries shown to be incomplete. These observations are reported to us and demand our attention and evaluation.

Depending on the nature of what is studied, these observations realize the smallest impact from the noetic effects of sin. The noetic effects still operate; they keep the observers from giving God glory for what they see, and they make it impossible to *guarantee* the accuracy of the observations. Still, the negative results are smallest at the observational level, and we can have the highest confidence in the operations of God's common grace. But people never merely observe. They always provide meaning to what they see. This is where the next level of evaluation comes in.

The *interpretations* of psychologists are when they seek to understand the information produced by their observations. Science moves from observation to interpretation, which Kuyper referred to as the move to science in "its more exalted and nobler sense." The belief that someone could make an uninterpreted observation is a myth. As John Frame has argued,

> There are no "brute facts," facts that are devoid of interpretation. All facts are what they are by virtue of God's interpretation of them. And just as facts are inseparable from God's interpretation of them, so our understanding of facts is inseparable from *our* interpretation of them. Stating a fact and interpreting it are the same activity.[10]

No mechanism exists to separate our observations from our interpretations. We seek to make sense out of the information we come to grasp based on the commitments we cherish.

The most significant commitment that any person will cherish has to do with his belief in God. We are either children of God or children of wrath. We are God's enemies or his friends. No more stark reality could characterize the human person. When unbelievers come to know facts, they interpret those facts as someone who does not love and trust the God of the Bible. When believers come to know facts, they will eventually interpret those facts as worshipers of the living God.

To use an example from outside psychology, geologists do not merely *observe* fossils. They make sense of those fossils by attempting to discern the time of their origin. Unbelieving geologists never trace

---

10. John M. Frame, *The Doctrine of the Knowledge of God* (Phillipsburg, NJ: P&R, 1987), 140, emphasis in original.

fossils to a personal God from several thousand years ago, but to impersonal forces several billion years ago.

It is the same with secular psychologists. They press their observations through the grid of a fallen worldview and will, inevitably, distort their observations with faulty interpretations. The difference between psychology and geology is that the implications for the human race are much more severe in an atheistic interpretation of counseling people than with an atheistic interpretation of rock formations. The interpretations of secular psychologists affect troubled people where they live and experience problems. It is in these interpretations where we see the largest impact of the noetic effects of sin.

The *interventions* of secular psychology are efforts to employ interpreted observations in helping people in counseling. It is at this point that the discipline of secular psychology produces the secular therapies. Secular psychology exists in large part because of an earnest desire to use these therapies to provide care to people experiencing difficulties in their lives. These counseling interventions used by various practitioners and theoreticians come at the end of the process I have been describing. Before a counselor can help someone with a problem, they must first have made an observation about what is wrong. After observing, they must interpret this data in a way consistent with their worldview commitments. After that, they develop an intervention that they believe will correct the problem.

Christians should always be suspicious of the counseling interventions of unbelieving therapists. Such suspicion should not be unique to biblical counselors, but to anyone who understands the importance of worldview commitments in our thinking. The counseling techniques of unbelievers are developed after processing their observations through the grid of an unbelieving worldview. The counseling interventions of unbelievers will be a collage of observations (some true, others untrue) and an atheistic worldview. In one way or another, secular counseling interventions will be distorted because of this unbelieving worldview. It could not be otherwise when you understand the way the noetic effects of sin operate regarding our interpretation of information as close to the center of existence as counseling is.

Secular Psychology: Three Responses

Biblical counselors use the information of secular psychology in at least three different ways.[11] Contributions from unbelievers can *inform* the work of biblical counseling. One obvious example of this helpfulness is medical knowledge. Because human beings have a body as well as a soul, and because the Bible is not sufficient for medical knowledge, physicians are a crucial adjunct to biblical counselors.[12] Our counseling is far inferior when we cannot pair our work with the medical competencies of physicians.

Another example of secular thinkers informing biblical counseling comes in the form of case wisdom. Many secular counselors have spent years talking to thousands of people with serious counseling problems. They have observed many difficulties that we have not. Biblical counselors will object to secular counseling interventions when they deviate from Scripture, but we should be eager to hear the observations they've collected from years of careful work.[13]

Secular contributions can also *provoke* biblical counselors to greater faithfulness in ministering the Scriptures. One great example of this actually has to do with the founding of the biblical counseling movement and the ministry of Jay Adams. Adams was teaching pastoral

---

11. I am indebted to David Powlison for his work on this issue that has been deeply influential on my own thinking. See David Powlison, "Questions at the Crossroads: The Care of Souls and Modern Psychotherapies," in Mark R. McMinn and Timothy R. Phillips, eds., *Care for the Soul: Exploring the Intersection of Psychology and Theology* (Downers Grove, IL: InterVarsity, 2001), 23–61.

12. Here, when I say that the Bible is not sufficient for medical knowledge, I am referring to sufficiency in the particular sense as I discussed in the last chapter.

13. In a chapter I wrote on postpartum psychosis, I made clear that I have counseled a few women who have struggled with this problem, but there are psychiatric professionals who have counseled hundreds of such women. It has been very helpful to me to study their observations of such women to add to my case wisdom. I was able to take my growing wisdom from such analysis and apply the biblical teaching on how to respond to such difficulties in a way that was characterized by greater information. Heath Lambert, "Sarah and Postpartum Depression," in Heath Lambert and Stuart Scott, eds., *Counseling the Hard Cases: True Stories Illustrating the Sufficiency of God's Resources in Scripture* (Nashville: B&H, 2012).

counseling at Westminster Seminary and set out to read all of the counseling literature he could find. The dominant thinkers whose works were influential at the time were Sigmund Freud and Carl Rogers. Adams read these works and became convinced as a Christian theologian that the Scriptures provided better care to hurting people than these secular thinkers did. Pushed by Freud and Rogers into careful biblical reflection, Adams began studying the Scriptures and producing the notes for his course, which were eventually published as *Competent to Counsel*.

Today biblical counselors can and should be spurred by the efforts of secular psychologists to more careful biblical reflection about any number of counseling difficulties. Problems like obsessive compulsive disorder, borderline personality disorder, the response to sexual abuse, and scores more are all in need of careful use of biblical resources. Biblical counselors with a calling for the work will benefit the church when they are informed by the observations of secular psychologists and provoked to dive into the Scriptures for God's solutions.

The provocative function includes a biblical call to critique wrong secular approaches. When biblical counselors go to Scripture and find superior information and interventions, they need to point out the differences and offer a call to faithfulness and more effective care. This critical function is not founded in a rejection of science or common grace. It is founded in a biblical commitment that the noetic effects of sin poison the worldview commitments of unbelievers and keep them from knowing information as correctly as they might.[14]

Finally, secular psychology can *demonstrate* the effectiveness of biblical counseling. I have two things in mind. First, I am thinking about the examples of secular counseling I used in chapter 1 when I referenced the counseling of Peter Kramer and David Burns, who each in his own way demonstrated the effectiveness of biblical counseling. Kramer's counseling failure demonstrated the superiority of biblical solutions to secular ones. Burns's counseling "success" inadvertently

---

14. See David Powlison, "Epistemological Priorities," in "Cure of Souls (and the Modern Psychotherapies)," sec. II, in *Journal of Biblical Counseling* (Spring 2007).

showed the wisdom and practicality of a biblical strategy like thought renewal. Reading the works of both men should encourage us, since they demonstrate the effectiveness of the Bible.

Second, research studies can measure the success of counseling strategies and provide some level of empirical evidence about the effectiveness of biblical interventions. For example, at least one research study provided some evidence that the Christian practice of meditation can reduce anxiety and minimize the experience of pain.[15] Such corroboration can be helpful in a world that increasingly demands empirical justification for counseling practices in general and for insurance reimbursement in particular. As I will make clear below, we need to be careful at this point lest empirical "proof" begins to displace the Bible as our standard of authority. As Christians, we are to be grateful for the common grace of outside corroboration concerning biblical principles.

Biblical counselors embrace common grace. They also embrace the noetic effects of sin. Biblical counselors embrace the observations of secular psychologists as being most readily attributed to God's common grace. Biblical counselors have objected to secular psychology when the noetic effects of sin cause the secular worldview of secular counselors to displace the Christ-centered worldview of the Bible. These two theological themes exist in tension and have been rightly held in tension by the biblical counseling movement in a way those themes have not been by other approaches to counseling.

This evaluation of secular psychology goes a long way toward explaining why biblical counselors have resisted including secular interventions in their counseling system. And yet we need to say more. The warping impact of the noetic effects of sin on the interpretations of secular observations does not corrupt all their observations. We saw in chapter 1 that the fallen worldview of cognitive behavioral therapists

---

15. A. Wachholtz and K. Pargament, "Is spirituality a critical ingredient of meditation?: Comparing the effects of spiritual meditation, secular meditation and relaxation on spiritual, psychological, cardiac, and pain outcomes," *Journal of Behavioral Medicine* 28, no. 4 (August 2005): 369–84.

still allows important elements of their observations to be included in their counseling interventions. Cognitive behavioral therapists rightly observe the importance of thinking. Those observations are helpfully included in their counseling interventions, like the triple-column technique, even though the Christ-centered nature of this approach has been stripped away. I have already argued that the stripping away of Christ is the removal of the most important part of the counseling intervention, and yet we must concede that something helpful remains in this counseling approach. Biblical counselors have been accused of rejecting common grace in general and science in particular for not using such findings. It is essential to our investigation to understand why this charge is untrue.

Rejecting Secular Methods While Embracing Common Grace

Some counseling interventions remain accurate and effective in spite of being filtered through the interpretations of unbelievers with a fallen worldview. Common grace makes it possible that these interpretations of secular observations do not corrupt every single secular intervention. Even when secular counseling interventions are oriented away from Christ, there will still be remnants of Christ's reality, unknown to the counseling practitioner, that remain in the counseling system. It has been the position of the biblical counseling movement that even though this is the case, such truthful interventions do not need to be included in a biblical counseling system. In this section I will advance four reasons why this position is correct and not at odds with a robust view of common grace.

The Sufficiency of Scripture

The Bible affirms that God's common grace in the intellectual realm makes it possible for unbelievers to know correct information. That does not mean that the correct information they come to know renders the Scriptures insufficient for counseling. In other words, no matter how accurate is the information of secular psychologists, their findings are not as valuable as sacred Scripture with regard to its authority and usefulness for counseling.

Biblical counselors contend that counseling is ministry of the Word in conversation just as preaching is ministry of the Word in proclamation. Christians do not accuse preachers of denying common grace because they avoid filling their sermons with scientific information. While hearing them preach, we may be aware of a research study that bears on what they are talking about, but we do not demand that they mention it as proof of their embrace of common grace. Instead, we realize that their job is to herald the Word of God in the ministry of proclamation. In the same way, counselors can believe in the doctrine of common grace to aid the minds of unbelieving secular psychologists while still remaining committed to counsel that is uniquely biblical.

The biblical counseling movement is based on the conviction that God has inspired the Scriptures in such a way that they really are sufficient for the kinds of problems that counselees reveal in counseling. A counselee can say, "Your word is a lamp to my feet and a light to my path" (Ps. 119:105). God intends his Word to shed real light on our path. He means to help us when we have serious problems. If God's Word is a light on our troubled path only when the problems are small, then— quite frankly—his Word is not worth much. God intended us to have light for the path when the problems are big as well as when they are small, and this light is his Word.

Christian counselors insist that psychological approaches can offer tangible help to people who are depressed, anxious, in conflict, and the like. They argue that Christian compassion demands that we use such interventions. Biblical counselors desire to have that kind of compassion. But we do not believe we have to go as far as the secular psychologies to find that compassionate and tangible care. We believe on the authority of Psalm 119:105 and ten thousand other verses that a compassionate God intended to care for his people in the pages of his Word. God wrote the Bible to offer compassionate and tangible care to people who are depressed, anxious, in conflict, and the like. Biblical counselors do not believe God intended to give his church the Bible and then make them wait 1,900 years for real help to come with the advent of modern psychology. The Word of God offers living, practical, and profound help that makes sense to people, that understands their problems, and that points to the power of the living Christ for change. When biblical counselors use the Word of God, they are not operating at a deficit but are offering the kind of relevant, caring, and practical wisdom that is available in no other source.

When biblical counselors emphasize the use of Scripture to the exclusion of other resources, it is not a denial that accurate information is available in other places. It is a statement that no other source of information, no matter how true, offers the kind of help for counseling that God does in his Word. Christians have always believed that we are to be people of the Book. We believe that it is our job to pay attention to the Christian Scripture to find correction for our sin and relief for our pain. It is a secular assumption that we must rely on the resources of secular psychology to get the tangible care in our trouble that is promised in Scripture. As Christians we must assert that we can learn how to offer counseling care when we carefully study the Scriptures. This assertion is not a rejection of common grace. It is an admission that there are things more important than common grace. It is not a rejection of compassionate care. It is an affirmation that God's intention all along was to show true care for his people through his revelation in the Bible.

Prioritizing Biblical Truth above Secular Articulations

The common grace that secular psychologists possess to know correct information does not mean that the articulations of secular psychologists about how to help people are *the* standard for what is true. The Bible, not the findings of psychology, is the standard for what people really need in counseling help. In fact, we will be able to judge which secular counseling approaches contain the most accurate counseling resources by discerning which approaches are the most similar to the strategies that God inspires in Scripture. If it were not for the Scriptures, which serve as our sufficient resource for how to help people in counseling, we would not be able to give thanks for common grace because we would not know when unbelievers were correct or incorrect in their prescribed interventions.

Christian counselors misunderstand this when they insist that counseling interventions must be ratified by some element of psychology before they are usable. There are two ways that Christian counselors do this. Each way places psychology in a position of authority over the Bible.

The first way is when counselors talk about biblical themes using the language of secular therapy. We have seen this in the triple-column technique from David Burns, who unwittingly wrapped a biblical teaching in his secular worldview. God knew about the importance of taking our thoughts captive well before Burns's book was published in 2008. God knew it because he created human beings to change as our minds change. The problem here is not that Burns is wrong. Indeed, we know that God was very kind to allow Burns that correct insight even though he is an unbeliever. The problem is that many Christian counselors will not use a legitimately biblical intervention until it has been articulated by a secular psychologist like David Burns.

One example is the work of Thomas G. Plante. Plante is a professing Christian and a counselor committed to a levels-of-explanation approach. This approach possesses a therapeutic worldview that psychology is the relevant field for the discipline of counseling. Advocates deny that it is necessary or even appropriate to make use of the Scriptures in counseling.[16] As Plante contends for this view in his own work, he makes

---

16. For further explanation, see David G. Myers, "A Levels-of-Explanation View," in Eric L. Johnson, ed., *Psychology & Christianity: Five Views* (Downers Grove, IL: InterVarsity, 2010), 49–75.

use of the "calling protocol."[17] Two elements of the calling protocol are detachment and discernment. Plante describes each of these:

> In the calling protocol, *detachment* refers to working to move away from problematic and sometimes debilitating behaviors, thoughts and attitudes that prevent someone from understanding and nurturing their gifts.[18]

A bit later he describes discernment, saying, "*Discernment* refers to thinking through how we can best live our lives and use our gifts that might lead us to experiences of consolation rather than desolation."[19] This language of detachment and discernment sounds like a very practical and helpful tool. I am thankful for the common grace that would lead to such a useful counseling strategy. The reason I know that it would be helpful is that, in a way similar to Burns, Plante has used secular language to articulate the idea of putting off and putting on, which God revealed a couple of millennia ago to the authors of Scripture. This helpful intervention is not true because a psychologist figured it out (even when that psychologist is a Christian, like Plante), though we are thankful for God's grace in allowing the discovery. This intervention is true—and we know it to be true—because the approach lines up in meaningful ways with the manner in which God made the change process to work, which he revealed in the Bible. No reason exists for Christians to articulate effective counseling techniques in secular language when we have the language of God's Word that makes it true.

A second way that Christian counselors insist that secular psychology must ratify biblical truth is by empirical research. Great pressure

---

17. Diane E. Dreher and Thomas G. Plante, "The Calling Protocol: Promoting Greater Health, Joy, and Purpose in Life," in Thomas G. Plante and Carl E. Thoresen, eds., *Spirit, Science, and Health: How the Spiritual Mind Fuels Physical Wellness* (Westport, CT: Praeger, 2007), 12–42.

18. Thomas G. Plante, "A Levels-of-Explanation Approach," in P. Greggo and Timothy A. Sisemore, eds., *Counseling and Christianity: Five Approaches* (Downers Grove, IL: IVP Academic, 2012), 75, emphasis in original.

19. Plante, "Levels-of-Explanation Approach," in Greggo and Sisemore, *Counseling and Christianity*, 75, emphasis in original.

exists in our culture to demonstrate the effectiveness of counseling interventions with empirical proof. This is an understandable reality when it comes to issues like insurance reimbursement. Insurance companies do not like paying the bills for uncertain treatments. It is one thing to demonstrate counseling effectiveness to unbelievers who do not care about God's testimony in the Scriptures. It is quite a different reality when believers speak to one another as though we cannot affirm a biblical approach to counseling until we have research studies to back it up.

A recent book entitled *Evidence-Based Practices for Christian Counseling and Psychotherapy* seems to make this case. The book seeks to demonstrate to therapists, researchers, students, teachers, and educated laypeople the therapeutic interventions with the best empirical evidence of success. On its own, such work has the possibility of great value. But the Christian editors make a troubling statement as they introduce the book:

> What if the advocate [of a particular therapy] says that the evidence for the efficacy of the treatment is simply that the treatment is consistent with Scripture? While this might be true, many questions remain. The Bible, for example, was written in everyday, lay-person language, rather than in scientific or professional-counseling discourse. Though inspired by God, it uses concepts and terms in a variety of unsystematic ways that do not yield the kind of precision and clarity that we strive for in science or modern professional counseling protocols. As a result, the appeal to Scripture can lead down many different, and sometimes even contradictory, paths. Moreover, how can counselors be sure that the success of their biblically based counseling is not due to factors other than Scripture, for example, the personality or interpersonal style of the counselor or the counselee? We need careful research to tease apart the influence of different factors that in everyday life are blended together and interact with one another. Also, the Bible reveals to us general helpful principles that apply to all people for all time. How can we find out which biblically-based treatments

work with different facets of human beings (e.g., rational, emotional, relational) or with different psychological problems or in different cultures? We cannot answer such questions without careful, empirical investigation.[20]

Two basic arguments advance the case that we need empirical research above biblical assertions. The first is that the Bible is not written using the language of scientific precision. This argument assumes that scientific language is or should be the standard in measuring counseling effectiveness. As I have argued elsewhere, this argument is very weak.[21]

The second argument asserts that without empirical research, we cannot tell whether the biblical interventions work, or whether success should be attributed to the effectiveness of the counselor or to something about the counselee. The problem here is that it wrongly assumes that the Bible teaches only disembodied counseling interventions not relevant to the needs of human beings. It does not do this. In a biblical understanding, effective counsel always springs from a combination of an appropriate biblical strategy used by a counselor with an effective manner and received by a counselee who is willing to hear—all working under the grace of God. The Bible does not base counseling effectiveness on one independent variable but on a combination of variables. There is no reason for man to separate with research what God has joined together.

In any event, the Bible never teaches that we must engage in empirical research to demonstrate the effectiveness of biblical ministry. This idea is actually grounded more in secular empiricism than in a belief in biblical authority. Empiricism teaches that something is not true until science has proven it to be true. Biblical authority teaches that something is true when God declares it to be true. Of course, knowing exactly what God declares to be true is often complicated. But in our

---

20. Everett L. Worthington Jr., Eric L. Johnson, Joshua N. Hook, and Jamie D. Aten, eds., *Evidence-Based Practices for Christian Counseling and Psychotherapy* (Downers Grove, IL: InterVarsity, 2013), 9.

21. Heath Lambert, "The Sufficiency of Scripture, The Biblical Counseling Movement, and the Purpose of This Book" in Lambert and Scott, *Counseling the Hard Cases*, 15–20.

effort to discern truth, God did not prescribe empirical research but gave us a Bible that serves as its own interpreter, a community of faith in which to understand the Bible, and pastors given the task of teaching.[22]

When the worldview of empiricism takes hold in the ministry of a counselor, it means death to the unique kind of counseling effectiveness that is grounded in faithfulness to the Scriptures. Thomas Plante demonstrates this in his defense of the levels-of explanation approach. As Plante explains his counseling approach based exclusively on secular psychology, he describes a number of counseling interventions that often closely resemble biblical approaches like meditation, prayer, forgiveness, gratitude, and acts of service. With every mention of these strategies, Plante is at pains to avoid grounding them in the Bible, but instead always points to secular research studies to indicate their effectiveness and the legitimacy of their use.[23] What must God think when his people talk about the principles of his Word only after they have been filtered through secular psychology?

To be clear, Christians are happy when empirical research demonstrates the truthfulness and effectiveness of the Bible. There are even some places where such information can advance the cause of Christ. But when counselors must demonstrate that everything God says has been empirically demonstrated to work, it undermines biblical authority by prizing the research that "proves" it to be true over God's authoritative statements that *make* it true. It makes empirical proof the authority instead of God's Word.

And what about the times when the biblical strategy does not *appear* to work? The prophet Isaiah was told,

> "Go, and say to this people: 'Keep on hearing, but do not understand; keep on seeing, but do not perceive.' Make the heart of this people dull, and their ears heavy, and blind their eyes; lest they see

---

22. That the Bible serves as its own interpreter is the issue of formal sufficiency that we discussed in chapter 2.

23. Plante, "Levels-of-Explanation Approach," in Greggo and Sisemore, *Counseling and Christianity*, 74–79.

with their eyes, and hear with their ears, and understand with their hearts, and turn and be healed." (Isa. 6:9–10)

Isaiah was given a ministry of hardening. He was told that his job was going to be to minister the Word to people who would not hear and repent. Did this mean that Isaiah's ministry was ineffective? Far from it. In fact, the same prophet who received this difficult summons to ministry would later say,

> "For as the rain and the snow come down from heaven and do not return there but water the earth, making it bring forth and sprout, giving seed to the sower and bread to the eater, so shall my word be that goes out from my mouth; it shall not return to me empty, but it shall accomplish that which I purpose, and shall succeed in the thing for which I sent it." (Isa. 55:10–11)

Any empirical research on the fruitfulness of Isaiah's ministry would have been devastating "proof" of the failure he was in ministry. If such evidence had been available in his day, no insurance company would have paid a dime to Isaiah for reimbursement. But God judges effectiveness based on the degree of faithfulness to the message, not always on the observable fruit. If counselors come to believe that a biblical counseling intervention must be "proven" to work before we can use it, we will move away from faithfulness to the divine message. Doing so will not demonstrate an embrace of common grace, but a compromise of biblical authority.

Assent to False or Debated Information

Common grace teaches that unbelievers can make true observations. It does not promise that every observation will be true. In fact, many of the observations of secular thinkers are false or debated. Before Christians can use those observations, they must know which ones are true and which ones are false. This is often a very challenging task.

One example of this is the problem of mental illness, which has become one of the most significant issues our culture has addressed in recent years. Many have addressed the nature of what mental illness is and how best to offer care to those who are diagnosed with these very serious disorders. The most common contemporary view is that all such disorders—depression, anxiety disorder, and the rest—are biological illnesses of the brain that must be treated medically and with professional secular therapy.[24] The biblical counseling movement has pushed back on this popular opinion, arguing that the problem of mental illness is more complicated than a simple biological explanation allows.[25] The belief that the problem of mental illness requires more complexity than a mere biological answer has met with stiff criticism from inside and outside the church. Some have charged those in the biblical counseling movement with simplicity and reckless disregard for the health and well-being of troubled people.[26]

Such criticism is unwarranted for two significant reasons. First, as I argue in chapter 7, the Bible teaches that human beings consist of both physical and spiritual aspects in one person. When the biblical counseling movement argues that mental illness is more complex than merely physical issues, they are not denying the existence of physical causation or physical complications for many problems. Nor are they denying the importance of physical care for physical problems. They are urging that people must receive the fullness of care they need in both body and soul and are pleading that we not reduce human beings to an exclusively physical element.

---

24. This popular belief has been regularly expressed by Ed Stetzer in articles at *Christianity Today* online. See Ed Stetzer, "Mental Illness and the Church: Some Helpful Honesty from Christian Leaders You May Know," *Christianity Today* (April 9, 2013), http://www.christianity today.com/edstetzer/2013/april/mental-illness-and-church-some-helpful-honesty-from.html. Ed Stetzer, "The Church and Mental Illness Part 1: Aspirations v. Reality," *Christianity Today* (October 2, 2014), http://www.christianitytoday.com/edstetzer/2014/october/church-and -mental-illness-part-1-aspirations-v-reality.html. Ed Stetzer, "The Church and Mental Illness Part 2: Medicine and Therapy," *Christianity Today* (December 9, 2014), http://www.christianity today.com/edstetzer/2014/december/church-and-mental-illness-part-2-.html.

25. Jay E. Adams, *Competent to Counsel* (Grand Rapids, MI: Zondervan, 1986), 26–40; Heath Lambert, *The Gospel and Mental Illness* (Louisville, KY: ACBC, 2014).

26. David Murray, "Dashed Hopes for Biblical Counseling," *HeadHeartHand* (March 28, 2014), http://headhearthand.org/blog/2014/03/28/dashed-hopes-for-biblical-counseling/. Kathryn Joyce, "The Rise of Biblical Counseling," *Pacific Standard* magazine (September 2, 2014).

This position is a reasonable one that comports with care for hurting people as well as with classic Christian theology.

The criticism is also unwarranted because it overlooks that many unbelieving professionals express the same concern about our culture's simplistic understanding of mental illness. A large body of literature exists that has taken great care to argue that the difficulties of those who struggle with mental illness are different and more complicated than the culture's conventional wisdom.[27] The point here is that many of the most well-informed unbelievers disagree about the nature and treatment of mental illness.

When secular authorities disagree amongst themselves about such complicated and technical matters, how are Christians to know which side of the debate is informed by a greater degree of common grace, and which side is informed by a greater degree of the noetic effects of sin? This is a truly challenging problem. The biblical counseling movement has tried to think through such a complex and debated issue, believing that the Bible gives us enough information about the nature of human problems, the function of the human heart, the importance of the body, and the relevance of Scripture to life that we can have meaningful wisdom as we care for people in counseling.[28] The biblical counseling movement's position is obviously controversial, but it is not characterized by reckless treatment either of the biblical text or of secular information. If biblical counselors are wrong, they are joined in their error by many unbelievers standing on a mountain of evidence.

The issue of mental illness is just one example. The point is that there is no demand that Christians must take the popular side in a

---

27. Peter D. Kramer, *Listening to Prozac: The Landmark Book about Antidepressants and the Remaking of the Self*; Irving Kirsch, *The Emperor's New Drugs: Exploding the Antidepressant Myth*; Allen Frances, *Saving Normal: An Insider's Revolt against Out-of-Control Psychiatric Diagnosis, DSM-5, Big Pharma, and the Medicalization of Ordinary Life*; Thomas Szasz, *The Myth of Mental Illness: Foundations of a Theory of Personal Conduct*; Herb Kutchins and Stuart A. Kirk, *Making Us Crazy: DSM: The Psychiatric Bible and the Creation of Mental Disorders*; Paula Caplan, *They Say You're Crazy: The World's Most Powerful Psychiatrists Decide Who's Normal*; Daniel Carlat, *Unhinged: The Trouble with Psychiatry—A Doctor's Revelations about a Profession in Crisis*.

28. One of the most helpful contributions in this regard is Edward T. Welch, *Blame It on The Brain?: Distinguishing Chemical Imbalances, Brain Disorders, and Disobedience* (Phillipsburg, NJ: P&R, 1998), especially 49–70. Here he helps Christians distinguish physical from spiritual issues on biblical grounds.

complex debate to demonstrate their belief in common grace or their compassion for hurting people. As human beings, all of our knowledge is limited. As fallen human beings, all of our knowledge is tainted. There are many dynamic and complicated issues that we are seeking to understand. Christians need to have humble patience with one another, do careful work, and kindly debate the merits of all legitimate perspectives. It is not a rejection of common grace to seek information, embrace biblical wisdom, and articulate a controversial position in the midst of hotly debated issues where some opinions are correct, others are incorrect, and many disagree.

Information That Is Peripheral to the Discipline of Counseling

The doctrine of common grace teaches that God allows unbelievers to know information about all kinds of things, including science. It does not mean that all of that information is equally relevant for all people and all disciplines. It is important to consider this idea in the face of accusations against biblical counselors that they shun certain kinds of scientific information.

In reality, some people, out of interest or necessity, will consume certain kinds of information that will be completely irrelevant to others because of different pursuits and requirements. We cannot judge someone's convictions about the goodness of common grace because they are interested in or require other kinds of information that is not significant for us.

For example, I am fascinated by science. Out of simple interest, I read a lot in the scientific area that I will never use in my ministry. Several weeks ago I read a fascinating study about twins who had been reared apart.[29] What the researchers discovered about the importance of biological factors in our development was fascinating to me as a twin

---

29. T. J. Bouchard, D. T. Lykken, M. McGue, N. L. Segal, A. Tellegen, "Sources of Human Psychological Differences: The Minnesota Study of Twins Reared Apart," *Science* (October 12, 1990): 223–29, 250. Stanton Jones has a fascinating and helpful interaction with this study in Stanton L. Jones, *Psychology: A Student's Guide* (Wheaton, IL: Crossway, 2014), 71–86

myself. Last week I read a very interesting article arguing that salt is not nearly as bad for you as previous government studies have reported.[30] I was so thankful for the information from that report that I added a little extra salt to my fries at lunch. And just the other day, as I sat at a table with some leaders in the biblical counseling movement, we discussed information we had read about public opinion polls for the 2016 presidential election. As far as I am aware, I have never talked about any of that information when doing counseling or when instructing others how to do it.

The point is that, like most biblical counselors, I have access to all kinds of information that I believe to be true and interesting but beside the point when it comes to counseling. The biblical belief in God's common grace does not require us to believe that all true information is equally relevant for the discipline of counseling.

This truth is seen in the connection many draw between counseling and the brain. The brain is an incomprehensibly complicated organ. Researchers have spent an enormous amount of energy studying it and, while we know a great deal more than we did in the past, we are still only at the beginning of what is possible to know. A lot of information about the brain has been coming out in recent years. An example of such information is in a recent book by William M. Struthers, *Wired for Intimacy: How Pornography Hijacks the Male Brain*. Struthers's book is fascinating, filled with great moral conviction about the sinfulness of pornography.

The most distinct element of Struthers's book is his use of copious amounts of research to demonstrate the negative impact that viewing pornography has on the male brain.[31] Struthers shows how pornography actually changes the "neural circuitry" of the human brain as the brain processes sexual images and releases powerful and pleasurable chemicals. Struthers makes it clear that the consequences of pornography are

---

30. Peter Whoriskey, "More Scientists Doubt Salt Is as Bad for You as the Government Says," *Washington Post* (April 6, 2015).

31. William M. Struthers, *Wired for Intimacy: How Pornography Hijacks the Male Brain* (Downers Grove, IL: InterVarsity, 2009), 83–111.

far more sinister than we can see with our naked eye. Christians should be grateful for the evidence of yet another layer of the intense damage from pornography.

As true, interesting, and helpful as the brain research is in *Wired for Intimacy*, and as thankful as I am for the manifold common grace that makes such information possible, that information is not what changes men who look at pornography. I have counseled many such men. I am relatively familiar with the problems they struggle with and with the most effective counseling strategies. In the thousands of conversations I have had, I have never seen a single man turn the corner from enslavement to freedom based on his access to information about the biological damage of pornography to the brain. This fact does not mean the information is untrue or has no value. It means the information is of very little relevance in the change process in counseling. I embrace as true the information that Struthers communicates. I do not believe that such information is the kind that counselors most need when they do their work.[32] We do not have unmediated access to the brain's neural circuitry in order to change the effects of pornography on the brain. We do have mediated access to the brain with the kinds of procedures for change that God has revealed in the Bible and which take place in counseling conversations.

Biblical counselors can be perfectly effective in their work even if they never know the information about the damage pornography does to the brain. They can also be perfectly effective if, knowing it, they never share it with a single counselee, as has been the case in my ministry. This position is true not because the information is incorrect or because biblical counselors do not believe in common grace. It is true because what is relevant in counseling is not the brain research that mankind discovers by common grace, but the principles of change revealed in God's Word.

What I have just said about counseling, the male brain, and pornography is equally true for other matters of human biology. Every biblical

---

32. This information is in my book *Finally Free: Fighting for Purity with the Power of Grace* (Grand Rapids, MI: Zondervan, 2013).

counselor agrees that counselees face medical and physical issues that exist in relationship to the spiritual issues on the table in counseling. Though they admit the existence of these other issues and even agree that they can be related to counseling problems, they nevertheless believe they can help counselees without knowing detailed information about or engaging with such biological information in counseling. This conviction is not unique to biblical counselors. It is also shared by the vast majority of those in the mental health field who do counseling without any medical training whatsoever.

When biblical counselors do their work, they are engaging in a conversation about the questions, problems, and troubles of their counselee and seeking to offer answers, solutions, and help. All manner of information may be true and available to a counselor that is not relevant for the answers, solutions, and help offered in counseling.

To illustrate this principle, it is helpful to think of what it takes to make a car move. The operations of a car require two very different kinds of information. There is practical information for the driver about how to steer the car, shift the gears, apply the gas and brakes, and follow the traffic laws. There is also technical knowledge about how the car's computer system works, how the transmission operates, and how the engine functions. Both kinds of knowledge are required for a car to operate properly, but it is possible to be very competent with one kind of this information without possessing any knowledge of the other. A driver's license is not necessary to replace a timing belt. It is not necessary to know how to rebuild an engine to pass a driver's exam. Car mechanics do not deny the importance of practical information about operating cars when they exclude defensive driving techniques while training other mechanics. Instructors at a traffic school do not reject the importance of the technical information by avoiding a seminar on spark plugs during driver education.

In the same way, counselors do not reject the existence and importance of neuroscience by excluding those details from their counseling any more than neurosurgeons reject the importance of biblical wisdom for living by not talking about the proverbs during a patient consultation for brain surgery. The issue is not the existence and importance of extra-biblical information made possible by the means of God's common grace. The issue concerns the nature of central information vital to a task, such as counseling, versus peripheral information. Biblical counselors do not reject neuroscience. Instead, they have rightly put their emphasis on certain practical knowledge to help them do their counseling. It is not a rejection of common grace to emphasize this information in counseling, while allowing others with scientific information to focus on their own work.

An Example: Cognitive Behavioral Therapy

I will return again to the example of cognitive behavioral therapy (CBT) used by Burns, because the method is so popular and several references in this book make it familiar to the reader. CBT seeks to help people with their problems in living by changing their thoughts and behavior. Much research has demonstrated the effectiveness of this approach and, as we have seen, it has many things in common with Scripture, which also emphasizes change at the level of thoughts and behavior. For these reasons, biblical counselors can affirm that many of the observations of CBT are accurate.

But CBT does not just make observations. Those observations are packaged in a worldview opposed to Christ. In particular, CBT possesses a materialistic worldview that rejects the existence of anything that is not physical in nature. They exclude all of the spiritual realities about mankind, which are so central to understanding and helping people. It means, ultimately, that they reject God, who is a spirit (John 4:24).

This gets to another worldview problem with CBT. Its system of change is amoral. The CBT system has a completely relativistic morality, with human behavior based on the preferences of the client and the counselor. There is no category for an objective moral code. The important categories of CBT are thoughts and behaviors that tend to work and those that do not tend to work. There is no category for right and wrong. CBT therapy will never address sin before a holy God, but will only be concerned with changing thoughts and behaviors to something more conducive to the counselee's comfort level.[33]

Many of the observations of CBT are true and are verified to be so by the Bible. But a fallen worldview compromises those observations and warps their counseling interventions away from God and his Word. Some would argue that we should evaluate secular approaches like CBT according to Scripture and strip them of their unbiblical observations, interventions, and worldview commitments. This is the goal of integrationists like Stanton Jones and Richard Butman in their book *Modern Psychotherapies*.[34] With such an approach, the Bible serves as the control of beliefs that filter out unbiblical elements, allowing the parts of the therapy that conform with Scripture to remain and be used by Christians. This is the approach of Christian compassion suggested by Jones as quoted earlier in the chapter. This approach, though popular, has two significant problems.

The first problem is that when Christian counselors use the Bible to evaluate the secular psychology they believe is so important to augment counseling ministry, it actually demonstrates the sufficiency of Scripture. Let me explain. Christian counselors have argued that we need secular approaches to fill in the gaps of Scripture concerning counseling care. Christian counselors have also argued that we must use the Bible to evaluate these secular therapies to determine what elements of them should be included or excluded in order to be faithful. But every time Christian counselors use the Bible as the standard to evaluate secular

---

33. For an example of this, see Arnold Lazarus, "Psychological Treatment of Dyspareunia," in Sandra Leiblum and L. Pervin, eds., *Principles and Practice of Sex Therapy* (New York: Guilford, 1980), 147–66. Lazarus reports on his work with a female counselee who was a serial adulteress and, as a result, has a growing opposition to sexual relations with her husband. Instead of leading her to repent of sexual sin and break off her relationships to pursue Christ and her husband, Lazarus used CBT to train her to become emotionally distant with her husband.

34. Jones and Butman review numerous secular counseling approaches and subject them to biblical critique. The idea is that the approaches are helpful and can be useful in counseling once evaluated by Scripture.

therapies, they demonstrate that the contents of Scripture address the counseling principles they claim it lacks. Using the Bible to evaluate secular therapies proves that the content of Scripture includes the information relevant to the subject matter of counseling.

It is not possible to have it both ways. It is impossible to claim that the Bible is insufficient to develop counseling principles seen in secular therapy, but then use the Bible to adjudicate which of those secular principles are faithful and which are unfaithful. Christian counselors have to choose. Either the Bible is insufficient for counseling, and we must evaluate the legitimacy of secular approaches on something other than biblical grounds, or the Bible is sufficient to develop counseling principles, and the secular therapies add nothing essential to the church's counseling wisdom. The middle position of claiming the insufficiency of Scripture for counseling while demanding biblical evaluation of secular therapy is untenable. If the Bible is sufficient to make a judgment about which specific elements of secular interventions are legitimate and which are illegitimate, then the Bible contains the resources to construct its own interventions.

The second problem with using the Bible to filter out the unbiblical practices and worldview commitments of secular therapy is that after you take away unbiblical observations and worldviews, you are no longer left with the secular therapy. When the materialistic, atheistic, and amoral worldview commitments of CBT are stripped away and replaced with Christ-centered and Bible-based commitments to practical change through mind renewal and behavior change, you no longer have CBT. You have *biblical* change. CBT makes some true observations about the way God made life to work for people, but it subtracts from its equation the God who made people to work this way. CBT then replaces God with its own God-suppressing worldview. When you take away all the godlessness in CBT and replace it with Jesus and the Bible, you have taken the very long route to creating a biblical approach to change.

There is no need to create a faithful model of change beginning with a faithless model of change. It is much better, and far more efficient, to unpack the principles for change that are already sitting there in Scripture, waiting to be applied to life and counseling.

The point of all this is that secular therapies give us three things: observations and interventions that reflect reality as God created it and revealed it in the Bible, observations and interventions that fail to reflect the reality God created and revealed, and a system of worldview commitments that misunderstands even those realities that they have correct. These therapies do not add anything essential to a robustly relevant and biblical counseling system. We simply do not need the secular therapies in order to have a meaningful counseling approach.

Common Grace, Counseling, and the Sufficiency of Scripture

I began this chapter on the resources for counseling outside Scripture by asking what is necessary to help Rick, Wendy, Gail, Trenyan, Jenny, Scott, Drew, Amber, Sean, and Sarah. To answer that question, we examined common grace and saw that, indeed, God does allow unbelievers to come to know true principles that are helpful in counseling. But the lesson of the chapter is that as wonderful and important as the doctrine of common grace is, it does not compensate totally for the noetic effects of sin, and it does not replace the doctrine of the sufficiency of Scripture for counseling. God gave us a Bible that is sufficient for counseling and does not need to be supplemented by the findings of common grace. Believers need common grace when it comes to numerous areas in life, but not when it comes to developing counseling approaches.

It is not a rejection of common grace to say that it is often held in check by the noetic effects of sin. It is not a denial of common grace to affirm that God's revelation in the Bible is more central to counseling than the realities he allows unbelievers to come to know. As wonderful as the doctrine of common grace is, and as much as we should be thankful for it, God never intended to provide the solution for life's problems in common grace. He intends Jesus Christ to fulfill that purpose.

The information unbelievers come to know by God's common grace is simply not as important for counseling as the truth God reveals in the Bible about how Jesus changes people. Troubled people can know much information about counseling through common grace, but what they most deeply need is the Bible to reveal Jesus and his special grace in salvation.

CHAPTER 4

BIBLICAL COUNSELING

and a

THEOLOGY OF GOD

I first met Jenny when she was twenty-two. She had learned about me from a previous counselee I had helped, and we began meeting together. Jenny was very shy when she first walked into my office wearing a sweat suit and looking tired. She found it very difficult to open up, but when she finally did start to share, she had a horrifying story to relate.

As far back as Jenny could remember, her father had sexually assaulted her. These assaults ranged from fondling to rape and would happen almost anytime her mother left the house. Jenny said, through tears, how she would plead with her mother to stay home rather than go out or to take Jenny with her. Sometimes her mom would heed these requests. Many times she would not.

One of the most painful memories of Jenny's life happened before she turned ten. Her father was raping her in his bedroom when her mom returned early from running errands. She became aware of her mom's presence when she and her father looked up during the attack and saw her mom standing in the open door to the bedroom. Jenny looked in horror as her mom stared and then returned down the hallway. Jenny's mom never brought this up. She even behaved normally at dinner that night. In Jenny's words, it was that moment when she knew that no one cared about her, that she was all alone and would have to figure everything out on her own.

Things only became worse. As Jenny grew, her father made her sexually available to his brother. This created an even more painfully complicated dynamic because, in addition to the sexual abuse, Jenny's uncle would physically harm her in other ways. Jenny would plead with her father not to let her be with her uncle. She learned during those years that she could sexually manipulate her father. If she would initiate sexual relations or behave in sexual ways she knew he liked, she could avoid being with her uncle, get things she wanted, and even "cheer up" her father when he was in a bad mood.

Around the time that Jenny turned fourteen, her father stopped having sex with her and, as it turned out, never did it again. Through high school her mom and dad were distant and "strange." She hated them and wanted to move out. She did her best to count down the days to the end of senior year. The summer after graduation, as she was preparing to move away to college, she was out with some friends when a guy from her school raped her. She was devastated.

The situation in Jenny's life became even more horrifying when she was raped again during her first semester at college. This time Jenny had no more strength left. She dropped out of college, quit her job, and began staying at whatever friend's house she could for as long as possible. She became involved in drugs and drinking. She was not interested in a long-term relationship, but would date episodically and would have sex with her boyfriends, though she did not enjoy it.

During this time Jenny began cutting her arms with razor blades. She often thought of suicide, though she never really contemplated it as a serious option, believing she would go to hell. It was at this point in Jenny's young twenties when she came to know Jesus Christ. A girl living in a house where she was staying was a Christian and invited her to church. Jenny decided to go and, after a few weeks, she trusted Christ. Her newfound brothers and sisters in Christ tried to do what they could to minister to her but quickly realized they were ill-equipped to help her and so reached out for help. That is when Jenny showed up in my office.

Jenny's story is painful and complicated. I counseled her for many months with the help of several young female counselors. There are all manner of things to talk about with regard to helping Jenny. In this chapter, however, I want to focus on one thing: whether the doctrine of God has anything to contribute to the kind of serious counseling case Jenny presented.

Knowing God

When I refer to the doctrine of God in the context of counseling, I am referring to what we know about God. We want to know what is true about him. We want to understand what it means to have a relationship with him. When we know who God is, we also know that he is the most wonderful being in existence. Knowing who God is changes your life. You cannot be the same when you realize that the God who fixed stars and planets in place directs his attention to caring for you.[1]

Knowing God is life changing. One of the ways we express that is in our words about God. Counseling is just one of the many places where our love for God overflows in words spoken about him to people who need to hear of him. We must talk about God in counseling, but not in the way we *must* clean out the gutters every spring. Instead, we must speak of him in the way we *must* hug our children when they draw us a picture. It is the requirement of delight. We are joyously compelled to speak of him because he has changed our lives, and we are eager to see him change the lives of others. In this chapter we will consider a few of the glorious realities about God that *must* inform our speech in counseling.

Theologians discuss a number of crucial issues that relate to the doctrine of God. These include the existence of God, his creation of the

---

1. A. W. Tozer famously said, "What comes into our minds when we think about God is the most important thing about us," in *The Knowledge of the Holy: The Attributes of God: Their Meaning in the Christian Life* (San Francisco: HarperCollins, 1961).

world, and the doctrine of the Trinity. Each of these could be mean-ingfully explored for their impact on the task of biblical counseling. As valuable as they are, however, I will focus in this chapter on the character of God. There is much that we can learn about God and how knowing God informs our counseling of others by exploring his attributes.

The Attributes of God

An attribute is a quality that is true of someone and which we use to describe that person. When you say your wife is beautiful, your neigh-bor is kind, or your boss is harsh, you are using attributes to describe them. One of the most wonderful things about the Bible is that it does not merely describe *that* God exists or *what* he does. The Bible tells us what God is like. It tells us about his likes and dislikes, the things he values and loves. It teaches us about the kind of being he is and what motivates his actions. This is so wonderful because God is under no requirement to tell us who he is. That God would give us so much infor-mation about himself is an indication of his desire for a relationship with us. He wants us to know more than facts about him. He wants us to know *him*. That adds enthusiasm to our search for understanding about these things. Let me explain.

When I was a senior in college, I met someone named Lauren. I thought she was the most beautiful woman I had ever seen, and though I did not know it at the time, she was the woman who would eventually become my wife. We began spending time together, and then we began spending more time together. We would sit up and talk late into the night about our families, our walk with the Lord, what made us laugh, what we wanted out of life, and a million other things. I loved talking to her. I loved hearing about what interested her. I wanted to know more and more about this girl who had so captivated my heart.

This is something of the spirit with which we should pursue our understanding of the character of God. The only difference is that no matter how wonderful my wife is, she is not in the same category as the God of heaven and earth. God is more wonderful than anyone we have ever beheld. We should pursue knowing him with unequaled enthusiasm. I am praying for that exact spirit as we look together at the attributes of God.

It is not enough to study the attributes of God. We have to know *how* to do it. When studying the attributes of God, systematic theologians break up the divine attributes into categories, or classifications. They do this because it is impossible to speak about all of God's attributes at once; you must take them one at a time. A classification system allows you to do that in an organized way, which helps to avoid overlooking any of God's attributes. Different theologians break up these attributes into different categories. Throughout history, theologians have used several different categories, including communicable and incommunicable attributes, moral and nonmoral attributes, absolute and relative attributes, and attributes of transcendence and immanence.[2] None of these divisions is perfect. They have all been criticized in one way or another.

There is no single biblically faithful way to organize God's attributes. Christians throughout history have organized information about the attributes of God in many different ways. They have simply done their best to discuss God's character in ways that contribute to effective communication and clarity in understanding.

---

2. See Louis Berkhof, *Systematic Theology: An Introduction to Christian Belief* (Grand Rapids, MI: Eerdmans, 1996), 55, 57–81; John M. Frame, *Systematic Theology: An Introduction to Christian Belief* (Phillipsburg, NJ: P&R, 2013), 231–420; Wayne A. Grudem, *Systematic Theology: An Introduction to Biblical Doctrine* (Grand Rapids, MI: Zondervan, 1994), 156–225; Norman L. Geisler, *Systematic Theology*, vol. 2 (Minneapolis: Bethany House, 2002), 17–422; Augustus Hopkins Strong, *Systematic Theology* (Charleston, SC: Bibliolife, 2010), ch. 1, part 4. The most common way to divide the attributes of God is into the categories of communicable and incommunicable attributes. Communicable attributes have to do with God's attributes that he shares with people. Incommunicable attributes are those qualities he has only within himself. Though this is the most common way to designate the attributes, it is far from the only one. Some theologians break up the attributes of God into moral attributes and nonmoral attributes. According to this distinction, nonmoral attributes refer to who God is. The moral attributes refer to what he does. Other theologians make a distinction between absolute and relative attributes. The absolute attributes have to do with who God is in himself, while the relative attributes have to do with who God is with reference to his creation. Still others make a distinction between the attributes of immanence and transcendence. In this distinction, transcendence has to do with God's distinction from his creation, and immanence has to do with God's nearness to his creation.

As we think about theology from the perspective of biblical counseling, we have some freedom, then, to categorize the attributes in ways that might be different from what others have done. Rather than replicate the categorizations of others, I will begin by making a division between God's attributes of *strength* and God's attributes of *care*. There are limitations with these designations just as there are with other ones used by classical and contemporary theologians. As will become clear, however, I think this distinction is helpful in communicating theology to counselors and counselees.

Because this is a theology of biblical counseling, our goal is to see how the theology we confess from the Scriptures explodes with relevance in counseling ministry. We will see how these truths make a relevant impact in the lives of people experiencing problems. That is where the story of Jenny comes in. The doctrine of God framed my counseling experience with her. As we progress through the divine attributes, I want to show you how each of them applied directly to her story. We will begin by looking at God's attributes of strength.

God's Attributes of Strength

God's attributes of strength refer to the qualities of his person where his unmatched power is on display. One of the most significant ways that God is different from us has to do with his might. God is strong. We are weak. When we come to know God by examining his attributes of strength, we encounter a God who is very different than we are.

Human beings are *always* weak, but when they seek out the kind of help we offer in biblical counseling, they *feel* their weakness in particular ways. It is essential for those who offer biblical counsel to know of God's strength so they can offer this strength to counselees. In this section we will examine six attributes of God's strength.

Self-Sufficiency

God is self-sufficient. He does not need anything outside of himself.[3] Consider for a moment how unique (even strange!) this can sound to us. As human beings, we are defined by our needs. We are astonishingly weak. If you think you are tough, try going a few minutes without any air! And we need far more than air. We need food, water, sleep, shelter—and that is just to keep us alive. When you start talking about being reasonably comfortable, the list gets much longer. One of the most defining features of humanity is our weakness, our dependence.

God does not need anything that exists outside of himself. As I write these words, I am tired and hungry. Food and sleep will have to come soon. God *never* feels this way. This is one of the characteristics of what it means for God to be God. It is one of the key distinctions between God, the creator of all, and humanity, his creation. God did not need anything to bring himself into existence because he never came into existence. He has always existed. Neither does God need anything to maintain his existence because he is forever *self*-sufficient. Many passages in Scripture teach these facts about God (Ex. 3:14; Pss. 50:12–13; 102:25–27; John 5:26; 1 Tim. 6:16). One classic passage relates Paul's words to the people of Athens in Acts 17:24–30:

> "The God who made the world and everything in it, being Lord of heaven and earth, does not live in temples made by man, nor is he served by human hands, as though he needed anything, since he himself gives to all mankind life and breath and everything. And he made from one man every nation of mankind to live on all the face of the earth, having determined allotted periods and the boundaries of their dwelling place, that they should seek God, and perhaps feel their way toward him and find him. Yet he is actually not far from each one of us, for 'In him we live and move and have

---

3. Other terms, which systematic theologians use for this attribute of God, include the self-existence of God, God's independence, and *aseity*—a word which derives from Latin and means "from himself."

our being'; as even some of your own poets have said, 'For we are indeed his offspring.' Being then God's offspring, we ought not to think that the divine being is like gold or silver or stone, an image formed by the art and imagination of man. The times of ignorance God overlooked, but now he commands all people everywhere to repent."

There are at least three things we can learn about God's self-sufficiency from this passage.

First, God is sufficient in himself with no needs outside of himself. We are told that God "does not live in temples made by man, nor is he served by human hands, as though he needed anything" (vv. 24–25). Paul is making a shocking statement about the nature of idolatry. Idols receive service from the people who make them because they have needs. These idols are made in the image of needy people. The self-sufficient God is very different. Paul upends these pagan categories by saying that, unlike every other being, God stands in need of nothing outside of himself.

Second, the self-sufficiency of God creates our dependence on him. God has no needs, but he gives to humanity life and breath—indeed everything. We are the opposite of God in this way. He needs nothing from us. We need everything from him. As Louis Berkhof has observed, "God is not only independent in Himself, but also causes everything to depend on Him."[4]

Third, God not only made us dependent on him but demands that we acknowledge this dependence. God has "determined . . . that they should seek God" (vv. 26–27) and repent. For God's human creation, it is not enough that it be true that God is sufficient and we are dependent. We must confess this relationship if we are to relate to God in the proper way. God's self-sufficiency, combined with our need, requires that we turn to God in humble dependence.

The implications of this truth for counseling are huge. Man's

---

4. Berkhof, *Systematic Theology*, 58.

dependency creates the very need for all counseling. God's self-sufficiency forms the basis for every counseling solution. There can be no ultimately helpful counsel that is devoid of reliance upon the self-sufficient God. God is the one who has no needs; we are the ones who find all our needs met in him.

This was certainly the case with Jenny. Jenny's painful story is one of a young woman who is weak, frail, needy, and dependent. Many different people might suggest many different needs for her: justice in the court system, a safe relationship with a friend she can trust, psychiatric hospitalization for some of her more extreme behaviors like cutting. Some would suggest that she needs to be on medication for her severe emotions. Each of these is on the table and needs to be considered. But which of Jenny's needs is the most crucial?

Be careful in answering this question. How you respond will determine whether you are thinking as a Christian or as an unbeliever. A Christian will agree about the importance of justice, friendship, and medical intervention for her physical symptoms. But are any of those important issues the *most* important one?

As Christians we must insist that her greatest need is God. This is not a cliché. It is a profound and unalterable reality that is grounded in God's attribute of self-sufficiency. The most pressing need Jenny has is to come to know the living God and to grow in wisdom, love, and knowledge of him. This is not at odds with the other kinds of care, which are also important. But those other important issues must be framed according to the controlling issue of her need for the only Person who can ultimately address all of her weaknesses.

Faithful Christians do not have the option to help Jenny in all kinds of "practical" ways while refusing to point her to a self-sufficient God. Counsel that does not send Jenny flying to the completely self-sufficient God is not only unchristian but also ineffective. The fastest way to become guilty of counseling malpractice is to refuse to reference, to rely upon, and to summon counselees to depend upon the self-sufficient God in whom "we live and move and have our being" (v. 28).

Infinity

God's infinity has to do with his freedom from any limitations to be God. Theologians often speak of God's infinity in three ways. God's infinity with respect to time is called "eternality." God has existed from the eternal past and will continue to exist into the eternal future. Human existence is constrained by time. God's existence is not.

God's infinity regarding space is called his "immensity." God is not limited by any spatial consideration. It is the very nature of humanity to be limited by space. We cannot be any other place than where we are at any given time. God's infinite immensity means that this is not true for him.

As important as these are and as much as they fuel our worship of God, they are not the aspects of divine infinity which will consume our attention here. Instead we will focus on God's perfection. God's infinite perfection means that all of his attributes are his infinitely. God is not just self-sufficient, he is infinitely self-sufficient. With respect to God's goodness, God is not just good. He is infinitely good. To use another example, God is not just loving, he is eternally loving.[5]

The Bible teaches us about God's infinite perfection, as in 1 John 1:5: "God is light, and in him is no darkness at all." In the Bible light and darkness are typically used as analogies for righteousness and sin. This text of Scripture is saying that the infinite God is defined exclusively by righteousness and has no sin in any aspect of his infinite being.

Jesus exhorts his hearers to "be perfect, as your heavenly Father is perfect" (Matt. 5:48). Jesus is making the point that it is not enough to love only those who love you. His command is to love even when you are hated. He commands to never be lacking in love. This is the standard

---

5. This area is one of the most common objections to the division of God's attributes between communicable and incommunicable attributes. God's goodness—to select just one element of God's character—is listed under God's communicable attributes. God is good, and human beings can be too, so his goodness is communicated to his people. The problem is that, while it is true that we can know some measure of God's goodness, the fullness of this moral attribute can never be fully shared with human beings. As much as Christians can grow in goodness, and as much as they will grow in goodness in heaven with Christ, they will never be infinitely good.

of perfection held by the infinite God. For Jesus, God's perfection has to do with his limitless virtue. God's love, like all of his other virtues, is inexhaustible.

In counseling, God's infinite perfection is of crucial importance. When a person experiences the kind of pressure that leads them to seek counseling help, there is always some negative circumstance at work. Something bad is happening. Some bad situation is unfolding in some bad place caused by, perhaps, a bad person. In such negativity, it is of great practical benefit to point to God's infinite perfection. This was certainly the case with Jenny.

Every man with whom Jenny had ever been close treated her in terrible ways. She had been violated, betrayed, and abused by her father. Think about a daughter's relationship to her daddy. It should be one of the safest and most sacred on earth. This was not the case for Jenny. The only dad she had raped her. The only uncle she knew raped her. Her boyfriends raped her. Rape is one of the worst and most painful things that anyone could experience. If Jenny had been subjected to the horror of only one of those relationships, we would say it was unspeakably bad. What do you say to a woman so overwhelmed by a multiplication of multiple tragedies? Where do you point her in the midst of the wickedness she has endured?

In counseling, I helped Jenny get to know a Person whose goodness, trustworthiness, love, mercy, grace, and patience are completely inexhaustible. I told her about God, who is the definition of perfection. As a Christian and as a man who just wanted to help her, I have no idea how I could have ministered to Jenny without sharing some of the knowledge of this God who is infinite in perfection.

It took me a long time to earn trust with Jenny. After I did, we were able to make a lot of headway in her life and to have a really good relationship. In one of our conversations, she was honest with me that, though she trusted me, she was often fearful that I would do something to break her trust. I wanted to assure Jenny that I would never break her trust. I wanted to promise that I would never do anything to hurt her. Unfortunately, I could not do that. Had I tried to make that assurance, I would have robbed her of the opportunity to hear about the God who actually never will break her trust.

Instead, I told her the truth. I told her I cared for her, wanted to help her, and was going to try very hard to maintain her trust. I also reminded her that I am a sinner, and that if we were friends for long enough, I would likely disappoint her in some way. I reminded her that the goal of our relationship was not to have her find her confidence in me, but in the God who alone deserves her confidence and will never break her trust.

Omnipresence

That God is omnipresent means that he is always present everywhere with the fullness of who he is.[6] As I mentioned earlier, God's immensity has to do with the fact that he is not constrained by spatial limitations. Divine omnipresence is a very important balancing truth for that doctrine. Whereas God's immensity means that he is not constrained by space, omnipresence means that he is present everywhere in any place with his entire divine being.[7] There is no place where God is not.

David speaks of this in Psalm 139:7–10:

Where shall I go from your Spirit? Or where shall I flee from your presence? If I ascend to heaven, you are there! If I make my bed in Sheol, you are there! If I take the wings of the morning and dwell in the uttermost parts of the sea, even there your hand shall lead me, and your right hand shall hold me.

---

6. In this chapter we will talk about omnipresence, omniscience, omnisapience, and omnipotence. These are theological terms with the same Latin root, *omni*, meaning "all." So omnipresence means God is everywhere present. Omniscience means God is all-knowing. Omnisapience means God has all wisdom. Omnipotence means God is all-powerful.

7. Berkhof, *Systematic Theology*, 61.

This passage and others teach us that God is always with us (see Jer. 23:23–24; Acts 17:28; Col. 1:17).

The omnipresence of God is a truth we need for counseling because it is a truth people need when they require help. The fact that God is always present with you in the fullness of his deity is a strong comfort when you are suffering. God shares this truth of his existence with us because he wants us to have the comfort that an infinitely good God is always with us no matter where we are. Consider Psalm 23:4: "Even though I walk through the valley of the shadow of death, I will fear no evil." Why? "For you are with me."

The fact that God is always present with you in the fullness of his deity is also a strong encouragement to you when you are sinning. God tells us this truth about himself to provide the accountability we need when we are tempted to sneak off alone and sin. You can never hide your sinful actions from God because he is always there with you.

Think of how this applies to Jenny. Though Jenny could not have articulated it at the time, one of her greatest difficulties was her experience of aloneness. As I listened to her, I came to see that much of her behavior was related to her being lonely. Jenny did not want boyfriends for the sex she detested. She wanted them for companionship. Jenny went around staying with different friends only partially because she needed a place to stay. Most of the time her selection of place was controlled by where she thought she was most likely to be around the maximum number of people. Even her cutting relates to this, since most people cut only when they are alone.

The doctrine of the divine omnipresence is a profound cure for the problem of loneliness. Omnipresence does not mean that it is unnecessary to be around other people since that reality is biblical too (e.g., Rom. 14:15; Eph. 4:15–16; Heb. 10:24–25). But omnipresence teaches that God's presence, though unseen, is just as real as any human being we might be with. God's presence is also more important than any other person we might be with.

Jenny needed to know that the self-sufficient God who is infinitely good was powerfully present with her. When she came to know that, and believe that, and be comforted by that, she changed the way she thought about where she would stay, what boys she would spend time with, and even whether she would cut herself.

Omnipresence teaches that Jenny is never alone. *You* are never alone. God is always there, wherever you are.

Omniscience

God's omniscience means that he has complete knowledge of everything. There is no event in the past, no situation in the present, no possibility in the future, and no element of his infinitely holy character of which God does not have perfect knowledge. This is a staggering amount of information, considering what is possible even with human knowledge. As powerful an instrument as the human brain is, our knowledge of the past and present is severely limited, and we have no knowledge whatsoever of the future. It is impossible for us to grasp knowledge about God without his saving grace, and even with that it will take an eternity to grow in the knowledge of the eternal God. Even when we can attain some limited knowledge of some of these things, it is not possible for us to have more than a few things in our mind at once. God, by contrast, knows all things perfectly.

This element of God's character, omniscience, is taught throughout the Old and New Testaments (1 Sam. 2:3; 2 Chron. 2:10–11; 16:9; Job 12:13; 28:24; Pss. 90:4; 94:9;139:1–4; 147:4; Isa. 29:15; 40:27–28; 42:8–9; 46:9–10; Matt. 6:8; 10:30; 1 Cor. 2:10–11; Heb. 4:13; 1 John 3:20). One significant place is in Psalm 139:1–6.

> O LORD, you have searched me and known me! You know when I
> sit down and when I rise up; you discern my thoughts from afar.
> You search out my path and my lying down and are acquainted
> with all my ways. Even before a word is on my tongue, behold, O

LORD, you know it altogether. You hem me in, behind and before, and lay your hand upon me. Such knowledge is too wonderful for me; it is high; I cannot attain it.

The description of God's knowledge in this passage is nothing other than exhaustive. God knows us. He knows when we sit and when we rise. He is acquainted with all of our ways. God knows everything we will say before it comes out of our mouth.[8] This truth means that God's knowledge of us is one of intimacy and familiarity.

In fact, God knows far more about us than we will ever know of ourselves. Even as the passage exalts the knowledge of God, it points out our own very limited knowledge: "Such knowledge is too wonderful for me; it is high; I cannot attain it" (v. 6). We do not know these things because we are not God and not as wonderful as he is. God's omniscience underlines his glory as creator and our neediness as creatures.

These verses are in the same passage of Scripture we looked at when examining God's omnipresence. This is significant. This passage, which exalts God's omnipresence, is the same passage that exalts God's omniscience. For David, the two go together. God is always with him and knows everything about him.

It is not enough to have the presence of God but have him lack intimate and exhaustive knowledge of you. Think of a husband who is present but emotionally distant. A wife in such a situation is with her husband, but his presence is cold comfort because he does not know her. He does not understand her. In some cases, such a presence can actually become a burden.

God is not just *with* Jenny. He *knows* her. Consider how important this knowledge is in counseling. No counselor can offer meaningful help to a counselee without accurate and careful knowledge of the

---

8. This observation brings up the issue of whether God knows the future. Open theism is a belief that the future is unknown to God because God knows all that exists and the future does not yet exist. See Gregory A. Boyd, *God of the Possible: A Biblical Introduction to the Open View of God* (Grand Rapids, MI: Baker, 2000). Evangelical Christians have rejected this view as unbiblical. See Bruce A. Ware, *God's Lesser Glory: The Diminished God of Open Theism* (Wheaton, IL: Crossway, 2000).

counselee's problem. Biblical counselors know the importance of careful listening in counseling.[9]

As counselors seek to gain knowledge about their counselees, they have two obstacles to overcome. The first obstacle is competency. Biblical counselors must grow in the skill of gleaning information in the context of counseling. The second obstacle is their natural limitation as a person. The most skilled biblical counselor will never be able to access all of the information relevant to a counselee's situation. It is simply not available to us. The doctrine of divine omniscience means that God faces none of these limitations.

The truth of God's exhaustive knowledge—not just of things in general but of people in particular—made all the difference to Jenny and to me, her counselor. My knowledge of Jenny's situation was and always will be limited. Even Jenny lacks the ability to know all of the information relevant to helping her. That God has none of these limitations gives us confidence in his ability to care for her.

Omnisapience

Omnisapience means that God always understands what is best. This is a very important element of God's character that builds profoundly on divine omniscience. In fact, we could say quite strongly that omniscience would come very near to being worthless if God did not understand what is best.

To prove this, let's try a thought experiment:

Imagine that you have been offered two jobs at two different companies. You know who your boss will be at each place, you know your job description, your salary and benefits, and you know what your spouse thinks about each option. You know all the facts, but you still cannot decide which of the two positions you should take. We experience such indecision all the time. It demonstrates that knowledge without wisdom

---

9. See John F. MacArthur Jr. and Wayne A. Mack, *Introduction to Biblical Counseling: A Basic Guide to the Principles and Practice of Counseling* (Nashville: Thomas Nelson, 1994), 210–30; Jay E. Adams, *The Christian Counselor's Manual: The Practice of Nouthetic Counseling* (Grand Rapids, MI: Zondervan, 1986), 249–93. See also Proverbs 18:13; James 1:19.

is often meaningless in practice. All the information in the world is worthless without the wisdom to know what to do with that knowledge.

It should be very encouraging to us that God not only knows all things, according to his omniscience, but he also knows what is best, according to his omnisapience. The apostle Paul exalts God's omnisapience in Romans 11:33–34 when he says, "Oh, the depth of the riches and wisdom and knowledge of God! How unsearchable are his judgments and how inscrutable his ways! 'For who has known the mind of the Lord, or who has been his counselor?'" Notice how the apostle Paul praises not just God's knowledge but also his understanding. Paul asks rhetorically who has been the Lord's counselor. The assumed answer is that no one has because God does not lack wisdom. Since he does not lack any wisdom, he does not need anyone to help him weigh options as we do almost every day of our lives.

When we are in trouble, we need to be sure that God knows everything—all of the facts. We need to be certain that he knows how to understand those facts. The Bible assures us that he does. For Christians, this news gets even better. God not only has comprehensive wisdom, but he promises to share that wisdom with us just for the asking. "If any of you lacks wisdom, let him ask God, who gives generously to all without reproach, and it will be given him" (James 1:5).

Jenny, like every person who seeks counseling help, is in desperate need of wisdom. Christians have no other option out of their faithfulness to the Bible, confidence in God, and love for people like Jenny, but to point to the promise of passages like James 1 and spend time praying for God's wisdom. As we seek to help Jenny find wisdom, there are many things we might choose to do. The one thing the Bible requires us to do is to help her find wisdom by leading her to pray to the God whose wise resources are inexhaustible.

Omnipotence

Omnipotence means that God is able to do anything consistent with his desires as God. When we think of God's attributes of strength, his omnipotence is the one that is often foremost in our mind. As we have seen, however, it does not stand alone. Omnipotence would be reckless and horrifying without being informed by omniscience and omnisapience. Power that is not guided and informed by knowledge and wisdom would be disastrous. On the other hand, if God has knowledge and wisdom but lacks the power to do what he knows is best, his knowledge is worthless. So while omnipotence is not the only attribute of God's strength, it is a crucial aspect of it.

One passage that teaches us about God's omnipotence is Ephesians 1:11, which says that God "works all things according to the counsel of his will." (See also Pss. 33:10–11; 115:3; Prov. 16:9; Isa. 14:24–27; 43:13; 55:11; 63:17; Jer. 1:5; Rom. 11:33–36; Rev. 3:7.) Paul emphasizes that all things are under the omnipotent control of God. God is the source of all power, and he does not relinquish that power at any point as he runs the universe. Such power requires us to make two observations regarding God's power.

The first concerns a question I was asked when I was a young child. One of my friends came up to me and said, "If God can do anything, then can he make a rock that he cannot lift?" I did not know how to respond because of the apparent dilemma. Answering with either a yes or a no would seem to limit God's comprehensive power. If God could make a rock so heavy that he could not lift it, then his failure to lift the rock would demonstrate his weakness. If he could never make a rock so heavy that it would be impossible for him to lift it, then his failure to make a rock that was sufficiently heavy would also demonstrate his weakness. I remember thinking about this question a lot and posing it to many people, trying to find an answer.

Years later, after I had become a Christian, was grown up, and was a student of theology in college, I learned that the correct answer to the question is that it is indeed impossible for God to make a rock so heavy that he cannot lift it. That answer does not limit God's power but actually emphasizes it. Remember that omnipotence means that God can do anything *consistent with his desires as God.* That is an important qualification on the power of God.

It is not true that God can do *anything.* There are things that God cannot do. For example, the Bible makes clear that God cannot lie (Titus 1:2; Heb. 6:18). And God cannot stop being God. Both of these are inconsistent with God's desires as God. God would never do them.

Now back to answering the question about the heavy rock. It is impossible for God to make a rock so heavy he cannot lift it because it is impossible for anything to exist outside of the omnipotent control of God.

If there were anything that existed outside of his control, then God would not be God over that thing. It is impossible for this to happen. That means it is just as impossible for God to make a rock he cannot lift as it is for God to lie. Both of these things would require God to stop being God.

The second observation raised by God's omnipotence concerns a debate that has perplexed Christian thinkers (indeed, all humanity) for millennia. How can God be sovereign while preserving the fact that human beings can be responsible and held accountable for what they do? This is the question that Paul poses in Romans 9 when he asks how God can find fault with human beings when it is impossible for them to resist his powerful will (Rom. 9:19). People make real decisions for which they are held responsible, but God is omnipotent, holding the world in his complete control. How can each of these things be true?

We will not solve these problems in one section of one chapter of one book. These are issues that consume entire volumes.[10] We also need

---

10. Some of the books that I have found particularly helpful in my own journey to understand these issues are D. A. Carson, *How Long, O Lord: Reflections on Suffering and Evil*; R. K. McGregor Wright, *No Place for Sovereignty: What's Wrong with Freewill Theism*; Jonathan Edwards, *Freedom of the Will*; and Bruce A. Ware, *God's Greater Glory: The Exalted God of Scripture and the Christian Faith.*

to be careful. In Romans 9 when Paul poses this hypothetical question, he urges caution: "But who are you, O man, to answer back to God? Will what is molded say to its molder, 'Why have you made me like this?'" (Rom. 9:20). We need to be sure that there is no arrogance in our consideration of these questions, but rather a willingness to embrace joyfully how God has made us and eagerly submit to what he has revealed in Scripture about who we are. We might be perplexed, but we should always be submissive.

None of these considerations mean that we cannot consider the issue of human responsibility and divine omnipotence that are addressed in Scripture. One good example is the story of Joseph in Genesis. You will recall that Joseph's brothers sold him into slavery because they were jealous of him. After a long service of slavery in Egypt, he was placed second in command under Pharaoh. It was at that point that Joseph's brothers came to Egypt seeking help in the midst of a famine. They appeared before Joseph, but they did not know he was their brother. Joseph finally revealed who he was to his brothers. Genesis 45:4–8 records what Joseph said:

> "I am your brother, Joseph, whom you sold into Egypt. And now do not be distressed or angry with yourselves because you sold me here, for God sent me before you to preserve life. For the famine has been in the land these two years, and there are yet five years in which there will be neither plowing nor harvest. And God sent me before you to preserve for you a remnant on earth, and to keep alive for you many survivors. So it was not you who sent me here, but God."

This is a fascinating text that affirms the work of God and men in the same action. We know from the previous chapters of Genesis that the brothers were guilty of selling Joseph into slavery. Genesis 45 affirms that fact, saying, "I am your brother, Joseph, whom *you sold* into

Egypt," and, "Do not be distressed or angry with yourselves because *you sold me* here." There is no doubt about the responsibility of the brothers.

And yet that is not all the passage says. It also affirms the sovereign hand of God in these events. It says, *"God sent me* before you to preserve life," and *"God sent* me before you to preserve a remnant for you on earth," and finally, "So *it was not you* who sent me here, *but God"* (emphasis added). Joseph says that in and through, over and above the working of the brothers, the sovereign hand of God was orchestrating these events.

This is the way the Bible consistently deals with these matters (Gen. 20:1–6; Lev. 20:7–8; 2 Sam. 24:1–17 (cf. 1 Chron. 21:1–7); Isa. 10:5ff; Acts 2:23; 4:27–28; 2 Thess. 2:11–12). It affirms that human responsibility exists underneath the sovereign omnipotence of God. Both are true. When my family drives to Pennsylvania to spend Christmas with my in-laws every year, we drive north on Interstate 71. For a while that interstate intersects with Interstate 75. For several miles the signs on the road have the names of two interstates on them. If my kids ask where we are (and believe me, they do), I might say that we are on Interstates 71 and 75. In the same way, God has chosen to create a world where human responsibility exists underneath his comprehensive sovereignty. Just as it is possible for my family to be on one road and two interstates at the same time, so in every single human action, there is the human actor and God, the divine actor. Human responsibility and divine omnipotence are each preserved.

We need to remember that the focus here is God's unmatched omnipotence. God is sovereign, doing all that pleases him. This is a fundamental aspect of his character. And it is God's omnipotence that matters when doing counseling with Jenny. Like all counselors, I want to be effective in my counseling with Jenny. I also want her to work to do what she needs to do to get in a better life situation than her current one. The doctrine of God's omnipotence teaches us that any power we have is derived from the sovereign God, the source of all power. As much as I want to work hard and as seriously as I desire Jenny to work hard, faithfulness in biblical counseling requires that we look to the only One whose power is inexhaustible. There can be no effective counseling without the powerful working of the omnipotent God. Faithful counselors believe that, confess that, and point their counselees to that.

The implications of these attributes of God's strength build upon one another in counseling. God is self-sufficient; he does not need us, but we need him. God is infinite; the God we need possesses perfection. God is omnipresent; the perfect God we need is always there for us. God is omniscient; God knows what is wrong and what we need. God is omnisapient; he is wise and understands what to do with that knowledge. Finally, God is omnipotent; he is able to bring about what we need. Such truths about our mighty God require us to be the kind of counselors who point to the God who alone provides this kind of strength. This is strength that Jenny needs and strength that every other counselee needs. Counselors need it too.

God's Attributes of Care

We have seen a picture of God, who is mighty in strength. There is no way to understand the character of God without appreciating that he is strong. The Bible also presents a God who cares for us. This is very encouraging for God's people. We often see pictures in our day of people who are *either* strong *or* caring. There are "macho" guys who are not very gentle, and there are caring people who lack muscle. The Bible teaches us that God is both tender and tough, caring and strong. This is good news for counselors who need to offer to struggling people a God who is powerful and a God who is gentle. We will look at six attributes of God's care.

Holiness

God's holiness is his devotion to himself as God above every other reality. In the Bible, something is holy when it is set apart for exclusive dedication to God and his service. The Sabbath day is holy because it is the day of the week devoted exclusively to the Lord (Ex. 20:8–10). Israel was called holy because the Israelites were a nation devoted exclusively to the Lord (Lev. 20:26). As Christians devote themselves to God, they are called holy (Rom. 12:1). In biblical terms, something is holy when it is given wholly over to God and devoted exclusively to his service.[11]

When we say that God is holy, we are saying that God is devoted to himself. Many have pointed out that the only threefold repetition of an attribute of God in the Bible is that he is holy, holy, holy (Isa. 6:3; Rev. 4:8).[12] Such repetition is the way biblical authors emphasize the importance of this attribute of God. We are to learn that it is a matter of central importance that God is devoted to himself.

Theologians commonly highlight that holiness has to do with separation, and they point out that holiness is that which serves as the

---

11. Since my definition of holiness differs from a popular understanding of the term, some explanation is in order. Since the time of the Reformation, the traditional view of God's holiness is to associate it with his moral purity and transcendence. During the last one hundred years, especially, the meaning of holy has been defined as "separateness" based on research analyzing the use of the word in Hebrew and in the literatures of the peoples surrounding Israel (e.g., Akkadian and Ugaritic). In that context, the basic meaning of the word is "consecrated to / devoted to." But in Exodus 3, the first instance of the adjective or noun *holy*, the word has to do with the meeting of God and man, not being separate. Moses becomes someone who belongs to God, who is devoted to God as an obedient servant. In Exodus 19, Moses as mediator brings the entire nation of Israel into a covenant relationship with God in which Israel belongs to God as a devoted and obedient son (Exod. 4:22). In Isaiah 6, the triple occurrence of holy is a form of extreme emphasis describing Yahweh as emphatically holy because he is completely devoted to the instruction, or Torah, in his covenant with Israel at Sinai. This instruction represents his own character and the faithful loyal love of the persons within the Godhead to each other. Thus God is holy in the sense that he is completely devoted to himself. Within the triune being of God, the Father, Son, and Holy Spirit are 100 percent devoted to each other in faithfulness and loyalty and trust. Since righteousness refers to the way people treat each other in relationship, God is holy in his righteousness. This all has implications for what it means for human beings to be holy. Human holiness has to do with only moral purity as a result of the primary focus, namely, our devotion to God. Moral purity and separation from sin is not the meaning of the word *holy* but the result of being devoted to God. In Isaiah 6 the holiness and transcendence of God are mentioned not because they are linguistically related but because God is 100 percent committed to the instructions for righteous living in the Mosaic Covenant. The fact that God is transcendent means that no one will escape his judgment. Thus God's transcendence backs up and supports his holiness, i.e., his commitment to his own righteousness and character. I am profoundly thankful for the work of Peter Gentry in helping me to develop my understanding of these matters. For an excellent treatment of this issue, see Peter J. Gentry, "The Meaning of 'Holy' in the Old Testament," *Bibliotheca Sacra*: BSAC 170:680 (October 2013), http://www.galaxie.com/article/bsac170-680-02.

12. R. C. Sproul, *The Holiness of God* (Carol Stream, IL: Tyndale, 2000), 25–26.

fundamental distinction between creature and Creator.[13] The definition I am offering here is not opposed to this understanding. The separation of holiness has to do with having complete devotion to God and being separated from a world that disregards God. Holiness creates one of the fundamental distinctions between God and his people.[14] That distinction is one of devotion to God. God is supremely and infinitely holy because he has supreme and infinite insight into his own awesome character. God's insight in this regard leads him to the ultimate devotion to himself. God's holiness—his devotion to himself—is a necessary attribute. If God were ever more devoted to something other than himself, that something, as the primary object of his worship, would make God an idolater. God's holiness means he is not an idolater and is not tempted to be one.

The holiness of God is an important attribute of care. To love something in the proper way, you must love it in the proper order. Our care for something will always be distorted unless we care for it in its proper place. Consider a few examples: Imagine a man whose life at home is in trouble because he is always at work. His wife feels lonely and isolated, and his kids see him as a distant figure. We might say to such a man that it is not wrong for him to love his job, but his love for work is out of order, which has brought pain into his life and the life of his family. Or imagine a college student failing out of his courses because he only wants to hang out with his friends. His parents are angry, and he is stressed about the situation he is in. The problem is not that the student loves his friends. It is rather that he has not loved his friends in the proper order, over and against his devotion (or lack of devotion) to his studies. Disordered love is not really love at all.

Christians believe that the most glorious person in the universe is God. Because he is so wonderful, we should love him more than anyone

---

13. One example of this is John Frame's excellent discussion of holiness in his *Systematic Theology: An Introduction to Christian Belief* (Phillipsburg, NJ: P&R, 2013), 276–79.

14. I would hesitate to say that this is *the* distinction between creature and creator. I think there might be several contenders for this spot, including self-sufficiency. The attribute of holiness is certainly a significant one in this regard.

else. We should be holy, devoted to God. When we do not love God, we are not equipped to love anyone rightly because we have not put first things first.

God's holiness requires us to see that Jenny's greatest and most important need is holiness. Even in the face of all the concerns and problems we must address in counseling Jenny, the most pressing need she has is to live a life of holiness. Since Jenny's greatest need is to be holy, we would say that the most important requirement in our relationship with Jenny is that counseling be holy. This makes sense. As counselors we want to help people who have problems. The greatest problem a person could have is not being supremely devoted to God. When that is the case, they need help to become holy. Counseling that fails to address the most significant problem that people face is counseling that is, in the grand scheme of things, not of value.

It is easy in counseling to focus on obvious issues that led someone to seek counsel in the first place. In Jenny's case, this would be her tragic past and her difficulty in living life in the aftermath of it. But Christians reading their Bibles understand that the most significant counseling problem is often one that counselees did not know was a problem. Our counseling must be holy because Jenny must be holy. Faithfulness in counseling requires biblical counselors to help people grow in their devotion to the holy God. Counselors who fail to do this are choosing the path of counseling failure.

Faithfulness

God's faithfulness means that what God knows and what he says are true. No one has said this better or more concisely than Jesus himself. In John 17:17 he says of God, "Your word is truth." This pithy statement overflows with profundity in a world full of lies and deception. God tells the truth (see Num. 23:19; 2 Sam. 7:28; Prov. 30:5; Titus 1:2; Heb. 6:18). Knowing this is of great significance in a world where the truth is hard to discern and where dishonesty often prevails. That God is faithful means we can trust that what he says is true and that the actions he promises will come to pass. God reveals this to us in the Bible because he wants us to have confidence in him.

God's faithfulness is a major issue in counseling. As we think about God's faithfulness, we realize that this element of God's character has just as much to do with biblical counseling as the sufficiency of Scripture does. The sufficiency of Scripture guarantees that the Bible is about counseling. The faithfulness of God promises that the words we speak to counselees from the sufficiency of Scripture are completely trustworthy.

In the introductory chapter, we looked at several different examples of counsel offered to people facing difficulties. Those examples are just a few of the thousands of different kinds of counseling wisdom that can be offered. Humility requires that all of us committed to being counselors ask how we can be so sure that the counsel we offer is faithful counsel. How can we be sure that our words to counselees are faithful words? An understanding of the faithfulness of God must encourage us to have our words remain as close to God's own as possible. That requires a counseling approach that is uniquely biblical.

Jenny is in obvious need of faithful counsel. After decades of faithless words from faithless people behaving in faithless ways, our sister Jenny needs to hear something trustworthy. As her counselor, I wanted to say faithful words. That meant that I had to be committed to say what God said to her through the Bible. Because I wanted to give her faithful counsel, I tried very carefully to help her think about her past the way God instructs, to offer the kind of comfort and encouragement that God offers, to help her believe the things that God says, and to do the things that are in God's Word. Helping Jenny means directing her to the God of truth and faithfulness.

Goodness

God's goodness means that everything God is and does is the standard in the universe for what is best. Wayne Grudem says, "God's being and actions are perfectly worthy of his own approval."[15] God's character and behavior do not need to conform to any external standard of good in the universe to be approved. If it did, that thing would be the standard of good in the universe. The Bible teaches us that something is good when it conforms to God (Ps. 34:8; Luke 18:19; Acts 14:17; Rom. 12:2; James 1:17).

Psalm 119:68 says, "You [God] are good and do good." What God does is good because he *is* good. The character of God serves as the standard for good. As sinful people, we get so confused about this. We often think *we* should be the standard for goodness. We think words that conform to our standards are good. We believe that sexual behavior that meets with our approval is good. We think our great ideas about how to treat others are good. The Bible teaches, human history illustrates, and our own sinful lives prove that there is no good without God. Everything else might look good, but it ultimately fails to satisfy.

Think how mistaken notions of goodness have burned Jenny. Jenny has been the victim of people whose behavior met their own approval but was not good. Her dad, uncle, and boyfriends raped her. Other boyfriends participated with her in sexual immorality. Her mom looked the other way when faced with horrifying abuse. Because people always do the things they do for reasons that seem good to them, we could say that it was mistaken notions of goodness that caused Jenny's problems.[16]

---

15. Wayne A. Grudem, *Systematic Theology: An Introduction to Biblical Doctrine* (Grand Rapids, MI: Zondervan, 1994), 198.

16. For example, Jonathan Edwards says, "To appear *good* to the mind, as I use the phrase, is the same as to *appear agreeable*, or *seem pleasing* to the mind. Certainly, nothing appears inviting and eligible to the mind, or tending to engage its inclination and choice, considered as *evil* or *disagreeable*; nor indeed, as *indifferent*, and neither agreeable nor disagreeable. But if it tends to draw the inclination, and move the Will, it must be under the notion of that which *suits* the mind. And therefore that must have the greatest tendency to attract and engage it, which as it stands in the mind's view, suits it best, and pleases it most; and in that sense, is the greatest apparent good: to say otherwise, is little, if any thing short of a direct and plain contradiction" (emphasis in original). Jonathan Edwards, "Freedom of the Will," in *The Works of Jonathan Edwards*, ed. Patrick H. Alexander (Peabody, MA: Hendrickson, 1998), 6.

Helping Jenny means introducing her to a new standard of goodness. Jenny is in desperate need of an encounter with a higher standard of goodness. She is in desperate need of coming to know the God who is good. This is one of the great needs of abuse victims in general. People who experience harsh treatment over time can lose their perspective on justice and injustice, right and wrong, cruelty and kindness. Clarity about what is good comes only when we focus counseling on the God who sets the standard for goodness.

Love

God's love means that he gives himself to benefit others. Theologians often discuss God's love under the category of God's goodness. We do not need to feel any pressure to conform to such conventions. The love of God and the goodness of God have some overlap in the concepts, which is why the Bible authors often place the two ideas together (e.g., Pss. 100:5; 106:1; 107:1). Still, there is a distinction between these two attributes. For our purposes, we can understand the distinction as the one between God's essence and God's compassion. That God is good in his essence means that God is objectively praiseworthy in and of himself. God's love has to do with the overflow of that good character in his desire to do good for others.

God's giving himself for the benefit of others is seen throughout the Bible. Indeed, the most famous passage of Scripture testifies to this: "For God so loved the world, that he gave his only Son, that whoever believes in him should not perish but have eternal life" (John 3:16). God's love motivates him to act for the benefit of the world even at the expense of his Son's life. We should be overwhelmed that the eternally self-sufficient God, who does not need us and is alone the universal standard for good, would move toward us with his compassion to benefit us.

Counseling someone as broken as Jenny means that we dare not ignore God's love. God's goodness—that God is the standard for what is best—is wonderful and precious but not enough. Jenny needs to know not only that God does what is best, but that as he does this he is *for her*. She needs to know of God's compassion for her. Jenny needs to know that God loves her. John 3:16 gives us the authority and the mandate in counseling to tell Jenny that God loves her. The consideration of such a reality was life-changing for Jenny. She had never experienced the love of someone else. At first, Jenny had a hard time believing that she could be the recipient of such love, but once it began to sink in, it revolutionized her life.

Mercy and Grace

When we speak of God's mercy and grace, we are referring to God's kindness to undeserving people who need help. As we examine these two attributes of God, we focus on characteristics of God's nature that can be very hard to differentiate. In spite of the difficulty, many systematic theologians do make the distinction. Mercy is often understood as a manifestation of God's goodness to those who are in trouble (2 Sam. 24:14; Matt. 9:27; 2 Cor. 1:3–4). Grace is often understood as a manifestation of God's goodness to those who do not deserve it (Ps. 119:132; 1 Peter 5:10; Rom. 3:23–24; 11:6).[17] I have addressed both in my definition because of the difficulty in my mind of making a hard-and-fast distinction between the two terms, which often overlap.[18]

Though dividing these two attributes is common, the Bible often places them together (see Ex. 33:19; 34:6; Ps. 103:8; Rom. 9:15; Heb. 4:16). Still, it is not as though we can make no distinctions in the terms. Paul says, "Blessed be the God and Father of our Lord Jesus Christ, the Father of mercies and God of all comfort" (2 Cor. 1:3). This passage is talking about God comforting people going through serious hardship (2 Cor. 1:3–7), and his mercy is what is highlighted.

---

17. Grudem, *Systematic Theology*, 200; Berkhof, *Systematic Theology*, 71–72. Frame discusses the challenges of understanding the meaning of the various terms used. See John M. Frame, *Systematic Theology* (Phillipsburg, NJ: P&R, 2013), 242, 248. The attribute of God's patience is also in the mix here. When God is good to people over a long period of time in spite of their sin, this is a demonstration of his patience. Understood in such a way, patience is one specific manifestation of his mercy and grace, so I shall not cover it separately.

18. The matter gets even more complicated when you consider that there are times in the Bible when grace takes on the meaning of "power" (cf. Rom. 1:5). See Heath Lambert, *Finally Free: Fighting for Purity with the Power of Grace* (Grand Rapids, MI: Zondervan, 2013), 21–22.

Then there is Paul's teaching in Romans 3:23–24: "For all have sinned and fall short of the glory of God, and are justified by his grace as a gift, through the redemption that is in Christ Jesus." Here guilty sinners receive the priceless gift of justification, which they could never deserve, and it is seen as a manifestation of God's grace. So, though grace and mercy are each a manifestation of the kindness of God that often overlap with one another, there is biblical warrant for seeing mercy as emphasizing God's kindness toward the needy and grace as emphasizing his kindness toward the undeserving.

Everyone who comes to counseling needs to know God's mercy and grace because people usually do not seek out counseling unless they need help, and as sinners they will never deserve such help. This is as true for Jenny as it is for anyone else who receives counseling. Jenny needs mercy and grace. Jenny is a victim of terrible crimes and needs help and comfort to recover from those experiences. Jenny is also a sinner who, like every one of us, deserves to be punished for her sin. Jenny needs the mercy and grace of God more than she needs air. It is encouraging for Jenny and other counselees like her to discover that God loves to grant grace and mercy out of his inexhaustible riches. Counseling that is even remotely biblical must emphasize the grace and mercy of God.

Wrath

God's wrath is his anger toward and punishment of wickedness. This is an attribute of God that often makes people feel uncomfortable. People do not like to think about a God who gets angry and punishes people when they disobey. It makes us feel better to think about God's love, mercy, grace, and goodness. But the truth of God's wrath is actually a crucial element of God's care for people. The doctrine of God's goodness reminds us that all God is and all he does is the standard for what is best. We can know that a desire to punish evil is a good thing, rather than bad. Jenny's situation is actually a remarkable proof of this.

Not many people have been mistreated the way Jenny has been. There is something deep inside of us that screams to have her attackers be punished for what they did. This desire springs from the fact that we are made in the image of God and have some faint longing for his justice to be displayed. It would be evidence of corruption and wickedness to sense no desire for just punishment to come to Jenny's father, uncle, boyfriends—and even her mother.

We can encourage Jenny with Paul's words in Romans 12:17–19:

> Repay no one evil for evil, but give thought to do what is honorable in the sight of all. If possible, so far as it depends on you, live peaceably with all. Beloved, never avenge yourselves, but leave it to the wrath of God, for it is written, "Vengeance is mine, I will repay, says the Lord."

This passage has a command and a promise. The command to all who have been wronged and suffered injustice is to live peaceably with all people and to avoid vengeance. This command, however, is grounded in a promise that God, in his wrath, will exact vengeance. The command not to avenge is not grounded in a reality that sees vengeance as bad. It is grounded in the reality that vengeance is something that only God, who is both good and wrathful, knows how to do.

In a world where crimes go unreported and unpunished, we need to know that God's care includes a promise to punish wrongdoers in his wrath.

Counseling and the Attributes of God

By God's grace, Jenny is doing much better today. By the time counseling ended, she had grown in her trust and her confidence and was truly growing as a Christian. She had come to believe that through all that happened to her, a God who was both good and strong was working to bring good out of her situation and to make her like Christ. Jenny was becoming a truly joyful woman.

Throughout this chapter I have tried to show the relevance of each of God's attributes to counseling by relating them to Jenny's story. As this chapter concludes, I would like to offer several summary applications about the doctrine of God and biblical counseling. I will suggest five responses for biblical counselors.

First, biblical counselors should be humble and should seek to engender humility in counselees. God is everything we are not. We need to be wise, but we are not. God is. We want the power to change, but we do not have it. God does. We want to be faithful and good, but we are not. God is. The very best counselors would have all of the characteristics that only God possesses. That is why he is called the "Wonderful Counselor" (Isa. 9:6)! All of these characteristics are ones we lack because of our sin or because of our limitations as creatures. Growing in knowledge of who God is should humble us, knowing we are far from possessing the attributes most crucial to success in our work. Those attributes, which do not characterize us, describe who the perfect God is in his essence.

Second, biblical counselors should be people who worship and who lead counselees to worship. When we catch a small glimpse of the glorious God we have been examining in this chapter, we should be motivated to exalt him. The overflow of that exaltation should be words that lead our counselees to worship him too. A counselor who could even consider a counseling session without pointing to the glories of God is a counselor whose heart is further from him than we would wish, since we always speak out of the abundance of the heart (Matt. 12:34). Everyone who comes for counseling has a worship deficit. Counseling is about restoring troubled people to proper worship. Biblical counseling exists because worship does not.[19] The job of counselors is to work themselves out of a job by restoring worship in the hearts of hurting people.

Third, biblical counselors should be people who trust in God and lead counselees to trust him as well. Organizing God's attributes according to strength and care allows us to see something of huge

---

19. John Piper, *Let the Nations Be Glad!: The Supremacy of God in Missions* (Grand Rapids, MI: Baker, 1993), 11. In this book Piper makes the claim that missions exist because worship does not. Here I am simply appropriating the same idea to counseling.

significance in the character of our God. We have seen that God has unmatched power. Many Christians love to emphasize God's attribute of strength as motivating our trust in him. But God's strength alone does not motivate trust. Just as the imposing heft of an abusive husband inspires terror, so the strength of God could be a hindrance to our trust rather than a help. Other Christians love to emphasize God's attribute of care as motivating our trust in him. But God's care alone does not motivate trust. A close relationship with a very kind person who has no power to help you when you are in need can dampen trust. Trusting God requires a God who is mighty in strength and gentle in care. We can trust God and point our counselees to do the same precisely because God is powerful and loving.[20]

Fourth, biblical counselors should be people who orient their counseling around gratitude for this God who is both strong and caring. Counseling is about change. The attributes of God point out that as sinners, counselors and counselees often lack the level of care required to be involved in such efforts. Even when we have the presence of some level of care, we always lack the strength to bring about the change required. Whenever change happens in counseling, we have our good and strong God to thank for it. In light of the doctrine of God, one of the goals of counseling is to engender profound thankfulness for God in both counselor and counselee.

Finally, God sets the counseling agenda. When counselors talk about the counseling agenda, they are talking about the kinds of things that get discussed in the process of counseling. The doctrine of God teaches us that God is the one who has the right to set the agenda for counseling. It is God who made us to operate in certain ways and has revealed them to us. It is God's standards that are on the table in creating the difficulties that lead to counseling. It is God's holy moral character

---

20. There are many helpful resources counselors can use to grow in trusting God and to help their counselees do the same. Two good ones are Jerry Bridges, *Trusting God: Even When Life Hurts* (Colorado Springs: NavPress, 2008; J. I. Packer, *Knowing God* (Downers Grove, IL: InterVarsity, 1973).

that serves as the standard for counseling change. It is God's strength and care that make possible this required change.

For decades Christians have disagreed about whether God is a legitimate topic in counseling. Far too many Christians think that the God of the Bible is a negotiable subject in the conversations we call counseling. Far too many believe that secular standards of ethics can force God from the counseling room. We all need to grow in our faithfulness to God in the work of counseling. I pray that we can come to agree that one of the most central ways we can grow is by including more, not less, of the character of God in our counseling. It is knowing God—his character and his Word—that is the only way we could ever know what faithfulness is.

CHAPTER 5

BIBLICAL COUNSELING

and a

THEOLOGY OF CHRIST

So far I have introduced you to two former counselees of mine I have called Jenny and Trenyan. Jenny is the young woman who was terribly abused over decades, and we talked about the relevance of the doctrine of God to my counseling with her. As we saw in that chapter, Jenny needed—among other things—to know that God loves her, that he is with her, that he is powerful to help her, and that he will uphold justice in a world where she experienced profound exploitation. The truths the Bible teaches brought more comfort and help to her than anything the world had to offer.

Trenyan is the teenager who began cutting herself during her parents' marital collapse. I demonstrated the relevance of Scripture to Trenyan as she faced her challenging and dangerous problem. I showed how Psalm 55 sprang into life in her situation, identifying with her pain and pointing to her need for divine dependence in a desperate struggle for faith. It was this passage of Scripture that, more than anything else, made the difference in Trenyan's life.

The doctrines of God and Scripture were each of crucial importance for these two women. And yet we must pose a crucial question: Why did these two women have a right to be comforted by these two truths of

Christian theology? The doctrine of God teaches Jenny that she needs the mercy and grace of God if she is to avoid the wrath of God. But how is Jenny to know that she will receive the mercy and grace of God and not his wrath? The doctrine of the sufficiency of Scripture comforts Trenyan that the Bible shows her how to call out to God to help and save her from her pain and turmoil. But how is she to know that such a promise is for her? On what basis can Trenyan have confidence that the God who drew near to David in his difficulties will draw near to her?

These are very important questions. They may be the most important ones in all of life and counseling. Their importance is found in the reality that, as counselors, we want to help people and offer them comfort when they seek us out. We want to point our counselees to authentic and genuine comfort. We do not want to say nice things that do not apply to them or make no real difference in their life. We need to be very sure that we understand why the truths we have discussed are for the counselees we meet. When a "Jenny" comes to you for counseling, how can you be sure that God's grace and mercy are for her? When a "Trenyan" comes to you, how can you have certainty that passages like Psalm 55 and others are relevant in that conversation?

In biblical counseling, we cannot answer these questions without a theology of Christ. It is Jesus Christ alone who makes the truths we are discussing apply to the people we want to help. It is in Jesus Christ that God affirms all of his promises (2 Cor. 1:20). At the center of all truly effective counseling is Jesus, the Son of God. Jesus is at the center of biblical counseling because he occupies the center of Christian theology. He is at the center of Christian theology because he is at the center of all of life.

We cannot talk about a theology of counseling without talking about Jesus, who is the glorious epicenter of all existence. He is the Savior with whom all people must reckon. For good or ill, every person who has ever drawn breath will one day bow their knee as they stare agape at this exalted King. Knowing him is foundational to life, and so it is foundational to counseling. When discussing the doctrine of Christ in Christian theology, it is customary to talk about the person and work of Christ. We will talk about each of these as we look at the relevance of the doctrine of Christ for biblical counseling.

Who Christ Is

The Bible teaches that Jesus Christ is dramatically different from any other person who has ever existed. Christians believe that Jesus is fully God and fully man—two distinct natures in one whole person. Each of the propositions in that statement is important. Jesus has two distinct natures: divinity and humanity. He is both fully divine and fully human. He is not partially God or partially man. He is not one to the exclusion of the other. He is both. Even as he has the fullness of each of these natures, he is not two people. He is one person with two natures, and each nature is the fullness of itself. Christians believe this about Jesus because it is the inescapable conclusion of mountains of biblical texts. We will look at a few.

Jesus Is God

From the very beginnings of Christianity, the church has believed that Jesus Christ is God. This is one of the longest, most enduring, and most central elements of the church's confession. One of the earliest false teachings the church had to confront concerned objections about the full humanity of Jesus rather than the full divinity of Jesus. His humanity was one of the first truly contentious issues about Jesus. The church's confession in this regard has been long.[1]

The reason for the church's certainty on this matter is that so much biblical support exists to demonstrate that Jesus Christ is God.[2] Here we will look at three textual proofs.

---

1. See Alister McGrath, *Heresy: A History of Defending the Truth* (New York: Harper-Collins, 2009), 101–34.

2. There is not space to unpack the voluminous evidence for the deity of Jesus Christ in the limited space of this chapter. We can summarize briefly the evidence for Christ's deity here. Christ is called Lord as a translation for the divine name, Yahweh (Matt. 3:3 [cf. Isa. 40:3]; Luke

First, Jesus Christ is identified as God by the authors of Scripture. In Romans 9:4–5, Paul writes:

> They are Israelites, and to them belong the adoption, the glory, the covenants, the giving of the law, the worship, and the promises. To them belong the patriarchs, and from their race, according to the flesh, is the Christ, who is God over all, blessed forever, Amen.

Paul describes Jesus as the God who is over all and is to be blessed forever. Such an assertion would be a horrifying example of blasphemy if Jesus were a mere human being. That Paul, writing under the inspiration of the Holy Spirit, would identify Jesus in this way exalts Jesus beyond being a mere human to the God who is deserving of our eternal praise.

Second, Jesus Christ is described as doing things that only God can do. One example has to do with the creation of the heavens and the earth. The Bible is clear that God alone is the creator of all that is (Gen. 1:1–31; Ex. 20:11). The New Testament is also clear that Jesus made the heavens and the earth. Colossians 1:15–17:

> [Jesus] is the image of the invisible God, the firstborn of all creation. For by him all things were created, in heaven and on earth, visible and invisible, whether thrones or dominions or rulers or authorities—all things were created through him and for him. And he is before all things, and in him all things hold together.

Something of tremendous significance is happening here. The Old Testament identifies God as the maker of heaven and earth. The New Testament speaks specifically in identifying Jesus as the member of the Trinity whose agency actually brought this creation into existence (John 1:1–3; Heb. 1:1–2).

1:43; 2:11). Other names given to God are applied to Christ (Titus 2:13; Heb. 1:8). Christ is described using attributes that belong to God alone (John 1:3–4; Heb. 1:10–12; 13:8). Christ receives the worship that is due to God alone (Matt. 2:11; 28:9–10; John 5:23; 9:35–39; Phil. 2:10–11; Heb. 1:6; Rev. 5:8–14).

A final evidence of Jesus' divinity is that Christ makes the actual claim that he is God. He does this many times (e.g., Matt. 26:63–64; John 5:18; 17:5), but one significant place is John 10:30 where Jesus says, "I and the Father are one." In this astounding statement, Jesus is saying that he and God the Father are so much of the same essence that they are one. It was very clear to his Jewish audience that Jesus was making himself equal to God. In fact, they picked up stones to kill him because they did not recognize the presence of the One they were claiming to honor (John 10:31).

We have to decide what we will do with Jesus' words here. We cannot affirm that Jesus is a good teacher and reject his own claim to deity. Either Jesus is a good teacher and is God, as he stated, or he is not God and, therefore, a bad teacher.[3]

According to Scripture, God is three and one. He is Trinity. There is a sense in which God is one because there are not multiple gods (Deut. 6:4; James 2:19), and yet God's oneness is not simplistic but is complex. There is plurality in God's oneness. The Father is God, Jesus Christ is God, and the Bible affirms that the Holy Spirit is also God (Mark 3:28–29; Acts 5:1–4). The church believes that these three members of the Trinity are distinct persons. So all three are God, yet the Father is not the Son, the Son is not the Spirit, and the Spirit is not the Father.

It can be challenging to understand the complex distinction within overall unity that is the biblical teaching on the Trinity. One way to think about this is by considering the government of the United States of America. The United States has one federal government. Yet within this one government are three branches. The executive, legislative, and judicial branches are each fully the government, yet they are each distinct in that the executive branch is not the legislative branch, the legislative branch is not the judicial branch, and the judiciary is not the executive.[4]

---

3. See C. S. Lewis, *Mere Christianity* (London: Collins, 1952), 54–56. Here Lewis poses his famous "trilemma" that Jesus is either a lunatic, a liar, or Lord.

4. Many analogies have been used for the Trinity, and all of them break down at a certain point. So does this one. While the federal government of the United States illustrates the

All of this is an important qualification as we consider Jesus' claim to deity in John 10:30. When Jesus is saying that he and the Father are one, he is not saying that there is no distinction between his personality as a member of the Trinity and the Father's personality. He is rather endorsing that he and the Father are of the same divine essence. Christians believe that Jesus is God because the Bible records that Jesus said he is God.[5]

Jesus Is Human

Jesus is God, yet the Bible is equally clear that he is also a human being. Here we must talk about the doctrine of the incarnation. The incarnation means that the eternal Son of God took on flesh, being born of a woman, and became a human being. Galatians 4:4–5 teaches this doctrine:

> But when the fullness of time had come, God sent forth his Son, born of woman, born under the law, to redeem those who were under the law.

In the incarnation something new, different, and astonishing happened. The infinite and holy Son of God took on human flesh. Bruce Ware says that the incarnation is

> the uniting of the divine and human natures in Jesus, such that this one would be born the son of Mary (Luke 1:31) and the son of "his father David" (v. 32) while also being "the Son of the Most High" (v. 32), "the Son of God" (v. 35).[6]

---

complex unity that exists in the Godhead, it is a poor example of the cooperative and loving relationship that exists among the members of the Trinity. The various branches of government often exist in an adversarial role, which is in no way true of God, who is Father, Son, and Spirit.

5. For more information, see Robert Letham, *The Holy Trinity: In Scripture, History, Theology, and Worship* (Phillipsburg, NJ: P&R, 2004).

6. Bruce A. Ware, *The Man Christ Jesus: Theological Reflections on the Humanity of Christ* (Wheaton, IL: Crossway, 2013), 16.

The incarnation requires us to believe and confess that Jesus Christ was not limited to being a divine person but was a human one as well.

Jesus' humanity is quite obviously the case in the picture of Jesus that we have in the Gospels. First, we read that Jesus was born (Matt. 1:25–2:2). Though Jesus was the product of a virginal conception (Matt. 1:18–23), his experience of physical birth was that of every other human being who has come into the world. We are also told that Jesus became hungry just like any other person (Matt. 4:2). After a long journey, Jesus was tired and needed to rest (John 4:4–6). When he was parched, he needed a drink of water (John 19:28). Finally, Jesus endured terrible pain, gave up his physical breath, and died (Luke 23:46–56).

Jesus was, therefore, a man. He had rather obvious human limitations, weaknesses, and physical needs. Without food and water, Jesus would have died. When he was crucified, he *did* die. Our belief in the Scriptures given to us by God requires us to believe the teaching about Jesus Christ as being fully human as well as fully divine.[7]

The Crucial Importance of the Two Natures of Jesus

Of all the truths of Christian theology, I find this one the most challenging to wrap my mind around. It is very difficult to grasp how Jesus could possess the fullness of two distinct natures in one person without any mixture or dilution of either one of those two natures.

---

7. The biblical truth that Jesus has two natures in one person has been called the "hypostatic union" and was first articulated by the church in 451 at the Council of Chalcedon. This was how Chalcedon described this theological reality: "We all with one accord teach men to acknowledge one and the same Son, our Lord Jesus Christ, at once complete in Godhead and complete in manhood, truly God and truly man, consisting also of a reasonable soul and body; of one substance with the Father as regards his Godhead, and at the same time of one substance with us as regards his manhood; like us in all respects, apart from sin; as regards his Godhead, begotten of the Father before the ages, but yet as regards his manhood begotten, for us men and for our salvation, of Mary the Virgin, the God-bearer; one and the same Christ, Son, Lord, Only-begotten, recognized in two natures, without confusion, without change, without division, without separation; the distinction of natures being in no way annulled by the union, but rather the characteristics of each nature being preserved and coming together to form one person and subsistence, not as parted or separated into two persons, but one and the same Son and Only-begotten God the Word, Lord Jesus Christ," International Society of Christian Apologetics, http://www.isca-apologetics.org/creeds.

Though the truth is hard to understand, we should not experience that difficulty as a serious problem. There are lots of things we do not understand that are true. My brother works in a part of the world where it is regularly 115 degrees. I do not understand what that kind of heat feels like, but I believe that he experiences it. My wife enjoys broccoli. I cannot understand how that is possible, but I believe she does. Our ability to understand something is not the standard that renders it true. All kinds of things are true without our having the commensurate ability to understand them. In fact, it is an encouragement to know that we cannot fully understand this doctrine. If it was easy for us to grasp that God took on human flesh and became a man, we would be suspicious that perhaps it was *too* easy. When the truths we confess are larger than our minds can grasp, it should encourage us about the immense glory of the God we worship. At a certain point, it is good to cease our pondering, realize that God is pleased with our faith (Heb. 11:6), and direct our confidence toward this God who came in the flesh.

The truth that Jesus Christ is fully God and fully man is not an abstract truth with no practical value. It is precious beyond words that God came in the flesh and revealed himself to us. It is crucial to our salvation that this is true. Five passages of Scripture emphasize why:

Isaiah 43:11 asserts, "I am the LORD, and besides me there is no savior" (cf. Pss. 3:8; 62:7). The Scripture is clear that there is no savior available to the human race other than the God of heaven and earth. It is impossible for there to be any other savior from sin because only the infinite God could bear the infinite penalty of sins for the human race (Rom. 8:3–4; Heb. 10:12). If Jesus Christ were a mere man and not God, he could not have been the Savior we need.

First Timothy 2:5 says, "For there is one God, and there is one mediator between God and men, the man Christ Jesus." When Paul speaks of a mediator, he is describing the need for someone to stand in the breach that exists between God and man. That breach is caused by sin. Isaiah 59:2 says, "But your iniquities have made a separation between you and your God, and your sins have hidden his face from you." That Jesus is fully God assures that he alone is the mediator to overcome sin. In his deity, Jesus provides the spotless sacrifice needed to apply forgiveness to humanity. In his humanity, he reveals God to us. It requires both natures of Christ's singular person to accomplish each of these and to be the required mediator.[8]

Hebrews 2:17 says, "Therefore he had to be made like his brothers in every respect, so that he might become a merciful and faithful high priest in the service of God, to make propitiation for the sins of the people." Propitiation means that Jesus bore the weight of God's wrath and paid the penalty for all sin. We saw, above, that only God can bear sin's infinite penalty for the human race. If Jesus were only God, he could not have been like his brothers in "every respect," nor could he have been a merciful and faithful high priest. He also could not have died as a human being to pay the penalty for our sin. Propitiation required a Savior who is fully God and fully man.

Romans 5:19 says, "For as by the one man's disobedience the many were made sinners, so by the one man's obedience the many will be made righteous." Paul is teaching that we need a representative. Just as humanity was represented in sin by Adam, so humanity must be represented in righteousness by Jesus. Again, as we saw above, only God can bear the penalty for sin and so be the Savior. Here we see that, as true as that reality is, God cannot represent man as man. Such representation requires humanity. Christ's divinity and humanity are both essential for him to be the representative of righteousness required for the forgiveness of our sin.

First John 2:6 says, "Whoever says he abides in him ought to walk in the same way in which he walked." We saw from Romans 5 that we need Jesus' righteousness as a human being to represent us in the righteousness we lack. First John teaches that we also need Jesus' righteous humanity to provide the moral example that we should follow. It is the clear teaching of this passage that those whom Jesus has represented

---

8. Louis Berkhof, *Systematic Theology* (Grand Rapids, MI: Eerdmans, 1996), 282–83. Berkhof talks about the "two-fold mediatorship of Christ."

as Savior and who abide in him will be the people who walk as Jesus walked. As we do this, we can have confidence that the same Spirit who empowered obedience in Jesus (Acts 10:38) will empower that same Christlike obedience in our lives as well (Rom. 8:11).

It is of crucial importance to embrace that Jesus Christ possessed, in one person, a fully divine nature and a fully human nature. Without this belief, our salvation from sin would be impossible. Without this belief, it would have been impossible to help Jenny and Trenyan, as we shall see. Now, having seen who Jesus is, we must now investigate what he has done.

What Christ Has Done

The person of Christ is inseparable from the work of Christ because it takes the character that Jesus possessed to complete the work he accomplished while on earth. We can summarize Jesus' work by saying that he came to save us. As was demonstrated above, only Jesus in his dual natures of God and man could have worked this salvation. In this section we will talk about the salvation that Jesus worked in three categories: earning our righteousness, paying sin's penalty, and rising from the grave and ascending to heaven.

Earning Our Righteousness

In the discussion above about the dual natures of Christ, I emphasized that Jesus Christ was fully human. From the time of the very early church until today, Christians have affirmed the humanity of Jesus by asserting that Jesus is of "one substance with us as regards his manhood; like us in all respects, apart from sin."[9] In other words, Christians have affirmed that there is only one thing about the humanity of Jesus that makes him distinct from every other human being: "For we do not have a high priest who is unable to sympathize with our weaknesses, but

---

9. This is from the language used to describe the humanity of Jesus at the Council of Chalcedon.

one who in every respect has been tempted as we are, yet without sin" (Heb. 4:15).

Jesus' sinlessness makes him distinct from every other human being, but that does not make Jesus less human. Indeed, the lack of sin in Jesus makes him *more* human than any other person. You do not have to sin in order to be human. Far from it. In fact, human beings were not designed to sin. They were created to glorify God with all of who they are. Sin, as it warps our design to honor God, actually dehumanizes us. Jesus' sinless perfection—far from minimizing his full humanity—actually maximizes it. We will not realize the full potential of our own humanity until we are free from the scourge of sin. The absence of sin in Jesus allowed him to experience the fullness of what it means to be a human being. It also was required for him to accomplish his work of redeeming the human race.

Unlike Jesus, other human beings are plagued with sin in every part of their existence. To overcome this problem of sin, we need the presence of positive righteousness that we could never earn in our sinfulness. We saw from Romans 5:19 that Jesus Christ served as a representative for us as he lived a righteous life before God. Paul describes himself as "not having a righteousness of my own that comes from the law, but that which comes through faith in Christ" (Phil. 3:9).

Paul writes that the only righteousness he has is the righteousness that is through faith in Jesus Christ. What is true for Paul is true for everyone else. As sinful people, we do not have any righteousness that we earn on our own by following the law. Jesus lived every moment of his life free from sin. He was tempted, but he never gave in. He never gave way to any moral weakness. Every day of his life he obeyed every word of his Father, earning the righteousness that becomes the property of every person who, as Paul said in Philippians, has faith in Jesus.[10]

---

10. Theologians often refer to this work of Jesus as his active obedience.

Paying Our Penalty

The obedience of Jesus solves only part of the problem we face as human beings and sinners who must confront a holy God. To be acceptable to God, we need positive righteousness. Additionally, we need to be rid of the penalty of God's wrath that is due to us because of our sin. Without the payment for our sin, we could never be acceptable to a holy God who cannot look upon sin.

That is why it is such good news that Jesus Christ not only earned our righteousness through his perfect life but he also paid our penalty through his painful death on the cross.[11] The apostle Peter describes this aspect of the work of Christ when he says, "He himself bore our sins in his body on the tree, that we might die to sin and live to righteousness. By his wounds you have been healed" (1 Peter 2:24).

Peter uses the powerful language of wounds and healing to describe the work of Jesus and its effects. Jesus' wounds, which he sustained on his cross, are what heal our otherwise incurable problem of sin. Jesus, as the perfect man and infinite God, offered himself as that One who received the painful penalty in the place of all who have disobeyed God and would trust in his work.

Jesus' work of paying our penalty on the cross is inseparably related to his work of earning our righteousness in his perfect life. Had Jesus not lived a blameless life, he would not have had the moral perfection necessary to take away the sins of those who believe in him since sin can only be cleansed away by a spotless sacrifice (1 Peter 1:19). Because Jesus' life was characterized by moral perfection, his death accomplished the necessary sacrifice that makes believers acceptable to God. As death loomed, Jesus announced, "It is finished" (John 19:30). Those words signify that Jesus had accomplished all that he had been sent by God to do, all that was necessary both to earn obedience and to pay the penalty for all who would trust in him as their Savior.

---

11. Theologians often refer to this aspect of the work of Christ as his passive obedience.

Rising and Ascending

If the work of Jesus Christ had ended after living his perfect life and dying his brutal death, it would have been bad news. His execution would have been the final word, and Jesus would have been proven ineffective in doing the work he came to do. He would have been defeated by the grave (1 Cor. 15:17). Jesus did not experience such a defeat. Instead, Jesus was victorious over sin, death, and the Devil. Jesus rose from the dead, and after he had appeared to many people as evidence of his resurrection (1 Cor. 15:1–8), witnesses observed him ascend into heaven to be installed as the victorious King of kings and Lord of lords (Acts 1:9–11).

Paul speaks of this in Ephesians 1:19–22:

> The immeasurable greatness of [God's] power toward us who believe, according to the working of his great might that he worked in Christ when he raised him from the dead and seated him at his right hand in the heavenly places, far above all rule and authority and power and dominion, and above every name that is named, not only in this age but also in the one to come. And he put all things under his feet and gave him as head over all things to the church.

This passage describes the incredible realities of resurrection and ascension. Consider that modern medical technology can work wonders on human beings who are very near the point of death and restore them to health. But there is no person, procedure, medicine, or machine that can restore life to someone who has passed the point of death. It is beyond the capacity of human beings to accomplish that. Consider also that it far surpasses any of our powers to take a person and elevate them to heaven. We do not even know where heaven is and are far from possessing the energy to get someone there. Such accomplishments are impossible for us. But God can do them, and he did do them for Jesus.

The apostle Paul tells us why:

Have this mind among yourselves, which is yours in Christ Jesus, who, though he was in the form of God, did not count equality with God a thing to be grasped, but emptied himself, by taking the form of a servant, being born in the likeness of men. And being found in human form, he humbled himself by becoming obedient to the point of death, even death on a cross. Therefore God has highly exalted him and bestowed on him the name that is above every name (Phil. 2:5–9).

Jesus Christ was in the "form of God" and yet "born in the likeness of men." In that state as the God-man he was obedient even to the point of "death on a cross." God the Father exalted Jesus in resurrection and ascension because of who he is and what he did. The person and work of Jesus are, therefore, of one piece. The God-man who was obedient in our place, earning our righteousness and paying our penalty, is the Christ who is exalted as King. This truth gives us great encouragement and confidence in the Christ we are called to worship.

Jesus, Trenyan, and Jenny

The theological understanding of the person and work of Jesus that we have surveyed in this chapter is not just of interest in counseling. It is *required* in counseling. Jesus is the key to the help and hope that our counselees need. He is the key to the care that I offered to Trenyan and Jenny. Jenny, on her own, is not entitled to the grace of God. Trenyan has no intrinsic claim to the comfort of God's presence in Psalm 55. Counselees in themselves do not deserve access to any of God's goodness. The grace of God and the comfort of God's presence—and much more—come only through Jesus Christ. They require what theologians have called "the doctrine of union with Christ." The doctrine of the believer's union with Christ teaches that God considers to be true of those who trust in Jesus Christ all that is true of Christ himself. When a person comes to have faith in Jesus, God views them as though they lived his life and earned his benefits.[12] The implications of this for counseling are enormous. There are at least three truths that we must consider here that every counselee needs.

Counselees Need the Person and Work of Christ for Forgiveness

Every human being needs God's forgiveness because every human being is guilty of sin. Every counselee needs God's forgiveness of their sins. Counselees also struggle with other problems besides their own sin, so the sin of a counselee will not be the only thing addressed in counseling. Sin often will not even be the first thing addressed. Leaders in the biblical counseling movement have been rather clear about this.[13] And yet the Bible teaches that the fundamental problem with every human being is our sin. It is this sin that occasions the need for Christ. To obscure this reality of sin in counseling—or anywhere else—is to obscure the central problem that Jesus came to solve with his person and his work.

Ephesians 1:7 says, "In him we have redemption through his blood, the forgiveness of our trespasses, according to the riches of his grace." This passage teaches that the forgiveness of our sins is found in the person ("In him") and the work ("redemption through his blood") of Jesus. Trenyan and Jenny are in desperate need of this forgiveness. Because Trenyan and Jenny are victims of the terrible sins of others, their own personal sinfulness is not the obvious factor in counseling them, but it does need to be addressed at some point. They each are guilty of sins that are not connected to any of the reasons they came for counseling. Sin is also in the picture for reasons directly related to their need for counsel. They have each responded to the sins of others with sins of

---

12. See Lewis B. Swedes, *Union with Christ: A Biblical View of the New Life in Jesus Christ* (Grand Rapids, MI: Eerdmans, 1983); Anthony A. Hoekema, *Saved by Grace* (Grand Rapids, MI: Eerdmans, 1994), 65–67.

13. Jay E. Adams, *More Than Redemption: A Theology of Christian Counseling* (Grand Rapids, MI: Baker, 1980), 139–40l; David Powlison, "Crucial Issues in Contemporary Biblical Counseling," *Journal of Pastoral Practice* 9, no. 3 (1988): 61–63; Edward Welch, "Exalting Pain? Ignoring Pain? What Do We Do with Suffering?" *Journal of Biblical Counseling* 12, no. 3 (1994): 4.

their own. Jenny responded to the violent sexual immorality of others against her with her own sexual sins as she lived promiscuously with numerous men. Trenyan's mom sinned against her in her own adultery, and Trenyan sinned against her own body by cutting her legs. Loving Jenny and Trenyan means more than being a comforting presence in their lives. Love requires that we point them to the person and work of Jesus to cleanse them from their sin.

The need for forgiving grace in the lives of Trenyan and Jenny is an example for us with our other counselees. Even when we are ministering to counselees who have been horrifyingly victimized, the Christian theology of Jesus reminds us that they also need to be forgiven for their sin. Sometimes the sin of counselees will be obvious to them, and other times it will not be. Sometimes their sin will be connected to their search for counseling help, and other times it will not. Sometimes counselors will confront sin earlier in one counseling context and later in another. But all counselees are sinners who need to hear of the forgiving grace of Jesus. They need God's grace. The doctrine of the person and work of Jesus moves a confrontation of sin from a mean-spirited attack to a deeply loving expression of care. We never merely confront people with a sin, but with the work of Jesus Christ to take away that sin by his own blood. When we confront a sin, it should always be done with compassion, care, and hope and always with the promise of Christ's forgiveness when the confrontation is met with repentance.

Counselees Need the Person and Work of Christ for Power

Just as every person needs Jesus for forgiveness, they also need him for the power to move away from sin and toward a holy life. Jesus Christ did not come merely to pay for our sin. He also came to help us to live a new life through his work as our ascended Savior. The resurrection of Jesus empowers a life of obedience for Christians:

What shall we say then? Are we to continue in sin that grace may abound? By no means! How can we who died to sin still live in it? Do you not know that all of us who have been baptized into Christ Jesus were baptized into his death? We were buried therefore with him by baptism into death, in order that, just as Christ was raised from the dead by the glory of the Father, we too might walk in newness of life. (Rom. 6:1–4)

An experience of the grace of Christ will not lead to more sin, but rather to righteousness (cf. Rom. 6:12–14). Paul grounds that fact in the resurrection of Jesus Christ. Christians can walk in newness of life because Jesus Christ has been "raised from the dead by the glory of the Father." The physical resurrection of Jesus leads to an ethical resurrection for Christians. We have the power to live according to Jesus' example because of the resurrection power purchased for us by Jesus.

The ascension of Jesus also empowers a life of obedience for Christians:

The former priests were many in number, because they were prevented by death from continuing in office, but he holds his priesthood permanently, because he continues forever. Consequently, he is able to save to the uttermost those who draw near to God through him, since he always lives to make intercession for them. (Heb. 7:23–25)

The author of Hebrews is demonstrating the superiority of Jesus to the Old Testament priests. He talks about the priestly element of Jesus' work as ascended Savior. A priest is one who speaks to God on behalf of the people. This passage contrasts the temporary nature of an Old Testament priest with the permanent nature of Jesus' priesthood. Jesus' priesthood is permanent because he lives forever. His priesthood is perfect because he always lives to make intercession for his people.

Jesus is always praying for his people. He is a priest who is always speaking to the Father on our behalf. One example of a priestly prayer of Jesus is found in John 17. In that passage Jesus prays numerous things for us, but one way to summarize his many requests is that he prays that the things God commands of his people would be true of them. It is astonishing that the things God calls us to do are the same things Jesus Christ is praying—even now—for us to have the power to do.

More than anything else, Jenny needs to know that through Christ, she has access to a Father who loves her and will always care for her. How is Jenny supposed to engage in the daily fight to turn to that Father in faith and trust when the only father she has ever known mistreated her worse than almost anyone else? The truth of the resurrection of Jesus Christ promises her that Jesus has secured for her the power to turn to God in faith and trust. The truth of the ascension of Jesus Christ assures that—even when she is not praying and nobody else is praying for her—Jesus is interceding for her as high priest. Biblical counselors will do many things to help Jenny experience change, but the most important is calling on her to trust in the power of her resurrected and ascended King.

Then there's Trenyan. She was experiencing all kinds of pain and difficulty as the cuts accumulated on her legs. In spite of that, when her parents were screaming and she was stressing, the thought of a break from the stress that a loss of consciousness would bring felt as tempting as a seat by a warm fire on a snowy day. How is Trenyan supposed to muster the resources to stop the cutting and break such a soothing cycle? There are many counseling interventions that the Bible would recommend for us to point out to her, but they are all grounded and founded on the resurrection resources of her ascended priest, Jesus, who prays earnestly for her to know a better way.

What is true for Jenny and Trenyan is true for your counselees and for you. There is a biblical process of care that we utilize in counseling, but in a book on theology there is no space to discuss the many issues of methodology that are of great import in counseling. Here we must affirm that no strategy, no intervention, no methodology or counseling system can ever produce the power our counselees need to change. The doctrine of Christ reminds us that the power we need is found exclusively in the person and work of Jesus of Nazareth.

Counselees Need the Person and Work of Christ for Comfort

As encouraging as it is to consider Jesus' grace to forgive us and change us, he gives us even more grace. We grow in holiness slowly and so still experience the consequences of our sin. We live in a world of other sinners who egregiously wrong us. We live in a world that experiences the bitter fruit of the curse of sin. All this ensures that in this life we will know pain and suffering. In a world like this, we need comfort. In chapter 8 we will consider the issue of comfort more fully, but here we examine the comfort we can know from the person and work of Jesus.

To see the comfort of Christ in this kind of pain, it is helpful to examine the promise of Hebrews 13:5: "I will never leave you nor forsake you." This promise is connected to the person and work of Christ found in Matthew 27:46, where Jesus cries out, "My God, my God, why have you forsaken me?" Many have wrestled with why Jesus, since he knew who he was and what he came to do, would ask that question. Jesus' question seems to indicate that maybe he was confused about what was happening. Such a suggestion forgets that Jesus is a teacher of the Bible who regularly quotes passages of Scripture to show his fulfillment of them. The question Jesus poses on the cross is actually a quote from Psalm 22:1. Psalm 22 is about a man who is forsaken by God, but who is eventually delivered by him (Ps. 22:19–21) and who spreads the fame of God throughout the world (Ps. 22:22–23, 25–31). Jesus quotes Psalm 22 to reference that he is the fulfillment of this passage. Jesus poses the question because the text he is quoting is written as a question.[14]

The point is that Jesus *was* forsaken by God. God the Father directed

---

14. John Stott is very helpful in understanding this issue. See John R. W. Stott, *The Cross of Christ* (Downers Grove, IL: InterVarsity, 1986), 82.

all of his hatred and revulsion of sin against Jesus and looked away from his own Son. For the first time in eternity, there was a break in the Son's relationship with the Father. Jesus was alone, abandoned, and forsaken. It was Jesus' payment of this element of sin's penalty that makes the promise of Hebrews 13 so incomprehensibly sweet. God can give the promise that we will never be forsaken because Jesus was forsaken on our behalf in his death on the cross.

Consider how this applies to Jenny and Trenyan. I pointed out the comfort that came into Jenny's life when she learned that the omnipresent God is always with her. I shared how encouraged Trenyan was by the promise from Psalm 55 that God will draw near to her in her time of pain. What we now see is that these promises are comforting only when those young women lay hold of them by trusting in the Christ who makes them true through his person and work.

Jesus Christ: The Key to All Counseling

Jesus Christ is the key to all counseling. Everything we need from God requires us to trust in Jesus to receive it.[15] In counseling, the only hope and help that matters in the long term is that which Jesus Christ brings. Other approaches can talk about strategies to minimize anxiety, exercises to reduce depression, tactics to stretch the fuse of anger, and medications to numb pain. None of these lead to real change, and none of them last. It is Jesus—and Jesus alone—who addresses the problems we face at a level of depth and power unavailable in any secular counseling intervention.

Jesus knows this is true. It is why he commanded us to tell others about him.

---

15. When counseling individuals, I always want them to be reading good books to grow in their knowledge of who Jesus is and what he has done. Some examples of books I use are John Piper, *Seeing and Savoring Jesus Christ* (Wheaton, IL: Crossway, 2004); C. J. Mahaney, *The Cross Centered Life: Keeping the Gospel the Main Thing* (Sisters, OR: Multnomah, 2002); Milton Vincent, *A Gospel Primer for Christians: Learning to See the Glories of God's Love* (Bemidji, MN: Focus, 2008).

Jesus came and said to them, "All authority in heaven and on earth has been given to me. Go therefore and make disciples of all nations, baptizing them in the name of the Father and of the Son and of the Holy Spirit, teaching them to observe all that I have commanded you. And behold, I am with you always, to the end of the age." (Matt. 28:18–20)

This passage is the Great Commission. Jesus said these words after his resurrection, after he had received "all authority" because of his obedient life and death. And just before his ascension, he promised that he will be with his disciples forever as their ascended King. That obedient, sin-paying, exalted, resurrected, soon-to-be ascended King gives the command to go and tell others about him.

The commission to speak of Jesus is a glorious command given to those who are beholding the only Person who can forgive, empower, and comfort them by virtue of who he is and what he has done. It is a command that Paul rejoiced in obeying: "I decided to know nothing among you except Jesus Christ and him crucified" (1 Cor. 2:2). It is a command that every Christian must obey. Jesus has not given us the freedom to avoid speaking of him to others. It does not matter whether we label our conversations "missions," "getting to know the neighbors," "lunch together," or "counseling." Christians are commanded by Jesus Christ to speak of him out of our overflow of love for him and our concern for those who need to hear of him.

That is why it is so sad to hear some Christian counselors say, for example,

I will only consider "spiritual approaches" for clients who have given informed consent and who are requesting such interventions. Further, I will not go beyond the boundaries appropriate to the setting in which I am practicing.[16]

---

16. Gary W. Moon, in Stephen P. Greggo and Timothy A. Sisemore, eds., *Counseling and Christianity: Five Approaches* (Downers Grove, IL: IVP Academics, 2012), 141.

As Christians we are simply not allowed to speak this way. It dishonors Jesus and his clear command, and it is a failure to love people who need Jesus more than anything else in the entire world. Such a statement betrays a greater deference to secular ethics boards than to the clear words of Jesus.

It is the privilege of every Christian to point to the unmatched glory of Jesus Christ as fully God and fully man, who has come to redeem humanity in his life, death, resurrection, and ascension. Refusing to speak of him is not only outside the bounds of biblical counseling, it is fundamentally unchristian. When we see who Jesus is, what he has done, and what that means for all who trust in him, we can do nothing but open our mouths and speak of him who, for our sake, died and was raised (2 Cor. 5:15).

CHAPTER 6

BIBLICAL COUNSELING

and a

THEOLOGY OF THE
HOLY SPIRIT

✝

Scott was furious. He was not angry, he was furious. He had been hostile toward me, his wife, and the entire counseling process from the moment he walked into my office four weeks previously. His hostility on that first day now seemed like gentleness compared to the way he was behaving.

Scott's wife, Renee, made the initial appointment to meet with me several months earlier. At that point she said her marriage, after a decade of misery, had become unbearable. Scott was *always* angry—sometimes violently. He had never used physical force against her, but he threw cups, plates, and chairs and punched his fist into the wall. He screamed and shouted profanities at her, their friends, people in traffic, servers at restaurants, and even his bosses at work. His tantrums at work put him in a perpetual cycle of looking for new employment. No one issue or person seemed to make Scott angry. He was just *always* angry about everything.

Unfortunately, that was not the only problem Scott had. He was also arrogant.[1] As far as Scott was concerned, he was never wrong about anything. Issues at home, work, church, and even driving around town were always the fault of someone else. Renee could remember no instance in their entire marriage when Scott had accepted responsibility for any of their problems. Instead, he constantly charged Renee with all of the blame.

Renee had reached a tipping point. She could not imagine enduring the situation any longer. Several weeks before she called to set up the counseling appointment with me, Scott and Renee were at dinner with friends when he blew up about something and left the table, telling her to get a ride home with their friends. Those friends were people I had counseled years earlier, and they gave Renee my number. Weeks later, Renee called, sobbing.

We arranged a time to meet at the earliest opportunity, but Renee was very uncertain about her ability to persuade Scott to come. He eventually did agree and came with Renee to the first meeting in my office. As soon as Scott came through the door, he confirmed everything Renee had shared with me in our phone conversation and on the intake form I had provided her. When I greeted Scott with a smile and an extended hand, he scowled, turned to sit, and said, in a raised voice, that he had no idea why they needed to see a counselor. He said Renee was being her usual hardheaded self, and if she would calm down and just listen to him, they would not be wasting anyone's time with a silly counseling appointment.

Through eight hours of meetings over the next four weeks, Scott's attitude never changed. I was never able to get through to him or to draw him into the counseling relationship in any way. When I prayed, he would sigh. When I read the Bible, he rolled his eyes. He evaded my questions, avoided work I gave him to do between sessions, denied fault, and snapped at Renee and me. When I would confront him with his

---

1. From a biblical perspective, arrogance and anger are inextricably related, since anger flows from unfulfilled selfish desires (James 4:1–2).

behavior, his frustration would increase. When Renee described painful incidents of their relationship, he would scoff.

By week four, we were no closer to progress than when Renee first called me. That meeting was particularly bad, and Scott's frustration was palpable. He began to yell at Renee and addressed her with a profanity. I told him that he must stop, that I would not allow him to speak that way to his wife in my office. He stared at me and repeated the profanity. I knew what he was doing. I appealed to Scott. I said I cared for him, his wife, and their marriage. I said I wanted to help him in any way I could, but that he must demonstrate a willingness to join the effort. I explained that one way he could do that was by not speaking in such a shocking, disrespectful, and sinful way. If he could not agree to this, he was going to have to leave. He looked at me again, repeated the vulgarity, stood up, and walked out, telling Renee to find her own way home.

As he thundered out of my office, his wife remained in my office, crying. Moving quickly, I got up and raced after him. I could not back off my standard and let him speak so terribly to his wife, but I wanted to make a final, private appeal for him to work with me. I chased him out to the parking lot. I pleaded for him to come back and try to be reasonable. I implored that his marriage to Renee was important and that he must work on it. I assured him that Jesus wanted more for his marriage than this, and that there was help and power to change if he would only trust Jesus. Scott never acknowledged me. He drove off, leaving me standing in the parking lot.

That was it. The meeting was over. I have stayed in touch with Renee episodically and learned that a few years after our meeting, they divorced. I have never seen Scott again. Our counseling ended abruptly and in tremendous failure.

The issue I want to address in this chapter is why counseling with Scott failed so miserably. I have many failings as a counselor, but I do not think those failings were responsible for the tragic ending of my counseling with this couple. I did many of the same things with Scott and Renee that have borne fruit with other counselees experiencing similar difficulties. I shared my notes from our sessions with two trusted counseling mentors who affirmed that I did the same kinds of things they would have done. My weaknesses as a counselor were not the cause of this counseling failure.

The reason that counseling with Scott and Renee failed is related to the biblical doctrine of the Holy Spirit. The Holy Spirit is vital to a biblical approach to counseling. In fact, if biblical counselors were to offer any qualifications to their theology of the sufficiency of Scripture, it would have to do with the doctrine of the Spirit. Biblical counselors do not believe that the Scriptures are sufficient without the ministry of the Holy Spirit. The Bible does not work automatically and on its own as the sacred words wash over people. The Word of God is only effective when the Spirit of God renders it effective in the lives of individuals. In this chapter on the doctrine of the Spirit in biblical counseling, I examine six elements of the Spirit's crucial role in counseling.

The Spirit's Work of Convicting

The crucial passage on the convicting work of the Spirit is found in John 16:8–11:

> When [the Spirit] comes, he will convict the world concerning sin and righteousness and judgment; concerning sin, because they do not believe in me; concerning righteousness, because I go to the Father, and you will see me no longer; concerning judgment, because the ruler of this world is judged.

The New Testament emphasizes the work of the Holy Spirit in believers, but this passage is unique in talking of the Spirit's role in the world. That work in the world is described as convicting and is developed in three ways.

The Holy Spirit works to convict people in the world of sin because they do not believe in Jesus Christ (John 16:9). The world needs the

The world needs the Holy Spirit [handwritten margin note]

Spirit for this work because these people would never experience such conviction on their own. Sinners are hardened into unbelief and disobedience and never feel the weight of their sin without the work of the Spirit.2

The Holy Spirit also convicts the world concerning righteousness (John 16:10). Following his work of convicting sinners of their sin, the Spirit works in the hearts of people to convict them of the righteousness they need. Jesus says the Spirit convicts of this righteousness specifically because he is going to the Father and his people will see him no longer. This is a powerful assertion that Jesus is the standard of righteousness in the Spirit's conviction of us. To see him is to behold the righteousness that he possesses and we lack. Because he has gone to heaven, we cannot see him. The Spirit miraculously convicts us of this righteousness. He does this by powerfully displaying Christ to us as our righteous and ascended King.3

Finally, the Holy Spirit convicts the world concerning judgment because the ruler of the world is judged (John 16:11). The Holy Spirit's convicting work is also seen working in the hearts of unbelievers to convince them of the judgment that is theirs because they follow the Devil, who has already been judged through the work of Christ on the cross (Col. 2:13–15). The world has been judged together with the Devil, and the Spirit works to convict them of this fact.4

---

2. Leon Morris says, "The Spirit brings the world's guilt home to itself. The Spirit convicts the individual sinner's conscience. Otherwise people would never come to see themselves as sinners." Leon Morris, *The Gospel According to John*, The New International Critical Commentary on the New Testament, ed. Gordon D. Fee (Grand Rapids, MI: Eerdmans, 1995), 619.

3. Leon Morris says, "The righteousness that is shown by Christ's going to the Father is surely the righteousness that is established by Christ. It is precisely this righteousness that requires the work of the Holy Spirit for people to be convinced about it. The Spirit shows people (and no one else can do this) that righteousness is not the acquiring of merit that they think it is; righteousness before God depends not on their own efforts but on Christ's atoning work for them." Leon Morris, *The Gospel According to John: The English Text with Introduction, Exposition, and Notes* (Grand Rapids, MI: Eerdmans, 1971), 620.

4. Andreas J. Köstenberger says, "When the evidence is properly weighed, it turns out that it is the world that is guilty of the sin of unbelief, convicted on the basis of Christ's righteousness (or his lack of unrighteousness) and judged *together* with the supernatural 'ruler of this world'" (emphasis added). Andreas J. Köstenberger, *John: Baker Exegetical Commentary on the New Testament* (Grand Rapids, MI: Baker Academic, 2004), 471. See also George Beasley-Murray, who says, "The Paraclete brings to light that this involves the judgment of the world in

The Bible is clear that the Spirit's work of conviction happens through human involvement. This is the teaching of Romans 10:13–14:

> For "everyone who calls on the name of the Lord will be saved."
> How then will they call on him in whom they have not believed?
> And how are they to believe in him of whom they have never heard?
> And how are they to hear without someone preaching?

Paul is clear that the kind of conviction that leads to crying out to the Lord requires someone to share the message for them to hear and ultimately believe. The Spirit's work of conviction works through the proclamation of Christ made by human beings. The point of John 16, however, is that there is no human proclamation that is effective on its own. Human words must be paired with the Spirit's activity to bring about conviction.[5]

For counseling to be successful, the Holy Spirit must take the words of our biblical counsel and press them into the hearts of people, convicting them in a way that only he can. Counseling will never ultimately be effective without the work of the Spirit. Our role as counselors is important. We are to nurture a set of effective skills and work hard at being faithful to the Scriptures when ministering to people. Our skills, however, are never effective on their own. They are effective only when paired with the work of the Holy Spirit to bring conviction.

---

that its submission to the 'prince of this world' led not only to its rejection of the Son of God, but to becoming the tool of its prince to his murder; its continued failure to acknowledge Jesus as the rightful Lord of the world, installed by God, implicates it in the judgment that took place in the cross and resurrection of Jesus. Like the prince of this world, its cause is lost; it has been judged." George Raymond Beasley-Murray, *John* (Waco: Word, 1987), 282.

5. D. Martyn Lloyd Jones says, "The Holy Spirit always works through the word of God. Now there are many people who claim that He works directly. That was what caused the Quakers to wander off from the main party of the Puritans. They said that the word was not necessary, that the Holy Spirit spoke directly to each person, in some secret mystical manner, by some 'inner light.' Not at all! . . . In order to do his work, the Spirit uses the word of God. And what does He do? . . . He presents and offers salvation in Christ; *through His people, He states the facts about Christ*" (emphasis added). David Martyn Lloyd-Jones, *God the Holy Spirit*, Great Doctrines of the Bible, vol. 2 (Wheaton, IL: Crossway, 1997), 51–52.

The Spirit's Work of Indwelling

The Spirit's work of convicting the world leads to his work of dwelling within believers. The Spirit's conviction in a person produces their confession of Jesus Christ as Savior and Lord. It creates a person who looks to Jesus Christ to provide the righteousness needed to be acceptable before a holy God. The Bible teaches that such a person, once convicted, comes to know the indwelling presence of God the Holy Spirit. Jesus says,

> "I will ask the Father, and he will give you another Helper, to be with you forever, even the Spirit of truth, whom the world cannot receive, because it neither sees him nor knows him. You know him, for he dwells with you and will be in you." (John 14:16–17)

Jesus states here that, for believers, the ministry of the Holy Spirit is present internally. The Spirit actually comes to reside in believers and consistently manifests the presence of Christ within them.

In the chapter on the doctrine of God, we saw that God's omnipresence means that he is present at all times in all places. The doctrine of God's indwelling presence means that he comes to dwell with believers in a very special way that leads them to call out to God in faith as their Father (Gal. 4:6).[6]

The Spirit's indwelling is full of powerful comfort that we must use in counseling. When Christians know that God is so intimately close, dwelling inside of them, it changes the trouble they experience. I have learned this truth as a father. My kids face situations that are relatively frightening all the time: unfamiliar kids on the playground, scary noises, nightmares, a basement with the lights off. When they face these scary situations, they come looking for me or their mom. Our kids know that it is easier to face scary challenges when accompanied by the comforting

---

6. Arthur W. Pink, *The Holy Spirit* (Grand Rapids, MI: Baker, 1970), 94. Pink says, "He is in believers not simply by the effects of common providence, but by His gracious operations and familiar providence."

presence of a parent who loves them and is with them. How much more helpful are the benefits of the Spirit who is not just with us but is *in* us, testifying that God himself is our Father who loves us.

The Spirit is not just in us, but is in us "forever." The Spirit's presence with us and in us, comforting us and pointing us to the Father, is permanent. He will never leave. Coming to trust in Christ as Savior means knowing the indwelling presence of God throughout an endless forever.

That God has given us the Spirit to be in us forever requires us to consider the Spirit's work of sealing believers. The function of sealing is mentioned three times in the New Testament. One is in Ephesians 1:13–14:

> In him you also, when you heard the word of truth, the gospel of your salvation, and believed in him, were sealed with the promised Holy Spirit, who is the guarantee of our inheritance until we acquire possession of it, to the praise of his glory.

When the Spirit comes to dwell in believers, he seals them, and this seal is a guarantee that the redemption promised in Christ will be theirs (cf. 2 Cor. 1:22; Eph. 4:30). The idea behind this language is that of an ancient king who would place his seal on a document, ensuring its safe arrival at the assigned destination. The Holy Spirit's presence with God's people is God's promise to them that they will receive their eternal inheritance.

Counseling is terrible work when people do not possess the powerful comfort of this indwelling and sealing Spirit. When our counselees do not have the Spirit, we can come up with comforting things to say, but that comfort is always superficial, transient, and fading. Only Christians sharing a theology of the Spirit's indwelling can offer the profound, permanent, and unfading hope of the presence of God the Spirit.

The Spirit's Work of Teaching

One of the first ways we see the Holy Spirit's ministry of teaching is in his inspiration of the text of Scripture.[7] The apostle Peter provides one of the clearest teachings on this in the Bible:

> No prophecy of Scripture comes from someone's own interpretation. For no prophecy was ever produced by the will of man, but men spoke from God as they were carried along by the Holy Spirit. (2 Peter 1:20–21)

Second Peter reveals that the Holy Spirit is the author of Scripture, but the Spirit does this in a very sophisticated way. The Spirit does not typically give Scripture to us in a unilateral way. There are times in Scripture when the Holy Spirit speaks words to people who merely record what they hear from him (Jer. 26:2; Rev. 2:1, 8). This work of the Spirit is called "dictation" but is not the main way he works.

The main way the Spirit authors Scripture is through a process called "accommodation."[8] This involves the Spirit using the unique gifts and individuality of human authors so that their personalities flow through the words of Scripture. The Spirit works in the effort of these authors so that they always communicate exactly what he wants them to communicate, and their words are protected from error. This is the process that Peter describes as being carried along by the Holy Spirit.

The Spirit desires to teach God's people, so he authors a dynamic, inerrant, and authoritative Word. This Word becomes the basis for much of the Spirit's ministry. When the Spirit convicts, he does it by the Word of God. When the Spirit teaches us as individuals, he does it by opening our eyes to the words of Scripture.

---

7. The Spirit's work of inspiring Scripture is typically addressed in the doctrine of Scripture. I am addressing it here because the chapter on Scripture focused on sufficiency, and I want to show how the Spirit's inspiration of the Bible is connected to his overall ministry of teaching believers.

8. For an explanation, see J. I. Packer, *"Fundamentalism" and the Word of God* (Grand Rapids, MI: Eerdmans, 1958), 79; also see Robert L. Saucy, *Scripture: Its Power, Authority, and Relevance* (Waco: Word, 2001), 127–44.

The Holy Spirit's inspiration of the Bible might be characterized as his general teaching ministry because the words in Scripture go out to many people in general. But the Holy Spirit does not constrain himself to that general ministry. He is specifically the teacher of the particular people he has come to indwell.

"These things I have spoken to you while I am still with you. But the Helper, the Holy Spirit, whom the Father will send in my name, he will teach you all things and bring to your remembrance all that I have said to you." (John 14:25–26)

When Jesus spoke these words, he was talking to the disciples gathered in the upper room on the night when he was betrayed. His declaration that the Spirit would bring to their minds all that he had said is, first and foremost, an encouragement to us that apostolic recollections of Jesus' words now recorded in Scripture are faithful to the statements he actually made.

Jesus' words apply directly and immediately to the gathered disciples, but they still have an application to his disciples today, who were not eyewitnesses of his earthly ministry.[9] Jesus' disciples in our contemporary culture need to be taught his words just as much as the ones in the upper room on that night so long ago.

"I still have many things to say to you, but you cannot bear them now. When the Spirit of truth comes, he will guide you into all the truth, for he will not speak on his own authority, but whatever he hears he will speak, and he will declare to you the things that are to come." (John 16:12–13)

---

9. James Montgomery Boice, *The Gospel of John: An Expositional Commentary* (Grand Rapids, MI: Zondervan, 1978), 212–13. "All this applies primarily to the disciples, but it also comes down to us in a much closer way. For we need to be taught also, and the Holy Spirit who taught the disciples, is our teacher as well. . . . Here the ministry of the Holy Spirit as teacher is explained. It was exercised, in the first instance, in the revelations of God to the apostles in the recording of what God had revealed to them in the pages of the New Testament. It is then exercised, in the second instance, as this same Holy Spirit teaches us from what they have recorded."

Jesus is clear here, as above, about the teaching function of the Spirit to speak what he hears and so guide the people of Jesus into all truth. The apostle Paul uses still different language to describe the Spirit's role as a teacher when he asks in prayer "that the God of our Lord Jesus Christ, the Father of glory, may give you the Spirit of wisdom and of revelation in the knowledge of him, having the eyes of your hearts enlightened" (Eph. 1:17–18). Believers in Jesus Christ can know the truth of God and have wisdom by the work of the indwelling Spirit who is our teacher. Let me explain why this is so crucial from a counseling perspective.

When people ask me what the hardest problem is that I have ever faced in counseling, I always respond by saying that there are no hard problems in counseling, only hard people. That is true because of the doctrines of the Spirit and the sufficiency of Scripture that I am advancing in this book. The Bible clearly and practically addresses the counseling problems we face. The Spirit opens our eyes to these realities. That is not only my confession. It is also my experience. I have seen the Spirit use his Word to change the lives of people who had the most overwhelming problems you can face in counseling. I am not intimidated by a hard problem when I am working with someone who sees his own difficulties, wants to work hard to change, and loves Jesus.

What is a significant challenge is when people do not see their issues, do not want to change, and want to blame someone or something for all their problems—as was true with Scott. Those are the hard people for whom counseling is so challenging. I have often felt sad and frustrated over repeated attempts to help someone see their problems and fruitless efforts to motivate them toward change. Given the choice, I would always prefer a counselee with an extreme problem who wants to change over one with a mild problem who does not.

The reason for the difficulties of counseling hard people who do not understand their problems is due to limitations that every human counselor faces. That limitation is the one mentioned by Paul in Ephesians 1. No human being can teach in such a way that they bring true understanding. Paul refers to this understanding as having the eyes of our hearts enlightened. Human counselors can talk, plead, pray, and even—at times—enforce consequences. We cannot open the eyes of a person's heart. There is only one Counselor and Teacher who can do that, and it is the Spirit of God.

The Spirit's Work of Empowering

If the indwelling Spirit served only as teacher to open our eyes to God's truth, we would be in a pitiful condition. It is one thing to understand what we are to do. It is quite another to possess the power to do it. That is why it is such good news that Jesus expands on the work the Spirit came to do: "If you love me, you will keep my commandments. And I will ask the Father, and he will give you another Helper to be with you forever" (John 14:15–16).

For Jesus, obedience is not optional. Jesus makes obedience the evidence of our love for him. Jesus knows, however, that obedience to his commands is so hard that it is impossible on our own. That is why as soon as he tells us we must obey as proof of our love for him, he promises a Helper in that obedience. One of the central functions of the Holy Spirit is to assist believers to obey Jesus (cf. John 14:21, 23).[10]

Another place where we see this is in Galatians 5 with Paul's instruction to walk by the Spirit and not the flesh, which are at odds with one another (vv. 16–17). He describes the "works of the flesh" as "sexual immorality, impurity, sensuality, idolatry, sorcery, enmity, strife, jealousy, fits of anger, rivalries, dissensions, divisions, envy, drunkenness, orgies, and things like these" (vv. 19–21). He says the "fruit of the Spirit is love, joy, peace, patience, kindness, goodness, faithfulness, gentleness, self-control" (vv. 22–23).

In this passage, when Paul describes sins and disobedience, he calls them the "works of the flesh." When he describes righteousness and

---

10. William Barclay, *The Gospel of John*, vol. 2 (Philadelphia: Westminster, 1975), 194. He says, "Obviously the love which issues in obedience is not an easy thing. But Jesus does not leave us to struggle with the Christian life alone. He would send us another *Helper*" (emphasis in original).

obedience, they are called the "fruit of the Spirit." The "works of the flesh" language is intended to attribute disobedience and sin to the sinful people who perform them. When they obey and do the righteous things listed in Galatians, those acts are called "fruit" and are attributed to the Holy Spirit. The clear teaching is that disobedience is what is intrinsic to sinful people, and obedient righteousness is what is intrinsic to the Spirit. When we obey, that is the fruit of the work of the Spirit, not due to our own moral effort.[11]

This subject of empowerment leads to a discussion of the filling of the Spirit. This idea comes from Paul's teaching in Ephesians 5:18 where he encourages Christians to "be filled with the Spirit." This passage has inspired much theological reflection because the exhortation to be filled with the Spirit is not repeated anywhere else in the Bible and contains no elaboration on its meaning in this context.

The Greek expression is *en pneumati*, which can be translated in English either as "Be filled *with* the Spirit" or "Be filled *by* the Spirit."[12] The dominant Christian interpretation of this phrase is the former translation, which means that the content of that filling is the Spirit. Interpreting the text in this way means that, though all Christians possess the Spirit by virtue of his indwelling believers at conversion, we must nevertheless pursue ongoing fillings of the Spirit for service and obedience.[13]

As popular as this translation has been, I doubt that it is the one the apostle Paul intends. I think the more likely translation is the second one: the Spirit is the one who fills, but he is not the content of that

---

11. Ronald Y. K. Fung says of the fruit of the spirit: "The phrase directly ascribes the power of fructification not to the believer himself but to the Spirit, and effectively hints that the qualities enumerated are not the result of strenuous observance of an external legal code, but the natural product ('harvest') of a life controlled and guided by the Spirit." Ronald Y. K. Fung, *The Epistle to the Galatians*, The New International Commentary on the New Testament, ed. Gordon D. Fee (Grand Rapids, MI: Eerdmans, 1988), 262.

12. Peter Thomas O'Brien, *The Letter to the Ephesians*, The Pillar New Testament Commentary (Grand Rapids, MI: Eerdmans, 1999), 391–92. O'Brien argues that it makes more syntactical sense to translate the phrase as "by the Spirit" because "there are no other examples in the Greek Bible of this verb 'to fill' followed by this prepositional phrase to indicate content."

13. Walter C. Kaiser, *Perspectives on Spirit Baptism: Five Views*, eds. Ralph Del Colle and Chad Brand (Nashville: B&H, 2004), 15–46. Kaiser makes a strong case for this view.

filling. This appears to me to be the case for three reasons. First, there is no grammatical reason to interpret the Spirit as the content of the filling. Second, it seems odd that Paul would talk about the need for more and more Spirit fillings, given Jesus' promise of the indwelling Spirit to be with us forever.[14] This is particularly true given that Paul, in his own teaching, does not seem to believe that Christians have any deficit of the Spirit (cf. Rom. 8:9–11; Eph. 1:13–14). Third, there is no other place in the New Testament where we are told that we need more of the Spirit. While it is true that a teaching has to appear only once in Scripture for it to be biblical, it is also the case that Christians are typically very cautious about building entire theologies around one verse. That is particularly the case when there is a simpler way to interpret the passage that would make it conform more closely to other clear teachings (as, in this case, the nature of the Spirit's indwelling).

In Ephesians 5:18, Paul tells Christians to be filled *by* the Spirit. Paul also speaks of Jesus filling all things (Eph. 1:22–23; 3:19; 4:10, 13). If the Spirit is the person who works to have us know the fullness of Jesus, then this would be consistent with the Spirit's work to exalt Christ, which we shall see below (John 16:14).

I am placing this discussion of the Spirit's filling under the heading of empowerment because I believe Paul is not asking us to seek more and more of the Spirit, but rather is asking us to depend on the Spirit to make us more and more like Christ. The spiritual fruit that the Holy Spirit empowers us to experience is not just more obedience. He also empowers us to know more and more of the love and fullness of Jesus Christ himself.[15]

---

14. Jim Hamilton has a very helpful discussion on this matter when he talks about the nature of Spirit fillings in the book of Acts. "In these passages where people are described as 'full of the Spirit' with *plērēs/pleroō*, something other than baptism in the Spirit is in view. Here is not a dramatic demonstration of God's approval, but a lifestyle marked by the Spirit's presence. The baptism terms do not overlap in meaning with *plērēs/pleroō*. The age in which believers can be indwelt by the Spirit, however, is broadly inaugurated by the baptism of the Spirit that took place at Pentecost." James M. Hamilton and E. Ray Clendenen, *God's Indwelling Presence: The Holy Spirit in the Old & New Testament* (Nashville: B&H, 2006), 198.

15. See also D. A. Carson, *The Gospel according to John* (Leicester, England: InterVarsity, 1991), 392.

Biblical counseling is about Christlike obedience. We want people to grow in their love of Jesus and in obedience to his commands. We want them to grow in obeying the command to love God, to love others, to seek reconciliation, to grant forgiveness, to speak more kindly, to listen more intently, to stop hitting their spouse, to read the Bible, pray, go to church, and many other things. The doctrine of the Spirit gives us confidence that all of these, and more, are possible through the Holy Spirit, who empowers believers to know Christ and obey him.

The Spirit's Work of Gifting

The Holy Spirit does more than empower Christians for obedience to the commands of Christ. He also offers a special empowerment for service in the body of Christ, the church. The New Testament teaches the gifting of the Spirit in several places (Rom. 12:3–8; Eph. 4:7–12; 1 Peter 4:10–11). Paul's instruction in 1 Corinthians is particularly significant for us:

> Now there are varieties of gifts, but the same Spirit; and there are varieties of service, but the same Lord; and there are varieties of activities, but it is the same God who empowers them all in everyone. To each is given the manifestation of the Spirit for the common good. For to one is given through the Spirit the utterance of wisdom, and to another the utterance of knowledge according to the same Spirit, to another faith by the same Spirit, to another gifts of healing by the one Spirit, to another the working of miracles, to another prophecy, to another the ability to distinguish between spirits, to another various kinds of tongues, to another the interpretation of tongues. All these are empowered by one and the same Spirit, who apportions to each one individually as he wills. (1 Cor. 12:4–11)

Though there is much we could say about spiritual gifts from this passage, I will make just two observations:

Paul says that it is the Spirit who sovereignly assigns the gifts. Any of the gifts listed in Scripture are gifts that God the Spirit has assigned to the person who possesses them. Second, after assigning the gifts, it is the Spirit who empowers their use. Because the Spirit assigns the gifts and provides the strength to exercise them, they are called "the manifestation of the Spirit." No Christians can take credit for their possession and use of the gifts.

After we know that the Spirit assigns the gifts for Christians to use, we are interested in learning how we can discover what our gifts are. The interest in knowing our spiritual gifts explains the existence of an entire cottage industry of spiritual gift inventories. I have never put much stock in those assessments. The same Bible that says the Spirit assigns and empowers the gifts does not say that we need to take an exam to figure out what he has given us.

A more biblical process of determining our gifts would consist of prayer. Believers should ask God to help them see where they could most fruitfully serve the church. Those are prayers God loves to answer. Believers should then consider which of the gifts in Scripture they desire to use in serving the church.[16] Christians can begin to narrow down some options by looking at 1 Peter 4:11. In that passage Peter provides two overarching categories for spiritual gifts, namely, gifts of speaking and gifts of serving. Many Christians will have an idea of which of those two categories sounds most appealing to them. Finally, since the gifts are to serve the church, believers should lean in to their local church for help in discerning their giftedness (cf. 1 Cor. 12:7; Eph. 4:12–13; 1 Peter 4:8). This process can begin with reaching out to church leaders, asking for advice about giftedness and seeking guidance about where to put it to use. This process culminates in the church's providing testimony that confirms the effectiveness of an individual with that particular gift.

---

16. God often uses our desires in determining our calling for service. First Timothy 3:1 is a great example where the qualifications for pastor are prefaced by considering whether a man desires the work.

The reason the Spirit's work of gifting is so important in counseling is because Christians have more spiritual power available to them than the power that strengthens them for Christlike obedience in their own lives. The Holy Spirit also strengthens them for service, to be a blessing in the lives of others. The Spirit of God wants Christians to minister to other Christians in the context of the local church.

One of the problems people often have when they come for help is that they are ineffective and unfruitful in serving the body of Jesus. When this is true, one of the goals of biblical counseling is to restore them to usefulness in ministry (2 Tim. 2:20–21). Biblical counselors know that a person has not been fully helped until they are actively involved in receiving the Spirit's empowerment for some kind of meaningful service to the local church. Because biblical counselors are alert to this, counseling will always be sensitive to discovering a counselee's areas of giftedness and placing that person in relevant positions of service to the church.

The Spirit's Work of Glorifying

As we examine this final element of the Spirit, we see that the Holy Spirit works to glorify Jesus Christ. When Jesus foretells the Spirit's coming, he explains this work of the Spirit as essential to his ministry. Jesus refers to this specifically in two places. The first is in John 15:26: "But when the Helper comes, whom I will send to you from the Father, the Spirit of truth, who proceeds from the Father, he will bear witness about me." In John 16:14 he says, "He will glorify me, for he will take what is mine and declare it to you." Christians have pointed to these passages to demonstrate that the Holy Spirit's ministry is Christ-centered. The Spirit's work is to highlight the person and work of Jesus.

As much as these passages relate the work of the Spirit to exalt Jesus Christ, we are able to see the same work in other places. In fact, we have already seen it in each of the functions of the Spirit we have examined in this chapter. The Spirit's work of convicting is Christ-centered because he convicts the world of the righteousness they need, which is found only in Christ. The Spirit's work of indwelling is Christ-centered because the Spirit comes to dwell only in those who have depended on Jesus Christ as Savior and Lord. The Spirit's work of teaching is Christ-centered because he works to remind people of the words of Christ. The Spirit's empowering is Christ-centered because he works to lead people to obey Jesus and to know his fullness. Finally, his work of gifting for service is Christ-centered, since the goal of spiritual gifts is that "God may be glorified through Jesus Christ" (1 Peter 4:11).

The Spirit's ministry is inextricably linked to the glory of Jesus Christ. The Spirit loves to exalt Jesus Christ. The greatest evidence that our churches and the people in them are spiritual is that we make much of Jesus Christ. This is no less true in counseling than in any other ministries of the church. Our counseling is Spirit-empowered when we use our conversations with troubled people to make much of Jesus Christ.

Counseling Implications of the Work of the Spirit

In this chapter I have tried to relate each of the Spirit's functions to counseling ministry, at least briefly. Before closing, I want to point out several ways that the doctrine of the Spirit urges us to respond as counselors.

Worship

Our first response in considering all of this incredible work of the Holy Spirit must be worship. We worship the Holy Spirit because he is God, the eternal third member of the Trinity. The early church had occasion to debate the deity of the Spirit, but this dispute was resolved very early on at the Council of Constantinople in 381.[17] The early church

---

17. Gregory of Nazianzus led the council to state, "And we believe in the Holy Spirit, the Lord, the Life-giving, who proceeds from the Father, who is to be glorified with the Father and the Son, and who speaks through the prophets."

confirmed the deity of the Spirit because he is called God in the Bible (Acts 5:1–4), because he is listed with the other members of the Trinity (Matt. 28:19; 2 Cor. 13:14), and because he does things only God can do. He is able to convict the world of sin and righteousness because of his own inexhaustible moral perfection. The Spirit can indwell all believers only if he possesses the attribute of omnipresence. He can indwell them forever because he has the divine attribute of eternality. He empowers for service by virtue of his omnipotence.

As counselors, we must worship God the Spirit, whose work is so crucial to what we are doing. We also must lead our counselees to exult over this Spirit, who is instrumental in their change in a way that only the Lord of heaven and earth could be. We saw in a previous chapter that one of the goals of biblical counseling is worship. Here we can affirm that this worship is often grounded specifically in the work of the Holy Spirit.

Humility

A second way we counselors must respond to the doctrine of the Holy Spirit is with humility. By the time a counselor has been ministering to people for any length of time, there will be some success stories to report: marriages are restored, the darkness of depression lifts, bad habits are broken, the tyranny of anxiety is overthrown. If we are not careful, it is easy for these successes to inflate our pride as we wrongly believe that our skills prompt change. A theology of the Holy Spirit is one of the most significant doctrines I know of to create the kind of humility required of a biblical counselor. The doctrine of the Spirit reminds us that we cannot make our counselees see their difficulties, we cannot make them understand the truth, and we cannot motivate them to change. This work belongs exclusively to the Spirit of God. We can and should seek to cooperate with what the Spirit is doing, but when our counselees change, that is no cause for pride. Instead it is an occasion to humbly thank the One who brought about the change.

Prayer

The doctrine of the Holy Spirit also points us to the importance of prayer in biblical counseling. Because the Holy Spirit is the eternal and powerful God who alone brings about the understanding and the change required, we must solicit his help in prayer. We must pray for counselees as a crucial element of our counseling preparation when we are trying to understand their dilemma, when we are planning what to say in counseling, when we are encouraged about how counseling is proceeding, and when we are discouraged about it. We also must pray with our counselees as a crucial element of the counseling process. Our counselees must learn not just by our words but also by our practice that they need the Spirit's work in their life if counseling is to succeed. One of the most effective ways to demonstrate this is to show, through prayer, that counselors are as dependent on the grace of God for help and change as counselees are.

Jesus

The Holy Spirit loves to glorify Jesus Christ. By doing all of his work with respect to Christ, the Spirit gives testimony to and exalts Jesus. This teaches us that if we want our counseling to be marked by spiritual power, we must work in the same areas the Spirit is working and be about the same project. We must be committed to exalting Jesus Christ in our counseling. Because the Spirit is the sovereign God who does as he wills, we cannot dictate where he will choose to operate or what he will choose to do. We can have some expectation of blessing when we are doing the same work of exalting Jesus as the Spirit is. If we desire to know the power of the Spirit of God in our counseling, we must be counselors who desire to make much of Jesus Christ with every counselee. We must pray that the Spirit will fill our hearts with love for Jesus and give us words to speak about him in our counseling. Biblical counseling is Spirit-empowered counseling. The only way to have Spirit-empowered counseling is to have Christ-centered counseling.

Bible

The doctrine of the Spirit also shows us that the Holy Spirit's ministry of teaching is based in the Word of God. The Spirit inspires the Bible, convicts people of sin and righteousness when the Word of God is preached, opens the minds of his people to understand what it says, and empowers them to do what it commands. The Holy Spirit is active when the Bible is being used. If a counseling ministry is to have any chance of being Spirit-empowered, it must be a counseling ministry based on the Word of God. The only kind of counseling that is Spirit-empowered is biblical counseling. I do not make that statement out of a desire to cheerlead for any one particular counseling approach, though I am deeply committed to biblical counseling. I make that statement out of deep theological conviction about the way the Spirit works. Counselors who desire to know a measure of the Spirit's power in their work must point to the Spirit's words in Scripture.

Trusting the Holy Spirit in Counseling Failure

My counseling with Scott was a heartbreaking failure. I so wanted to break through to him. I wanted to help him know a more joyful and fulfilling life than the one of anger and bitterness he was experiencing. I wanted to provide some relief to Renee in their desperate marriage. It was not to be. Even now as I write these words, I pray for Scott and desire that the Lord would change his heart and lead him away from his bitterness to an abundant life in Christ. Perhaps that has happened. But that day when I saw Scott driving away from me, it certainly was not the case.

As biblical counselors, when we experience a failure in our work, there are a couple of things we can do. First, we should evaluate our counseling and ask God to show us areas where we might have demonstrated more understanding of the counselee's problem, more insight into what God says about their difficulty, or more gentleness in our counseling care. I regularly evaluate my own counsel with a few men who have been counseling for decades longer than I have been. We should all avoid assuming our counsel is perfect and humbly submit to the evaluations of others who have counseling wisdom. When we do this, we typically discover ways that our counseling could have been more faithful.

Sometimes we discover that—though our counseling is never perfect—we got the large themes correct. We did understand their problem, we did offer biblical wisdom, we did care for them well. When counseling fails in spite of our faithfulness, that is where we need to trust in God the Holy Spirit. The Holy Spirit is the sovereign God who works in people's hearts according to his own wise and loving will (John 3:8). When our counseling is successful, we must give thanks to God whose Spirit gave the growth. When our faithful counsel appears to result in failure, we must trust in the wise and sovereign purposes of God. It may be his desire to harden their heart (Rom. 9:18). It may be his desire to have us do preliminary work while another person reaps the harvest (1 Cor. 3:5–9).

The doctrine of the Spirit that we have studied in this chapter underlines the fact that the Spirit is worthy of our trust. He is the omnipotent God who inspires a powerful Word, convicts by that Word, teaches that Word, brings about obedience to that Word, supplies gifts for service, and exalts Jesus Christ. He is the one who makes all real and lasting change possible.[18]

---

18. Resources on the Holy Spirit that I often recommend for counseling: Jerry Bridges, *The Pursuit of Holiness* (Colorado Springs: NavPress, 2014); J. C. Ryle, *Holiness: Its Nature, Hindrances, Difficulties, and Roots* (Peabody, MA: Hendrickson, 2007).

CHAPTER 7

BIBLICAL COUNSELING

and a

THEOLOGY OF HUMANITY

The doctrine of humanity concerns the biblical nature of what it means to be a human being. That topic has traditionally been referred to as the doctrine of anthropology, or the doctrine of mankind.[1] When Christians address this area of theology, they commonly address the design of man as God's image bearer, the essence and nature of mankind, and the issue of gender and human sexuality. I will address each of these three important categories as well as highlight their importance for biblical counseling. Before unpacking these issues, we will begin as

---

1. I have used the term *humanity* in the title of this chapter because it is more gender-inclusive, making it obvious that in addressing a theology of the human race, I am referring to both men and women. Theologians have typically talked about the doctrine of "man" or "mankind" in talking about this doctrine because these terms are perfectly legitimate terms to use with respect to the entire human race. There is biblical warrant for this practice. Genesis 1:27 says, "So God created man in his own image, in the image of God he created him; male and female he created them." God uses the term *man* (Hebrew: *adam*) to refer to both men and women. If God is completely comfortable referring to both genders of the human race with a term that connotes male headship in that creation, then we should be completely comfortable with it as well. In this chapter I will observe this practice on occasion. The title of this chapter uses the more gender-inclusive language for the communicative function of making it clear that I am talking about both men and women. It is not meant to express a principled objection against the use of "man" language, since I have no such principled objection. See Wayne A. Grudem, *Systematic Theology: An Introduction to Biblical Doctrine* (Grand Rapids, MI: Zondervan, 1994), 439–40.

we have begun other chapters, with a counseling case study. In order to demonstrate the practical importance of this doctrine for counseling, I want to share with you the story of Drew and Amber.

Drew and Amber

On the day of their wedding, Drew and Amber were overwhelmingly happy. Surrounded by family and friends in their Christian community, they felt that God had been uncommonly gracious in directing them to each other. This sense of an overwhelming extension of grace was particularly acute for Drew. Drew had grown up with a struggle against same-sex attraction. This attraction had been in place for as long as he could remember and had been a source of turmoil while he was growing up.

Drew had been sexually active a few times. The first was in high school, but his response surprised him. He did not enjoy it as much as he always thought he would. He appreciated the intimacy of the relationship, but found the actual physical part surprisingly unsatisfying. After a while the relationship ended and left him feeling empty and ashamed.

In search of help, Drew found a sexual recovery group that met weekly in the basement of a mainline church in his town. The group was a large one full of men and women who struggled with all kinds of problems other than homosexuality, but Drew managed to make a contact with an "ex-gay" who had found freedom from his homosexual lifestyle. Drew started to spend more time with this man and started to feel a deep connection with him. Drew was surprised at how quickly the emotional connection grew between them. He was caught off guard when the relationship became physical a few weeks after they met. Drew was disgusted. He did not enjoy the encounter at all and despaired that he would ever change. He did not understand how he could have a desire for something and then feel so guilty for doing it immediately afterward. He spent days in his room at his parents' house feeling sad and miserable.

The pain that Drew experienced in the aftermath of this experience eventually led him to an evangelical church down the street from his house. For the first time, he heard the Bible preached, the gospel proclaimed. He began interacting with Christians who showed care for one another and worshiped together. Drew had never experienced anything like it and, after several months, came to trust Jesus Christ.

After becoming a Christian, Drew's homosexual desires left. For the first time in his life, he felt free. He was growing dramatically in his relationship with God and was delighting in the close friendships he was developing at church. It was at this point when he met Amber at a retreat for singles in their church. The two hit it off. They talked for six hours into the night about everything—their parents, their interests, how they came to Christ, and even Drew's past struggle with homosexuality. Drew had never tried to keep his struggle a secret, but he was surprised by how freely he shared that information with Amber at such an early stage. He was even more surprised by Amber's kind and understanding response.

Within a few months they were expressing their love for each other, and a few months after that they were talking about marriage. With the blessing of the church leadership and their parents, Drew and Amber were married almost a year after they first met.

The joy of the wedding day extended into the joy of married life. Both had jobs and spent their free time decorating their small apartment and spending time with friends from church. For the first couple of years, things were great. Then, just before their second anniversary, Drew came to Amber and confessed through sobs that he was struggling again with same-sex attraction. He confessed that there were a few guys at work that he was attracted to and that—though he had not acted out with other men—he had been regularly looking at pornography. Together they decided to go to see their pastor.

Their pastor tried to be encouraging, but admitted he had no experience with this issue. He offered to find some help for them. He eventually connected Drew with a counselor in their area who specialized in reparative therapy. In the meetings with this therapist, Drew began to learn that, according to reparative therapy, he desired same-sex relationships because he lacked a close relationship with his father and desired to create that closeness in sexual relationships with other men.[2] This description rang true for Drew. His relationship with his father was distant. Yet Drew felt that his counselor's approach was missing something. He was also troubled by some of the elements of his therapy. One example was when his therapist asked him to view heterosexual pornography in an effort to help him change.[3] Drew told his pastor, who advised Drew to not continue the therapy.

Drew became even more discouraged. He started to doubt that there was any help. Eventually Drew, Amber, and their pastor learned that a better approach is in biblical counseling. By God's grace, Drew and Amber were able to grow in grace as they received biblical marriage counseling and individual biblical counseling to address some of the specific issues that there was not time to address in joint counseling sessions. I have provided a critique of reparative therapy as well as biblical guidance on counseling those with same-sex attraction in other places.[4] Here I want to show how the doctrine of humanity is relevant to the counseling issues faced by Drew and Amber. We will see this relevance as we evaluate the image of God in man, the constituent nature of man, and the creation of mankind in two genders.

---

2. This is a core claim of reparative therapy. Joseph Nicolosi says that the problem in homosexual boys is that they "envy the masculine bodies of other boys, in a compensatory (reparative) attempt to acquire other male bodies by erotically joining with them." Joseph J. Nicolosi, *Shame and Attachment Loss: The Practical Work of Reparative Therapy* (Downers Grove, IL: IVP Academic, 2009), 69.

3. This is a counseling intervention authorized by reparative therapy. See Joseph Nicolosi, "Identify Your Shame-Based Self Statement," a talk given at the Exodus International Freedom Conference in Irvine, CA, 2010.

4. Denny Burk and Heath Lambert, *Transforming Homosexuality: Living Faithfully with Same-Sex Attraction* (Phillipsburg, NJ: P&R, 2015). See also Heath Lambert, "What's Wrong with Reparative Therapy?," *Association of Certified Biblical Counselors Blog*, November 17, 2014, http://www.biblicalcounseling.com /blog/what-wrong-with-reparative-therapy. See also Heath Lambert, "Counseling Persons about Same-Sex Marriage" in Jeff Iorg, ed., *Ministry in the New Marriage Culture* (Nashville: B&H, 2015) 119–35.

Humanity: Made in the Image of God

God made human beings in his own image to be similar to him and to portray his character and work in the world. When God made mankind, the first thing he said was that human beings are to be made in the image of God: "Then God said, 'Let us make man in our image, after our likeness" (Gen. 1:26). This is not true of any of the other creatures that God made. God made the animals each according to their kind (Gen. 1:24–25).

God made man after his own image. The concern for Christians has been what it means that we are made in God's image. No one passage in Scripture says explicitly what the image of God is, so we must construct our understanding from various passages. We will examine three ways that human beings manifest the image of God, uniquely representing him in the world.[5]

Who We Are

Throughout history many have understood that the image of God in human beings has to do with some essential element of what it means to be human.[6] There are a few examples that we can consider. First, human beings, unlike any other creatures, are able to engage in complex reasoning. We can plan a budget, decide whom we want to marry, design and build a hospital, and set long-term life goals. No other creature has

---

5. Because there is no one passage that specifically lists all that it means to be made in God's image, theologians have often characterized the image of God in ways that are a bit different. For example, John Frame argues that the image of God is seen in three categories, which are analogous to God's attributes of lordship. The divine image is seen in mankind's qualities as a king, priest, and prophet. These three attributes are respectively analogous to the lordship attributes of control, presence, and authority. See John M. Frame, *Systematic Theology: An Introduction to Christian Belief* (Phillipsburg: P&R, 2013), 784–91. Wayne Grudem argues for numerous ways in which the image of God is seen in man and arranges those under five main headings: moral, spiritual, mental, relational, and physical manifestations of the image. See Wayne A. Grudem, *Systematic Theology: An Introduction to Biblical Doctrine* (Grand Rapids, MI: Zondervan, 1994), 442–49. Most theologians have seen the image of God in one, or some combination, of the manifestations I chronicle in this chapter.

6. Theologians have often referred to this as the structural view, since it finds the divine image located in some essential structure of mankind.

the ability to reason in such a profound and complex way. Other creatures have the ability to see, hear, and think, but not in the sophisticated way that we do. When I look at these words on the computer as I type, I see something very different than my dog, Simeon, who also just looked at the screen. God is a rational being with an amazingly complex ability to think logically and carefully. Our ability to reason pales in comparison to God's. Being made in God's image does not mean that we are identical to God. It means that we are like him and portray his nature to the world. We do this in our cognitive abilities.

Another way we see the image of God in who we are is in our moral life as human beings. Human beings are inalterably moral. Every person living or who has ever lived has some sense of basic right and wrong (Rom. 2:12–16). There has been remarkable overlap in this moral code throughout human history and in every human culture. Lying, stealing, and sexual immorality—to name just a few—are common themes of morality among virtually all people. This is true even among groups whose existence seems predicated on violations of these moral codes. C. S. Lewis pointed to pirates as an example. Pirates appear to be an exception because they do not seem to think it is wrong to lie and steal. Indeed, their existence depends on these activities. Lewis pointed out, however, that if you try stealing from a pirate, you will quickly discover that he thinks stealing is wrong.[7]

Human beings are inalterably moral creatures. This trait separates human beings from grass and wolves, for example, but makes humans similar to God, who is, of course, a moral being. Since God is the source of all morality and because we are sinners, God's morality is far superior to ours. Being made in the image of God does not require that we be exactly like God, only that we resemble him enough to portray who he is in the world he has made. One element of the divine image in mankind consists of who we are as human beings.

---

7. C. S. Lewis, *Mere Christianity* (San Francisco: Harper, 2009), 9–15.

The Relationships We Have

Another way humanity is similar to God and portrays him in the world is in our relationships.[8] We see these relationships in Jesus' teaching on the first and second great commandments.

> And one of them, a lawyer, asked him a question to test him. "Teacher, which is the great commandment in the Law?" And he said to him, "You shall love the Lord your God with all your heart and with all your soul and with all your mind. This is the great and first commandment. And a second is like it: You shall love your neighbor as yourself. On these two commandments depend all the Law and the Prophets." (Matt. 22:35–40)

Jesus' words here are commands for relationship never given to anything else in the natural world. These commands show two ways we are different from every other created thing. As human beings, we display God's image when we know and love God. No animal or tree can do this. Perhaps rabbits know that God exists. I really do not know. Even if they do, they have never built a cathedral or written a hymn. When human beings relate to God, they are doing something that only God's image bearers can do.

Human beings image God by knowing and loving other people. This is not possible for other creatures, even though it might seem as if it is. Think again of my dog, Simeon. Simeon is a Brittany spaniel and a delightful pet. Good friends of ours also have a Brittany. Its name is Monica. Simeon is always very happy when he is around Monica. They run around and play for hours. But as much as Simeon enjoys Monica, he has never written her a love poem or celebrated the anniversary of their meeting. Even though animals can have some measure of camaraderie, they never know the depth of relationship that human beings experience as we live life together. This a uniquely human experience

---

8. Theologians refer to this as the relational view of God's image in humanity.

that separates us from the animals and makes us like God, who enjoys perfect relationships within the Trinity.

What We Do

A final way that mankind is like God and represents him relates to the things we do in the world.[9] The chief way we see this is in the fact that mankind is given dominion over all of creation.

> Then God said, "Let us make man in our image, after our likeness. And let them have dominion over the fish of the sea and over the birds of the heavens and over the livestock and over all the earth and over every creeping thing that creeps on the earth." (Gen. 1:26)

Immediately after the divine counsel is revealed about God's making man in his image, we are told that man is given dominion over the other elements of creation. This dominion has often been referred to as the creation mandate. It may be the most textually obvious of our three categories: mankind is given dominion in the same moment God expresses his intention to make man in the divine image.[10]

Human beings demonstrate this element of the image of God whenever we exercise stewardship in the world. When we build a skyscraper, feed our dog, cut the neighbor's grass, pave a road, or adopt a highway, we are caring for the creation in a way that is reminiscent of God's care for the world. As with the other categories, our care for this world is greatly diminished from God's unmatched power and unfading goodness as the supreme caretaker of the universe. Still, we legitimately image God when we steward the areas of responsibility he has given to us.

---

9. Theologians refer to this as the functional view of the divine image.

10. This seems accurate to me even though some theologians doubt that dominion given to humanity is an obvious expression of the image of God. See Millard J. Erickson, *Christian Theology* (Grand Rapids, MI: Baker, 1998), 531–32. This functional view of the divine image is the most recent one to receive attention in the history of the church.

Many, Not One

The three categories I have just surveyed are fairly standard ways in Christian theology of talking about the image of God. It has been common for Christians to contend for one or two categories to the exclusion of others. Some have advocated that the image of God is based exclusively in what we do, others in who we are, others in the relationships we have, and others in some combination of two of the three. There is no reason to so limit the meaning of the divine image.

The Bible teaches that the image of God includes all the ways we are similar to God and portray him in the world. There is no reason to find one, and only one, way that we do this. The Bible teaches many ways that we image God, and we should embrace all of them. There is nothing to be gained from insisting that the image of God is manifested in only one way, rather than in a multitude of ways.

A Broken and Restored Image

The Bible teaches that the fall of the human race into sin significantly marred the divine image, though it did not destroy it. Mankind still carries God's image, though in a distorted form. Genesis 9:6 says, "Whoever sheds the blood of man, by man shall his blood be shed, for God made man in his own image."

God speaks these words to Noah after the fall, indeed after the judgment against fallen people in the flood. God's words make it clear that mankind still bears the divine image, and that this image forms the foundation for the command against murder and justifies capital punishment when murder is committed. It is the image of God in man, even in a fallen world, that is the foundation for the sanctity of human life.

But God's image is marred in fallen human beings. We see that the image is broken in all the ways we fail to represent him as we should. We demonstrate that God's image is broken in us every time we do not think as we should, obey as we should, love God and others as we should, or care for the creation in the way we should. In short, we see the defacing of God's image in all those places where sin distorts how we were created to function.

It is the purpose of Jesus Christ to come to restore the defaced image of God in fallen mankind. Jesus Christ is the perfect image of God (2 Cor. 4:4). He is the perfect image of God because he has no sin to distort his exact representation of who God is. We saw in chapter 5 that Jesus Christ came to take away our sin and give us his righteousness. Another way to say that is that we have been "predestined to be conformed to the image of his Son" (Rom. 8:29). A Christian understanding of the image of God is a Christ-centered understanding. The only way God's broken image can be fully restored in sinful people is through Jesus Christ, the perfect image bearer who came to conform us, by grace, to resemble God as closely as he does. The divine image shattered by sin is restored in Christ.

Biblical Counseling and the Image of God

The doctrine of the image of God has everything to do with how we counsel. People *are* made in the image of God. This fact is the most important reality about what it means to be a human being. We do not get to choose whether we represent God in the world. That is already true of us. The only issue that remains is whether we will acknowledge this fact and respond to it in a way that honors God.

When you understand the truth of the image of God, you can understand that counseling exists because we live in a world where the image of God has been distorted in all those created to bear it. Every counseling need traces back to a failure to fully image God. Rick and Wendy, from the introductory chapter, failed to image God in their relationships toward God and with one another. Their lives fell apart and they sought counseling. Trenyan and Jenny experienced a failure in the image of God when their fathers failed to love them and exert faithful dominion in caring for them. These failures created tragedy in their lives, and they required counseling help. Scott destroyed his marriage through his failure to image God in his marriage. We see the same thing in every other example in this book. The image of God has been shattered in every human being who seeks counseling. The goal of counseling should be to facilitate the restoration of the image of God to its proper functioning in all of the practical ways that it has been shattered in the lives of those who come to see a counselor.

I say the goal of counseling *should be* to facilitate restoration of the image of God because, unfortunately, most counseling approaches do not see it as the job in counseling to have anything at all to do with God and his image in man. This is tragic. As image bearers we refer to the God whose image we bear. It is wrong, corrupt, and ineffective to treat image bearers as though the one whose image they carry does not exist or is irrelevant to the problems they are facing.

We must never be guilty of ignoring such a crucial reality. It must occupy a central element in our counseling because it is central to who we are. Humanity is created in God's image. The Bible, which is God's Word, describes to us that we are made in the image of God and tells us what it means to be made thus. Since counseling problems are related to some failure to accurately represent God, we need the Bible to show us where we are off course and to help us know how to get back to where we ought to be. This *requires* biblical counseling.

This is the problem with the reparative therapy that Drew received. Though we can agree with reparative therapists that homosexuality is a problem and that change is possible, we must make clear that reparative therapists do not treat Drew and others like him as the image bearers they are. The therapist ignored the fact that God makes demands on Drew, and that God gives specific directions on how he can live out these demands. Though many consider reparative therapy to be a Christian option, it is impossible to agree with this when reparative therapists ignore the fundamental aspect of what it means to be human.

Drew is called to image God in his relationships. The only way Drew or any of us can know how to do this is to pay attention to God's normative standards for how we are to love others. God regulates Drew's relationships by forbidding intimate sexual relationships with anyone but his wife. The only way to help Drew is by working to restore him to be a more faithful image bearer. This requires acknowledgment of and obedience to the Bible.

The reparative therapist Drew visited did not just ignore key realities of God's image but actively worked to further undermine God's image in Drew. When he assigned Drew the task of viewing pornography, he was working to degrade God's image even more in Drew. This is just one example. We saw the same thing in the secular counseling that Rick, Wendy, and Gail received. I am personally not shocked that unbelievers ignore the image of God as a central element in counseling. What does concern me is when believers in Christ behave as though secular counseling approaches have something indispensable to offer the counseling process, when these approaches do not even understand or acknowledge the most fundamental reality of what it means to be a human being.

Humanity: Made with a Body and Soul

A second crucial reality the Bible teaches about what it means to be a person is that human beings are created with two essential aspects. When God explains what it is that makes up a human being, he says that we have both a body and a soul. In Genesis 2:7 the Bible records, "Then the LORD God formed the man of dust from the ground and breathed into his nostrils the breath of life."

When God made the first person, he paired the physical with the spiritual, and the combination created a living person. The spiritual aspect of humanity is described as God's own breath, which God has given to no other creature in his world.

Many other passages in Scripture teach this spiritual reality (Job 34:14–15; Eccl. 12:7; 1 Cor. 7:34; 2 Cor. 5:5). A person's dual qualities of body and soul are made clear in Matthew 10:28 where Jesus admonishes, "Do not fear those who kill the body but cannot kill the soul. Rather fear him who can destroy both soul and body in hell."

The Bible makes a distinction between these two aspects of humanity, but it never makes an ultimate division. In biblical terms, there is no such thing as a person who is not both a body and a soul together in one human being. This biblical reality is called "dichotomy," which refers to the fact that human beings consist of two aspects.[11]

These two aspects, though distinct, are so closely related that there is only one situation in which they can be separated. That one situation is the tragic reality where sin entered the world, bringing about death in the human race. Death in a human being is the horrifying separation of the body from the soul (2 Cor. 5:8). It is the literal destruction of a human being. But even that destruction is temporary. The eternal destiny of every human being is one of an eternal union between body and soul either in heaven or hell (Matt. 25:31–46).

Biblical Teaching on the Body

There are a few different terms in the Bible to highlight the physical element of human beings. The words "flesh" and "body" are each used in the Bible to translate one Hebrew word and two Greek terms.[12] This physical element is a crucial element of who we are. We see this in numerous places throughout the Scriptures. We will look at two, one in the Old Testament and the other from the New.

In the detailed narrative of the creation of mankind, God describes the process of making the woman from the man.

---

11. The word *dichotomy* comes from Greek and means, literally, to cut in two. This literal meaning is not ideal, since human beings are not designed to have the two aspects of their nature be cut at all. Rather, they were designed to stay together. Still, insofar as the language points to the two-sided nature of a human person, it is useful. Theologians have used other language, including, dualism, duality, duplex, holistic dualism, and psychosomatic unity. Many of these terms have their own baggage. My personal preference is to use the language of holistic dualism or psychosomatic unity since I think those terms are the most theologically precise in showing that human beings are a united whole of two aspects. I have chosen to use dichotomy, however, since that seems to be the most common term.

12. In the Old Testament, the Hebrew term is *bāsār* and is translated as "flesh." In the New Testament, the Greek terms are *sarx*, often translated as "flesh," or *soma*, which is often translated as "body."

The Lᴏʀᴅ God caused a deep sleep to fall upon the man, and while he slept took one of his ribs and closed up its place with flesh. And the rib that the Lᴏʀᴅ God had taken from the man he made into a woman and brought her to the man. Then the man said, "This at last is bone of my bones and flesh of my flesh; she shall be called Woman because she was taken out of Man." (Gen. 2:21–23)

In this passage we see that God makes the woman from one of the physical elements he took out of the man. Then, after God forms the woman and presents her to the man, the man is clearly overwhelmed and begins to speak out of the overflow of his joy at seeing the woman. It is significant that he directs his enthusiasm about the woman to the fact that they are made from the same physical matter: "This at last is bone of my bones and flesh of my flesh." Even the name of the woman comes from the fact that she is drawn from a physical element of the man. This passage points to the high honor that God assigns to our physical bodies.

A passage from the New Testament which honors the body is found in 1 Corinthians 6:15–20:

Do you not know that your bodies are members of Christ? Shall I then take the members of Christ and make them members of a prostitute? Never! Or do you not know that he who is joined to a prostitute becomes one body with her? For, as it is written, "The two will become one flesh." But he who is joined to the Lord becomes one spirit with him. Flee from sexual immorality. Every other sin a person commits is outside the body, but the sexually immoral person sins against his own body. Or do you not know that your body is a temple of the Holy Spirit within you, whom you have from God? You are not your own, for you were bought with a price. So glorify God in your body.

Paul is emphasizing the teaching on sexuality in this passage, grounding his instruction against sexual immorality in a theology of the body. He affirms that our physical bodies are members of Christ (1 Cor. 6:15), that sexual immorality is wrong because it is a sin against our physical body (1 Cor. 6:18), that our physical body is a temple of the Spirit (1 Cor. 6:19), and that we must glorify God with our bodies because they are not our own but have been purchased by Jesus Christ (1 Cor. 6:20).

I can think of no more exalted statements about our bodies than that Jesus purchased them with his own blood and that the Holy Spirit came to reside in them. When you add to this the truth that Jesus himself became incarnate, taking on a human body (Phil. 2:7–8) which will be his forever, it is clear that the Bible assigns very high honor to the physical bodies of human beings.

Biblical Teaching on the Soul

The Bible teaches the internal, spiritual dynamic of mankind using many different kinds of language. Sometimes the Bible uses language for the purpose of pointing to the existence of the internal aspect of who we are. The Bible also uses language to point to the specific functions of this internal reality. Four significant terms are used to indicate the existence of an immaterial soul.

One term is "soul": "My soul also is greatly troubled" (Ps. 6:3).[13] Another term is "spirit": "But Hannah answered, "No, my lord, I am a woman troubled in spirit" (1 Sam. 1:15).[14] Other language includes the "hidden person": "But let your adorning be the hidden person of the heart" (1 Peter 3:4). And "inner self": "Though our outer self is wasting away, our inner self is being renewed day by day" (2 Cor. 4:16).[15]

The Bible not only teaches the existence of the soul but also describes some of the functions performed by the soul. The function

---

13. Soul is used to translate the Old Testament term *nephesh* and the New Testament term *psychē*.

14. Spirit is used to translate the Old Testament term *rûach* and the New Testament term *pneuma*.

15. Notice that the language of "inner self" for the soul is contrasted with "outer self," which is another term for the physical body that, in this passage, is demonstrated as succumbing to the decay of life in a fallen world.

of volition is emphasized with the use of the term "will": "If anyone's will is to do God's will, he will know whether the teaching is from God" (John 7:17).[16] Cognition is emphasized with the term "mind": "And you, who once were alienated and hostile in mind" (Col. 1:21).[17] Our moral sense of right and wrong is highlighted using the word "conscience": "Thus, sinning against your brothers and wounding their conscience when it is weak, you sin against Christ" (1 Cor. 8:12).[18] The human seat of emotion is referenced with the popular term "heart": "Let not your hearts be troubled" (John 14:1).[19] Interestingly, in the New Testament the word for "flesh," which often refers to the physical body, can refer to an internal principle of indwelling sin that remains in the believer: "For those who live according to the flesh set their minds on the things of the flesh" (Rom. 8:5).[20]

That is an incredibly brief survey of nine different terms. That diversity of terminology points to the diverse functioning of the internal aspect of human beings. Sometimes the Bible emphasizes the cognitive element of our soul to think and reason. Sometimes the volitional element is used to emphasize our ability to choose. At other times the Bible emphasizes emotional language to highlight our ability to feel. The Bible also underlines the moral part of our soul that embraces or rejects good and evil.[21] The Bible uses language like heart, soul, spirit,

---

16. The Greek term here is *thelḗma*.

17. The Greek term here is *nous*.

18. The Greek term translated here is *suneidḗsis*.

19. The Greek word used for heart in the New Testament is *kardia*. The Hebrew word used in the Old Testament is *lēbh*. The term for heart referenced above at times highlights the emotional element of man but is also used very often to point to the spiritual aspect of man in general. Indeed, it is the term used most frequently.

20. See note 12.

21. Some in the biblical counseling movement have worked to try to articulate the various functions of the human soul. One attempt came from Mike Emlet, "Understanding the Influences on the Human Heart," in the *Journal of Biblical Counseling*, (Winter 2002): 47–52. This work was followed by Jeremy Pierre, "Trust in the Lord with All Your Heart: The Centrality of Faith in Christ to the Restoration of Human Functioning," PhD dissertation, The Southern Baptist Theological Seminary, 2010). Pierre follows Emlet in finding three essential functions of the human heart, namely, affection, cognition, and volition. The works by these men are well done and of crucial importance. I do think we should consider adding at least one more function of the heart, and that would be the moral function I mentioned earlier. The use of the language for "conscience" and "flesh" seems to point to approval and rejection of either good or evil. This seems to me as something a bit different from what is contained in the other three categories.

and inner man, which merely points to the existence of the spiritual without making a specific function explicit.

We should conclude from all of this variety in language that the Bible is teaching a diversity within an overall unity concerning the human soul. Though the various terms point to many different functions of the soul, the central reality is that we have one soul. We do not need to come up with a new and different aspect of humanity every time we encounter a different word referring to the soul. Instead, we should understand that the Bible will use different language to refer to the same thing, and that different language may highlight a specific function of the soul. This would be similar to a man speaking about his wife, his children's mother, and his best friend. With each new use of language, he is still talking about the same person while highlighting different things about her.

This is why I am not persuaded by the view that human beings, instead of being a union of body and soul, are actually a body, a soul, *and* spirit.[22] This view, known as trichotomy, does not seem to understand that the Bible can use different terms to speak of the same thing. In fact, one of the passages that, to me, poses the most difficulty for this position is one of the texts proponents of trichotomy commonly use to defend their position:

> For the word of God is living and active, sharper than any two-edged sword, piercing to the division of soul and of spirit, of joints and of marrow, and discerning the thoughts and intentions of the heart. (Heb. 4:12)

Trichotomists believe that this passage teaches that the soul is something different from the spirit because they are divisible by the Word of God. If we are going to create separate roles for the spirit and the soul because of this passage, then we also must make a separate role

---

22. Franz Delitzsch, *A System of Biblical Psychology*, trans. R. E. Wallis, 2nd ed. (Grand Rapids, MI: Baker, 1966).

for the heart, which is also mentioned in this verse. We would have the same problem with Luke 10:27: "You shall love the Lord your God with all your heart and with all your soul and with all your strength and with all your mind." Here the Bible talks about four different elements of the human person. Rather than believing that each item in the list refers to something different, we should allow the Bible to speak of the aspects of people using different language. In Hebrews, God is describing the penetrating power of the Bible. In Luke, God makes a statement about the comprehensive love we are to have for him.[23]

The Relationship of the Body and the Soul

In discussing the dichotomist nature of mankind, we must do more than observe the aspects of body and soul. Body and soul are tightly bound together, so we must have some understanding of how these two facets interact with one another. We can observe at least two interactions of body and soul.

First, God has designed human beings to be guided by their souls. God created people to work in such a way that their souls initiate the activity of their bodies. This is a clear teaching of Scripture in places like Proverbs 4:23: "Keep your heart with all vigilance, for from it flow the springs of life." Solomon conveys great importance to the heart in this passage. He urges us to protect it with great care because everything we do—all of the activity in our life—flows from our heart. We have an example of this in Exodus 25:1–2: "The LORD said to Moses, 'Speak to the people of Israel, that they take for me a contribution. From every man whose heart moves him you shall receive the contribution for me.'" When God speaks to Moses, he says that the people will give when their hearts motivate them to behave in that way.

This idea that the body is guided and steered by the soul is one that the biblical counseling movement has emphasized. One particularly

---

23. For a more thorough response to trichotomy, see Anthony A. Hoekema, *Created in God's Image* (Carlisle, UK: Paternoster, 1994), 204–10.

articulate expression of this came from Ed Welch in his book *Blame It on the Brain?*:

> The unique contribution of the body to the whole person is that it is the *mediator* of moral action rather than the *initiator*. In a sense, it is equipment of the heart. It does what the heart tells it to do; it is the heart's *vehicle* for concrete ministry and service in the material world.[24]

Welch's point is to make clear that in a biblical theology of humanity, we understand the heart as the "initiator" of moral action and the body as the "mediator" of moral action. It is important that we make clear that it does not demean the body to assert that the soul instigates behavior. Instead, it rightly locates the crucial importance of the body as the arbiter of the soul to the rest of the world.

The body not only mediates the soul to the rest of the world, it also conveys information to the soul. Human beings, as creatures, are dependent by definition. We need God, but we also need other things. We need food, water, sleep, and air in order to survive. Our bodies provide physical indicators for each of these necessities. This is something that is both assumed and taught in the Bible.

Matthew 12:1: "At that time Jesus went through the grainfields on the Sabbath. His disciples were hungry, and they began to pluck heads of grain and to eat." Matthew records here that the disciples needed food, and the way they knew this was by the sensation of hunger in their bodies. The bodies of the disciples instructed their souls, which then initiated the physical action of picking grain and eating it. There is then something of a two-way relationship between the body and soul where the body both mediates and informs the intentions of the soul.

A second reality we can observe about the interaction between body

---

24. Edward T. Welch, *Blame It on the Brain?: Distinguishing Chemical Imbalances, Brain Disorders, and Disobedience* (Phillipsburg: P&R, 1998), 40, emphasis in original. See also David Powlison, "Idols of the Heart and 'Vanity Fair,'" *Christian Counseling & Educational Foundation*, October 16, 2009, http://www.ccef.org/idols-heart-and-vanity-fair.

and soul is that, in a fallen world, our souls fail our bodies and our bodies fail our souls. On the one hand, the Bible is clear that our souls fail our bodies. When sin darkened the heart of the first couple, it made it possible for corrupt desires of the heart to guide the body into sinful behaviors. When Adam and Eve corruptly discerned that the fruit of the tree of the knowledge of good and evil was good, they each disobeyed and ate. In other words, they sinned against their own bodies by using them to do something against the command of God. We repeat their transgression every time we have a wicked desire that grows into wicked behavior. We betray ourselves and use the bodies God gave us to mediate the wickedness of our hearts to the world. God never intended human beings to use their bodies in this way.

This is what Paul is teaching in 1 Corinthians 6:16, 18. He instructs our hearts in this passage to turn away from sexual immorality. "Do you not know that he who is joined to a prostitute becomes one body with her? . . . Flee from sexual immorality." His argument in making this appeal is grounded in the honor of our physical bodies. He pleads with Christians to have sexually pure desires so that they will not sin against their bodies with sexually immoral acts. A world of sin creates a context where sinful people can betray their own bodies by misdirecting them with sinful desires.

On the other hand, the Bible is also clear that our bodies fail our souls. We live in a world of physical death where our bodies die and decay. The physical brokenness in the body leads to trouble for the soul.

> So we do not lose heart. Though our outer self is wasting away, our inner self is being renewed day by day. For this light momentary affliction is preparing for us an eternal weight of glory beyond all comparison, as we look not to the things that are seen but to the things that are unseen. For the things that are seen are transient, but the things that are unseen are eternal. For we know that if the tent that is our earthly home is destroyed, we have a building from God, a house not made with hands, eternal in the heavens. For

in this tent we groan, longing to put on our heavenly dwelling, if indeed by putting it on we may not be found naked. For while we are still in this tent we groan, being burdened—not that we would be unclothed, but that we would be further clothed, so that what is mortal may be swallowed up by life. (2 Cor. 4:16–5:4)

In this passage, our souls are discussed using the language of "inner self," and our bodies are discussed using the language of "outer self" and a "tent." Paul affirms here that in a world of physical decay, our spirits can be renewed even as our bodies waste away to ultimate death.

The Christian, therefore, experiences a world in which their body and soul are moving in something like different directions. As the Spirit within us drives the inner person toward life, a fallen world pushes our body toward death. Our body will often be unable to do the work that our soul beckons it to do. Physical weakness places an enormous burden on the soul. A potentially endless list of physical problems complicate the ability of our dying body to carry out the desires of our soul, which is being renewed. Problems like tumors in the brain, intense physical pain, dementia, Parkinson's disease, hormonal problems, Cushing's disease, chronic brain injury, hypokalemia, insomnia, and—literally—thousands of other problems all challenge the ability of the human body to carry out the commands of the soul.[25] And we have not even talked about the innumerable problems the medical community has not discovered yet,

---

25. It is beyond the scope of my work in this chapter to address what is called the biogenic theory of mood disorders, more commonly known as the theory of "chemical imbalance." This has to do with the debate about whether our mood disorders are due to imbalances of chemicals in our brain, like dopamine and serotonin. Christians aren't the only ones who have raised concerns about this theory. Many unbelieving experts have as well. Resources that I have found helpful in addressing this matter have been Daniel Carlat, *Unhinged: The Trouble with Psychiatry—A Doctor's Revelations about a Profession in Crisis*; Irving Kirsch, *The Emperor's New Drugs: Exploding the Antidepressant Myth*; Peter D. Kramer, *Listening to Prozac: The Landmark Book about Antidepressants and the Remaking of the Self*; Edward T. Welch, *Blame It on the Brain?: Distinguishing Chemical Imbalances, Brain Disorders, and Disobedience*; David Powlison, "Biological Psychiatry," in *Seeing with New Eyes: Counseling and the Human Condition through the Lens of Scripture*; and Charles D. Hodges, *Good Mood, Bad Mood: Help and Hope for Depression and Bipolar Disorder*. The first three on that list are secular thinkers; the last three are biblical thinkers. I believe the biblical counseling movement has added a very careful perspective on the matter with our understanding that the body cannot make us sin.

which cause countless people untold amounts of suffering as they await an accurate diagnosis and effective treatment. All of these constitute the "groaning" of our weak bodies, which await "a building from God, a house not made with hands, eternal in the heavens" (2 Cor. 5:1).

This does not mean that the body is bad. The body is very good and is declared to be so by God himself, who makes his home in it. It does mean that sin is very bad, and it weakens and decays the body. We long for the day, mentioned by Paul, when we will have glorified bodies not stained by sin and weakness (cf. 1 Cor. 15:35–49). In the meantime, this teaching justifies the use of medicine, medical procedures, and medical doctors who provide cures and symptom relief for the physical problems we experience.

Counseling Implications for Human Beings with Bodies and Souls

The Bible urges us to see humanity as created with both a body and a soul that have a complex—often mysterious—interaction. I think it is possible to explain at least four implications for biblical counseling.[26]

First, biblical counselors will address problems that are both physical and spiritual. It is a simplistic denial of a complex biblical teaching to insist that counseling problems could only be physical *or* spiritual. Counseling problems can be physical, spiritual, or combinations of the two. The complex interaction of body and soul, combined with our limited knowledge as human beings, may make it complicated or even impossible to identify a singular genesis of a given problem as physical, spiritual, or both.

This leads to a second implication that biblical counselors must utilize and cooperate with competent medical professionals as they counsel troubled people. Biblical counselors understand that in a fallen world,

---

26. For more information on this, you can see the "Statement Regarding Mental Disorders, Medicine, and Counseling" from ACBC. This statement is recorded in its entirety in appendix A. I was on the committee that drafted this statement and believe it to be a good summary of a Christian approach to counseling those who experience a medical element to their counseling problems.

the body both influences and weakens the soul. They also understand that the material sufficiency of Scripture extends to counseling but not to medical treatment.[27] Furthermore, they understand that the doctrine of God's common grace gives to many people rich knowledge in medical science.[28] All of this information leads us to an enthusiastic cooperation with medical science. My personal creed in counseling is: "When in doubt, check it out." When I am counseling someone who is experiencing a problem that is extreme, new, bizarre, or out of the ordinary in any way, I encourage that person to see a physician for a full medical exam. The information produced by such an exam greatly benefits counseling. It helps me to see all the potential problems in the counselee, both in body and soul.

A third counseling implication is that medical care, while important, is never sufficient to address the problems people have. Problems people have are never *merely* medical. People exist with a body and soul, so will always need the kind of care that we offer in counseling. Even when problems are obviously medical, the person still requires counseling. A person with cancer needs chemotherapy but also needs biblical counsel to offer encouragement in the diagnosis and prognosis. A person who has lost a limb needs surgery, rehabilitation, and a prosthesis. They also need conversation with a wise and caring person about how to address the spiritual trauma they face. Even a head cold often requires the kind of encouragement and service that biblical counseling knows how to offer. This is just another way of saying that whether our problems are extensive or mundane, we are called to respond to them in a community of care. That is why God made the most central institution on planet Earth to be the church, not hospitals. Since this need for counseling care is real even in obviously physical situations, consider how much more counseling is needed in situations that are less clear.

A fourth counseling implication is that biblical counselors must not practice medicine. We must honor the discipline of medical science

---

27. I explain the material sufficiency of Scripture in chapter 2. The content of the discipline of medical science and the content of Scripture do not overlap.

28. A theology of common grace is addressed in chapter 3.

by leaving it to the people trained and credentialed to practice it. The Bible offers sufficient resources to offer counseling care but not sufficient resources to offer medical care. Instead, the Bible's teaching on the importance of the body encourages medical care by those who are expert in providing it. As biblical counselors, we do not offer professional medical advice to counselees, but instead encourage them to see physicians to diagnose and treat any physical problems.

We need to make very clear what it does and does not mean to say that the Bible is not a sufficient resource to offer medical care. The Bible lacks an explanation of the details of how to perform cardiac bypass surgery, for example. Medical professionals learn this information from sources outside of Scripture. This does not mean that the Bible ceases to be the authority over medical practice. Medical procedures like heart surgery are warranted because of the Bible's teaching on the sanctity of human life. Interventions by physicians for assisted suicide, selective reduction during pregnancy, and use of the so-called morning-after pill are ruled out because of the same biblical principle—the sanctity of human life. Biblical counselors are required to weigh in with their counselees, to urge them to avoid such practices, when matters of such obvious biblical principle are at stake.

All of this is deeply related to the kind of counsel offered to Drew when he received reparative therapy. Reparative therapy is wrong because it has a wrong understanding of the nature of humanity. When reparative therapy focuses exclusively on behavior rather than desires initiated in the soul, it treats Drew in a way that is subhuman. In the same way, when reparative therapy tried to tinker with Drew's physicality by inducing him to watch pornography, it treated him as a body stripped of a soul accountable to God for its functioning. Treating Drew as fully human requires us to acknowledge his soul as well as his body. The example here is for reparative therapy as it related to Drew. Many other therapies fail to acknowledge the spiritual part of a person. Interventions such as biological psychiatry, cognitive behavioral therapy, and others strip human beings of one of their constituent aspects.

Counselors using these therapies need to learn from the Scriptures what it means to address human beings more fully in their problems in living.[29]

Humanity: Made Male and Female

The Bible teaches a third crucial reality about the existence of mankind. Not only are we made in God's image, composed of physical and spiritual aspects, but we are also made with two genders. This is stated in Genesis 1:27: "So God created man in his own image, in the image of God he created him; male and female he created them." This passage shows that God created the one human race to exist in two different genders, namely, male and female.

The human race is composed of two genders, but the individual gender roles are not identical. They are complementary. That is why Christians who embrace this teaching are called complementarians.[30] They believe the Bible teaches that God made two equivalent genders that complement one another. Each of these propositions—men and women are equal, and men and women are different—are important in understanding the biblical teaching on gender.[31]

Men and Women Are Equal

The Bible teaches that men and women are equivalent in at least two senses. First, men and women are equivalent in their status at creation.

---

29. For a critique on biological psychiatry, see David Powlison, "Biological Psychiatry" in *Seeing with New Eyes* (Phillipsburg, NJ: P&R, 2003), 239–52. For an engagement with cognitive behavioral therapy, see chapters 1 and 3.

30. Christians who deny that human gender roles are not identical are called egalitarians, arguing that there is no difference between the sexes in the roles they are to carry out.

31. For more information on this topic, see John Piper and Wayne Grudem, *Recovering Biblical Manhood and Womanhood: A Response to Evangelical Feminism* (Wheaton, IL: Crossway, 1991); John Piper, *What's the Difference?: Manhood and Womanhood Defined According to the Bible* (Wheaton, IL: Crossway, 2008); Wayne Grudem, *Evangelical Feminism and Biblical Truth: An Analysis of More Than 100 Disputed Questions* (Wheaton, IL: Crossway, 2012); Andreas J. Köstenberger, *God, Marriage, and Family: Rebuilding the Biblical Foundation* (Wheaton, IL: Crossway, 2010).

God made men and women as equivalent creations. This equivalence is seen in the Genesis 1:27 passage already noted: God made mankind in his own image as both man and woman. Both genders are created in the image of God, and neither can claim an exalted status that the other gender does not possess. Any brand of chauvinism that prejudices one gender over another cuts at the heart of God's creation of both sexes made in his own image.

Men and women are also equivalent in the redemption offered in Christ Jesus. Jesus Christ came to save men and women who both have equal standing in the kingdom of God. Galatians 3:28 says, "There is neither Jew nor Greek, there is neither slave nor free, there is no male and female, for you are all one in Christ Jesus." This does not mean that there is no longer any distinction between men and women, but rather men and women all have equal access to Jesus Christ as Savior and Lord, just as do Jews and Greeks, and slaves and freemen. The apostle Paul wants to make the point that there are no racial, economic, or gender barriers when it comes to calling upon the name of Jesus. Jesus saves all who come to him in repentant faith.[32] Because Jesus equally redeems men and women, we must be committed to an equivalent embrace of both genders. There is no room in Christ's church for prizing one gender over the other.

Men and Women Are Different

Men and women are equivalent in creation and redemption, but that does not mean there are no differences between them. The biological differences range from the obvious physical indicators of manhood and

---

32. This is a passage that has been hotly contested with the onset of evangelical feminism, or egalitarianism. Egalitarians argue that this passage means that in the redemption offered by Christ, all distinctions about gender have been removed. See Gilbert Bilezikian, *Beyond Sex Roles: What the Bible Says about a Woman's Place in Church and Family* (Grand Rapids, MI: Baker Academic, 2006), 95. I find the egalitarian argument completely unsatisfying for a variety of reasons. For a sound biblical response, see S. Lewis Johnson, "Role Distinctions in the Church," in John Piper and Wayne A. Grudem, eds., *Recovering Biblical Manhood and Womanhood: A Response to Evangelical Feminism* (Wheaton, IL: Crossway, 1991), 154–64; and Wayne A. Grudem, *Evangelical Feminism: A New Path to Liberalism?* (Wheaton, IL: Crossway, 2006), 187.

womanhood to the hormonal differences underlying those indicators. The distinctions the Bible emphasizes have to do with differences in the context of the home and in the context of life in the local church.

In the home, men are called to the role of servant leadership and are given charge over the operations of the home. Women are called to respond to this leadership with submission. Colossians 3:18–19 says, "Wives, submit to your husbands, as is fitting in the Lord. Husbands, love your wives, and do not be harsh with them." In the parallel passages in Ephesians 5, Paul makes clear that the submission of a wife to her husband should mirror the submission of the church to Christ himself (cf. Eph. 5:22–24). Paul also makes clear that the love of a husband for his wife should image the kind of loving leadership that sent Jesus to the cross to purify his bride, the church (cf. Eph. 5:25–30). We are assured in the Scriptures that the fall of mankind into sin corrupted this created order (cf. Gen. 3:16; 1 Peter 3:1–2), but we are never told that God's command to husbands and wives is wrong in itself or that God intends to change it.

A second area where we are told of differences is in the redeemed community of the church. Men and women are called to fulfill different functions in the Christian community. Men are called to a position of spiritual leadership in the church, and women are called to respond to this leadership. This distinction in church roles is located most obviously in the pastoral office of teaching.

> Let a woman learn quietly with all submissiveness. I do not permit
> a woman to teach or to exercise authority over a man; rather, she
> is to remain quiet. For Adam was formed first, then Eve. (1 Tim.
> 2:11–13)

This passage gives a command and a basis for the command. Women are instructed to learn and not to teach or to exercise authority over a man. This does not mean that a woman cannot be involved in teaching other women but that the teaching office of pastor is reserved for men.

Paul provides the basis for the command in creation. The reason Paul reserves the authoritative role of teacher for men is grounded in the creation of man before woman, indicating his authority over his wife, who is equivalent to him in her created essence.

God created a framework of authority within equality when he designed the complementary roles of manhood and womanhood. Men and women are created to equally image God, and yet as they do this together, they accomplish it by doing different things. The woman best images God as she responds to male leadership. In the family and among the body of believers, the man best images God as he exerts servant leadership—at home and at church.

Counseling Implications for Manhood and Womanhood

There are many implications of this truth for counseling. It is worth noting that counselors need to embrace this element of biblical teaching to be effective in marriage counseling. Over the years I have done more marriage counseling than any other kind, and every marriage has needed help in this area of manhood and womanhood. By the time married couples arrive for counseling, there has been some breakdown in the functional structure of headship and submission in marriage. Counselors who do not understand and embrace the biblical teaching on complementarity are not equipped to address the issues at the core of troubled marriages.

The most effective counseling happens in churches honoring God's creation design for manhood and womanhood. When churches engage in practices that undermine biblical gender roles, they undercut the created framework of gender in which God made us to function. Counselors and counselees need to be in a church that embraces and models God's good design for manhood and womanhood.

Yet another implication has to do with the actual meetings that counselors have with counselees. Here we must address how gender works itself out in the roles that counselors are called to play as they interact with their counselees.

First, Paul's prohibition against women teaching doctrine to men applies equally to counseling and preaching. Counseling is ministry of the Word of God, just as preaching is. The only difference is that counseling is the personal ministry of the Word in a conversation, and preaching is a public ministry of the Word in proclamation. Because biblical counselors believe in the sufficiency of Scripture, we believe that a substantial portion of counseling consists in teaching the Bible to counselees. Because women are not to teach men the Bible, they should not counsel married couples alone.

This has practical implications for Drew and Amber. Drew is not the only person in need of a counselor. Drew and Amber both need counseling. The counselor leading their marriage counseling when they are together should be a man since he would be the image bearer most equipped to discharge the teaching responsibilities to men and women in counseling. Of course this does not mean that a woman could not or should not be involved in marriage counseling. In my counseling ministry, I have counseled very few married couples without having a woman counselor present. Having a female counselor present in marriage counseling is incredibly helpful. The presence of a woman would help Amber to feel more comfortable in a room with two men. It also allows the opportunity for the woman to be taught the Bible by the female counselor. The female counselor can also help in making the male counselor aware of things he may have missed in the counseling session. She can also interact with the man being counseled, asking questions and helping him to understand certain things about his wife from the perspective of another woman. She must be careful in her interaction, however, not to engage in biblical instruction to the man.

Second, Paul's instruction to the Ephesians that sexual immorality, impurity, and covetousness "must not even be named among you, as is proper among the saints" (Eph. 5:3) is relevant for counseling. This passage makes us as Christians responsible for the appearance of our opposite-sex relationships. It is not enough that individual Christians strive for purity in their own relationships before God. They also must appear to be striving for purity in their relationships with other people. It does not require recent statistics to demonstrate that many pastors fail in ministry because of sexual sin that begins in counseling. The biblical teaching and this consequent reality force us to consider our responsibilities to the biblical teaching of gender in individual counseling.

The call to avoid any appearance of sexual immorality means that under most normal circumstances, it is wrong to counsel members of the opposite sex in an ongoing way. Men should not counsel women in an ongoing way, not because it is wrong to instruct a woman in counseling, but because the man must avoid any appearance of sin. Women should not counsel men, not only to avoid teaching men doctrine but also to avoid the appearance of impropriety in meeting consistently and alone without their spouses. Related to this is the lack of comfort that most men experience in being alone with and instructed by a woman. Let me make two important qualifications on this issue.

I am being very careful to say that men should not counsel women alone in an *ongoing* way. That is different from saying they must *never* meet with a woman or counsel them alone. Some have the conviction that a man must never meet alone with a woman who is not his wife. I appreciate that conviction and would never urge anyone who holds it to violate his conscience and do something different (cf. Rom. 14:23). Having said that, I also believe that saying this practice must be observed by all Christians at all times goes beyond what is written in Scripture.

At certain times pastors, in particular, will need to have a private meeting with a member of the opposite sex. I have typically observed three rules when meeting with a woman: I had a window cut in my office door so anyone can see in my office. I meet with women when a secretary or other staff person is present. The goal in the meeting is to transition the woman to the care of another woman as quickly as possible. I have never met alone with a woman in her home except in the case of elderly women.

The rationale behind this standard is to avoid any hint of sexual immorality. I have heard some people scoff at such standards, saying they seem to extend the worst possible motives to the counselor or counselee, as if, left alone for a moment, they will commit an act of sexual immorality. The basis for such careful standards for counseling meetings has nothing necessarily to do with the intentions of anyone in the meeting. Instead, the basis is to honor God by avoiding any hint of sexual immorality. An outsider looking in cannot see the intentions of our hearts but can see whether we are consistently meeting with someone of the opposite sex. Since they cannot know what is happening during those times when we are alone, we uphold the teaching of Ephesians 5:3 by avoiding time alone with the opposite sex as much as possible.

These principles apply to the counseling of Drew and Amber. They are experiencing a very difficult time, and they each need to meet alone with other people in addition to regular marriage counseling. The many issues they face that require conversation are more than one person could ever address in a weekly counseling session. In addition to her regular marriage counseling sessions, Amber needs to be meeting weekly with another person. Based on the biblical teaching on gender, the best person to do that is a wise and godly woman.

Drew also needs to meet with another person, and the biblical teaching on gender directs that this must be a man. But things are a bit more complicated with Drew. His same-sex attraction might make us wonder if it is risky to pair him with another man for counseling. This question is particularly relevant because one significant struggle Drew faced with his sexual desire had to do with a man he was meeting with in counseling. Several men in my ministry have wondered if it is wise to counsel someone of the same gender when that person is struggling with same-sex attraction. They asked this question because they do not want to be a temptation to the person they want to help, and they do not want to raise a suspicion about sexual immorality in violation of Ephesians 5:3.

The way to avoid both temptation and the appearance of sin is actually not to place same-sex-attracted people in counseling with members of the opposite gender. Instead, the best course is to offer counseling with a member of the same gender who is in no way tempted to homosexual sin. A member of the same sex who is a wise and growing Christian and who is marked by Christlikeness and chastity is the best choice. Such a counselor is best able to maintain the purity of the relationship and is best equipped to respond to and resist any potential attraction that exists on the part of the counselee.

Before leaving the issue of gender, there is one more matter that we must address. That concerns the transgender issue that has been so much in the headlines lately. News reports swirl of persons who believe themselves to be a different gender than the one indicated by their biological sex.[33] These people reject the so-called "gender binary" that makes room for only two genders of male and female. One very articulate expression of this rejection is found in a statement from the International Gay and Lesbian Human Rights Commission:

> We believe it is indispensable to deconstruct the binary sex/gender system that shapes the Western world so absolutely that in most cases it goes unnoticed. For "other sexualities to be possible" it is indispensable and urgent that we stop governing ourselves by the absurd notion that only two possible body types exist, male and female, with only two genders inextricably linked to them, man and woman. We make trans and intersex issues our priority because their presence, activism and theoretical contribution show us the path to a new paradigm that will allow as many bodies, sexualities and identities to exist as those living in this world might wish to have, with each one of them respected, desired, celebrated.[34]

---

33. Of the many stories, the account of Bruce Jenner adopting the persona of Caitlyn is only the most famous. See "Caitlyn Jenner: The Full Story," *Vanity Fair*, http://www.vanityfair .com/hollywood/2015/06/caitlyn-jenner-bruce-cover-annie-leibovitz.

34. International Gay and Lesbian Human Rights Commission, "Institutional Memoir of the 2005 Institute for Trans and Intersex Activist Training," 2005, 7–8, http://iglhrc.org/sites/ default/files/367-1.pdf.

Such a position must be rejected by any faithful rendering of Scripture. As we have seen, God creates the human race in two complementary genders and sovereignly assigns gender to human beings. That gender is revealed to us plainly at birth.

In a fallen world, our bodies are corrupted by sin, and one terrible consequence is the condition known as "intersex."[35] This is a physical condition where the normal biological indicators of gender are confused, making it challenging to identify whether one is a boy or a girl.[36] This physical condition is very different from transgenderism, where a person tries to reject the obvious indicators of gender in favor of a different one that God has not assigned. Such a posture constitutes a rejection not only of the goodness of gender but also of the goodness of the body. Biblical counselors must point persons, by the grace of Jesus Christ, to the goodness of their physical gender and help them to repent of a desire for a body God has not given. Biblical counselors will, therefore, resist any efforts to help counselees adopt the physical characteristics, clothing, and even the mannerisms of the opposite sex.[37]

Humane Counseling

The Bible tells us what it means to be truly human. There is no better way to honor human beings or to help them than to treat them in a way that corresponds to biblical teaching. The most humane form of counseling is biblical counseling, which intentionally approaches people as the image bearers they are, existing with a body and a soul

---

35. I will speak more about the impact of sin on our bodies in the next chapter.

36. For more information on intersex, see Denny Burk, *What Is the Meaning of Sex?* (Wheaton, IL: Crossway, 2013), 151–59.

37. This means that Christians cannot follow the counsel offered in books such as Mark Yarhouse, *Understanding Gender Dysphoria: Navigating Transgender Issues in a Changing Culture* (Downers Grove, IL: InterVarsity, 2015). Yarhouse offers a helpful survey of the most recent issues but ultimately refuses to close the door on transgender behaviors, including gender reassignment surgery. Such a refusal is at odds with the biblical teaching observed in this chapter. For more information regarding gender, sexuality, and counseling, see Appendix C, "The Standards of Doctrine of the Association of Certified Biblical Counselors" from the ACBC board.

and engendered as either male or female. It is unbiblical and unhelpful to treat people in counseling as though these realities do not exist or are not relevant. Any counseling approach that does not actively engage and acknowledge these realities is inhumane, regardless of intentions to be helpful.[38]

---

38. Books useful in counseling for the topics addressed in this chapter: Sebastian Traeger and Greg Gilbert, *The Gospel at Work: How Working for King Jesus Gives Purpose and Meaning to Our Jobs* (Grand Rapids, MI: Zondervan, 2013); Timothy Keller, *Every Good Endeavor: Connecting Your Work to God's Work* (New York: Riverhead, 2014); Matt Perman, *What's Best Next: How the Gospel Transforms the Way You Get Things Done* (Grand Rapids, MI: Zondervan, 2014); Timothy S. Lane and Paul David Tripp, *Relationships: A Mess Worth Making* (Greensboro, NC: New Growth, 2006); Edward T. Welch, *Side by Side: Walking with Others in Wisdom and Love* (Wheaton, IL: Crossway, 2015); Jonathan Holmes, *The Company We Keep: In Search of Biblical Friendship* (Minneapolis: Cruciform, 2014); Martha Peace, *The Excellent Wife: A Biblical Perspective* (Bemidji, MN: Focus, 1999); Stuart Scott, *The Exemplary Husband: A Biblical Perspective* (Bemidji, MN: Focus, 2002); Charles D. Hodges, *Good Mood Bad Mood: Help and Hope for Depression and Bipolar Disorder* (Wapwallopen, PA: Shepherd, 2013); Elyse M. Fitzpatrick and Laura Hendrickson, *Will Medicine Stop the Pain?: Finding God's Healing for Depression, Anxiety, and Other Troubling Emotions* (Chicago: Moody, 2006).

CHAPTER 8

BIBLICAL COUNSELING

and a

THEOLOGY OF SIN

As we turn to the issue of sin, we arrive at a consideration of the most horrifying reality in the entire universe. In fact, we must be careful in thinking and writing about sin, as it can be easy to think of it as an abstract concept instead of the ghastly reality it is, ruining everything it touches. In counseling, sin never appears in the muted gray of abstraction. It always comes in the shocking detail and alarming colors of names and faces experiencing real life, real consequences, and real pain. Sin is truly wretched. One of the greatest illustrations I know of this came in the life of a man I know named Sean.

Sean and Sarah were in their mid-twenties and had been married five years when their son, Coty, was born. Neither Sean nor Sarah was very mature when they married. They both loved to party late, sleep in, spend money, and skip work, which created many difficulties in the first few years of marriage. Still, they loved each other, and for each of them the decision to have children was the decision to make a fresh start and get serious about their life. When Sarah got pregnant, they did get serious. Sean got a "real" job, they quit partying, started trying to make some new friends, and even went to church a few times, though they never really got interested.

Coty's birth began a years-long period of happiness in their family. Coty grew like crazy, Sean excelled at work and received several promotions, and Sarah was able to take care of Coty most of the time while her mom watched him two days a week so she could work in a very lucrative part-time job. Sean and Sarah had a happy home and an affluent lifestyle. Neither could imagine how things could get any better.

All that changed one Saturday afternoon a few weeks after Coty's third birthday. Sean was running late for a round of golf with some friends when he hurried to his SUV and backed out of the garage. He was thinking of the apology he would offer to his friends for arriving late to the course when his car jolted, and he instinctively stopped. He wasn't sure what he had hit, but his worst fears were confirmed when he walked to the back of the car and saw Coty lying underneath the car.

The next fifteen minutes were a horrifying blur as Sean screamed for help and tried to revive his son while Sarah called the paramedics. The emergency personnel arrived, and Coty was taken to the hospital in an ambulance. A sheriff's deputy drove Sean and Sarah to the hospital a matter of moments after the ambulance left.

The couple raced into the ER and were met by a physician. She asked the couple to sit down and explained that Coty had died before he arrived at the hospital. Sarah let out a loud and guttural scream and collapsed into Sean's arms.

The next days and weeks were unspeakably awful. They did not seem real. Sean and Sarah made their way through questions from the police, the first night at home without Coty, the funeral home visitation, the burial service, visits from friends and family that were sometimes helpful and sometimes burdensome, selling the SUV, staring at pictures for hours through sobs, and the feelings of guilt that came in the aftermath of what happened.

Neither Sean nor Sarah blamed the other for what happened, but they each blamed themselves a lot. Sarah blamed herself for not keeping closer tabs on their son. Sean felt responsible for not checking more thoroughly behind him before backing away in a hurry. Sean, in particular, was merciless in holding himself responsible for the death of his son. In fact, the responsibility he placed on himself was more than he could bear. One night, eager for a break from the pain, he went back to drinking alcohol, but for the first time in his life, he drank alone.

Over the next two years, Sean's drinking increased dramatically. When he was home he would retreat to the basement, away from Sarah, and would drink all evening or all weekend. For a while he was able to keep his growing enslavement to alcohol contained to times when he was not at work, but it did not last. He started missing work, was demoted, and eventually fired. Through all of this Sarah was pleading to have her husband back. She felt alone and helpless without a son and now functionally without a husband. Sean would sometimes feel guilty but did not sense that he had anything to give to Sarah or any ability to stop drinking.

Sarah was growing increasingly tired of the isolation imposed on her by Sean. It was her son who died too, and she felt that Sean was leaving her alone to deal with matters by herself. One way that she experienced this was in having to pick up more hours at work to compensate for the loss in Sean's salary. Eventually she began to find relief in her growing responsibilities at work, her increased time on the road, and time with coworkers that she cared for. It gave her a break from being home with a husband who was drunk.

Over time Sarah grew very close to a man she worked with named Tom. Tom was a bit older than Sarah and had recently been divorced from his wife. The two began to grab dinner after work regularly and spent a lot of time together on business trips. Sarah loved receiving attention from a man again and appreciated how Tom seemed genuinely to care for her. One night when they were out of town, the two committed adultery. Their resulting affair was intense and began to consume an enormous amount of energy. They always roomed together on trips out of town, spent weekends together, and began to plan Sarah's divorce from Sean. Sarah did not believe Sean even noticed all that was happening. She was wrong.

Sean was suspicious that something was going on. At first, Sean was glad that Sarah was spending more time away since he wanted to be left alone. Eventually, however, he came to see that his drinking was making his life worse. He also was growing concerned about the state of his marriage. One night Sean asked Sarah if there was someone else. Sarah told Sean everything. She admitted there was someone else, that they were in love, and she was going to leave Sean.

Sean begged Sarah to give him another chance. He admitted that he had blown it after Coty died, but that he did not want to lose her too. He begged her to try to come to counseling with him to see if they could fix their many problems. Sarah made it clear that she did not think it would work, but she would give it a try. They agreed to meet with me and reached out for an appointment. Sean and Sarah had visited our church several years earlier and spent some time with me. They never responded to the gospel and eventually quit coming to church, but I really cared a lot about them. I had reached out to them after Coty died and spent some time in their home. They appreciated that time, and we had a good relationship. I was thrilled when they called about getting together and was eager to do what I could to help their very troubled marriage.

The Fall of Mankind

All of the problems that Sean and Sarah faced came about because they are two sinners living in a world tainted by sin. To help this couple, a counselor must understand the biblical teaching on sin. Sin is a disposition of human beings that leads to a failure to conform to the moral law of God. Notice that sin is a *disposition*. Human beings have a nature that is oriented away from God. Sin does not just describe the bad things human beings do or fail to do. More fundamentally, it describes who we are as wicked people.[1]

---

1. This disagrees with the Pelagian view of sin, which was condemned at the Council of Carthage in 418. Pelagius argued that man did not need the enabling grace of God to bring him to faith. He taught that mankind had a will of moral neutrality and could choose to do either

This disposition leads eventually to sinful desires and behavior. We can sin in our spirits and in our bodies, and we can sin actively and passively by engaging in sinful realities or by avoiding good things. Human beings were not created by God to possess this sinful disposition, to want sinful things, or to behave in sinful ways. Instead, God created mankind to be in a state of moral goodness.

After God completed his human creation in the garden, he pronounced everything he had made to be "very good" (Gen. 1:31). When Adam ate of the tree of the knowledge of good and evil against the command of God (cf. Gen. 2:16–17), he sinned against God and became a sinner (Gen. 3:7). Adam's disobedience instituted a spiritual separation from God and inaugurated his eventual physical death. Adam, his wife, and the serpent who tempted them each became cursed by God (Gen. 3:14–23).

When Adam sinned, the consequences rippled out from his own existence to the life of every person who would ever live, except Jesus. When Adam sinned, God considered the rest of humanity to have sinned with him:

> Therefore, just as sin came into the world through one man, and death through sin, and so death spread to all men because all sinned—for sin indeed was in the world before the law was given, but sin is not counted where there is no law. Yet death reigned from Adam to Moses, even over those whose sinning was not like the transgression. (Rom. 5:12–14)

Paul is teaching here about representation (cf. Rom. 5:15–21). He is indicating that the entire human race came to be sinners in Adam because he represented them in his own sinfulness.

This kind of representation happens all the time in our world. My kids attend school every day because I represented them by making a

---

good or evil. He disagreed that the Bible taught that man is inherently fallen and corrupt. He argued, instead, that because the Bible commands man to do good that man must be able to do good.

decision about their education. That decision affects them every day of their life, even when they are unhappy about it. A few years ago my senator, Mitch McConnell, led the United States Senate to pass a bill that I was diametrically opposed to. I registered my disagreement with a letter and a call to his Senate office, but Senator McConnell voted against my wishes. The bill passed, and President George W. Bush signed it into law. These men represented my interests even when I was opposed to what they were doing. The president and Congress can send troops overseas to fight in armed conflicts. Because of this principle of representation, the world understands the United States to be at war even when significant groups of Americans are opposed to sending our troops.

It is hard to imagine life functioning without the principle of representation. We are happy when representation works in our favor, as it does with Christ's representation of us in his life and death for sin. We are unhappy when the same principle works against us, as in Adam's work in the garden. The principle is in place, however, whether we are happy or unhappy with it. Because God created this reality, we can trust him that it is good.

Adam's sin in the garden created many consequences for the human race that impact us all today. In this chapter I will review seven tragic implications of sinfulness on the human race and show what this means for the counseling task.

The Effects of Sin

The fall of mankind in the garden has comprehensive implications for what it means to be a human being. Sin touches every element of our existence as people. In order to understand the impact of sin on people, we need to know who people are. That is why I examined a theology of humanity in the previous chapter. We will now look at the implications of sin on who we are as people made with a body and a soul.

The Effects of Sin on Our Standing before God

Adam represented the human race before God in his disobedience. Because Adam is guilty, every other person stands guilty as well. This guilt attaches to us from the very beginning of our existence. David can say in Psalm 51:5, "Behold, I was brought forth in iniquity, and in sin did my mother conceive me." From the very moment that we began to exist, we began to be guilty of sin because of Adam's representation of us (cf. 1 Cor. 15:21–22). This guilt destroys our relationship with a holy God with whom we have experienced separation because he cannot look upon evil (Isa. 59:2). Because of this guilty separation, as soon as human beings are able, we become sinners, not merely in being represented by Adam but through our own actions.

The biblical teaching that guilt resides in us from the beginning of our existence is called "original sin." Original sin does not refer to Adam's sin or to the first sin we commit, but rather to the fact that Adam's guilt before God is our guilt before God by virtue of his work of representation.[2] Original sin, or this inherent guilt and sinfulness, creates a desperate and hopeless situation for humanity. We stand condemned before a holy God and are separated from and opposed to his goodness, wisdom, and power.[3]

Sin not only exists but all of humanity knows it exists. Paul's teaching in Romans 2:14–15 proves this:

> For when Gentiles, who do not have the law, by nature do what the law requires, they are a law to themselves, even though they

---

2. Some theologians are uncomfortable using the language of original sin because the term can be so confusing. Some prefer to use the language of inherited guilt. I appreciate the clarity of an expression like inherited guilt, but original sin is the term that theologians have used for an incredibly long time, and I cannot tell that this practice is close to changing. I am therefore using the term *original sin*, attempting to carefully define what I mean by it. See Wayne A. Grudem, *Systematic Theology: An Introduction to Biblical Doctrine* (Grand Rapids, MI: Zondervan, 1994), 494–96. See also John M. Frame, *Systematic Theology: An Introduction to Christian Belief* (Phillipsburg, NJ: P&R, 2013), 856–58.

3. For more information, see Hans Madueme and Michael Reeves, eds., *Adam, the Fall, and Original Sin: Theological, Biblical, and Scientific Perspectives* (Grand Rapids, MI: Baker, 2014); Henri Blocher, *Original Sin: Illuminating the Riddle* (Downers Grove, IL: InterVarsity, 2000).

do not have the law. They show that the work of the law is written on their hearts, while their conscience also bears witness, and their conflicting thoughts accuse or even excuse them.

This passage uses two words to talk about the spirit of man that we reviewed in the last chapter. Paul uses the language of "heart" to teach that God's law is written on the soul, and he uses the language of "conscience" to highlight the soul's function of convicting us of sin. The point is to show that all human beings have some knowledge of God's law and a conscience that functions to convict them of their failure to keep the law. This heart function of convicting of sin develops beyond the threefold function of the human heart articulated by others in the biblical counseling movement.[4]

The Effects of Sin on Our Motivations

Another element of our inner person that is impacted by sin has to do with our motivations. We are speaking here about the function of our inner man that has to do with volition, choice, and desire. Sin not only warps our standing before God, it also distorts the motives of our hearts. It makes us desire the wrong things. James makes this clear in his epistle:

> But each person is tempted when he is lured and enticed by his own desire. Then desire when it has conceived gives birth to sin, and sin when it is fully grown brings forth death. (James 1:14–15)

James is very helpful here in showing that every sinful act is preceded by a prior distortion in the human heart that desires the wrong things. Sinful behavior grows out of sinful desires in the human heart. Whenever a person performs an action that incurs the wrath of God, it is evidence that they have a spiritual disposition to want the things God

---

4. See p. 195 and chapter 7, note 20

does not want. Human beings were created to be motivated by the same things that motivate God, but sin has twisted our desires away from God and toward ourselves.[5]

The Effects of Sin on Our Thinking

Sin impacts how our minds work. This refers to the spiritual function of cognition. Because of our sinfulness, we do not think as we should. Paul says that we were once "alienated and hostile in mind" (Col. 1:21; cf. Rom. 1:18ff; Eph. 4:17–18). Theologians sometimes refer to this as the "noetic effects of sin." The implications of this are huge.

Because of the influence of sin on our thinking, we cannot be honest about the existence of God (Rom. 1:18–24). Sin's corrupting influence on our thinking means that we can rationalize moral choices and make good things seem wicked and bad things appear to be acceptable. The noetic effects of sin even make us perplexed so that we are legitimately confused about the things we are to do.[6]

The Effects of Sin on Our Emotions

Sin not only affects our standing before God and our motivations and thinking but also our emotions. Sin influences our soul's ability to feel as we should. One of the functions of the soul is the ability to experience emotions, and this function has been severely damaged by human sinfulness.

Christians can sometimes sound as though emotions are a bad thing. This is not true. Emotions are good. God created human beings with the incredible capacity to experience emotion. This is a profound blessing. What is wrong is that sin causes our emotions to be disordered.

Over and again the Bible explains the disordered nature of our sinful emotions. Sinful people feel hatred when they ought to feel love. We

---

5. See David Powlison, "I Am Motivated When I Feel Desire," in *Seeing with New Eyes: Counseling and the Human Condition through the Lens of Scripture* (Phillipsburg, NJ: P&R, 2003), 145–62.

6. I address this issue in chapter 3.

see this in the very beginning with Cain's hatred of his brother Abel (Gen. 4:1ff). Sinners feel love for things they are called to hate. Solomon speaks of those "who rejoice in doing evil and delight in the perverseness of evil" (Prov. 2:14). The presence of sin creates the context for the emotion of sorrow, which would never be necessary in a world free of transgressions. Paul says, "I have great sorrow and unceasing anguish in my heart. For I could wish that I myself were accursed and cut off from Christ for the sake of my brothers, my kinsmen according to the flesh" (Rom. 9:2–3). Paul was right to feel sorrow for his lost fellow Israelites, but this painful emotion exists only in a fallen world. In a sinful world, we can experience emotions that are misplaced, emotions that are out of proportion to the occasion, and emotions that are wrong.[7]

The Effects of Sin on Our Bodies

Sin is not limited to the spiritual aspect of our existence but affects our physical bodies as well. Sin stains both the inner and outer man. We have learned that even as our inner self is being renewed, our outer self is wasting away.

Paul teaches this in 1 Corinthians 15:42–44. Even as he points to the hope of a resurrection body, he describes the terrible reality of our current physical body given over to decay. He characterizes it as perishable, dishonorable, and weak. Paul is not qualifying any of the good things the Bible teaches about the body, which we saw in chapter 7. He is instead underlining the terrible reality of sin that has so horribly corrupted a body created to be good. God created human beings to live forever in health. Sin ruined that ideal, creating physical weakness and, ultimately, death.

The effects of sin that we have seen so far all relate to humanity as they impact our inner person and outer person. Below, we will examine two more effects of sin as they radiate out from individual persons to our environment. Before we do that, however, we need to pause and

---

7. See Brian S. Bergman, *Feelings and Faith: Cultivating Godly Emotions in the Christians Life* (Wheaton, IL: Crossway, 2009).

evaluate the sinfulness we have seen so far as it impacts each individual. When we survey the impact of sin on the entirety of what it means to be a human being, we see an astonishing amount of corruption that comes into our life because of sin. Theologians have referred to this comprehensive corruption as "total depravity."

Total depravity means that every aspect of our human existence has been touched. In our inner man, our conscience, will, intellect, and emotions have been corrupted. In our outer man our bodies are given over to decay, weakening our ability to obey and tempting us to sin. Total depravity does not mean that every person is as bad as possible, but that sin touches all the elements of humanity.[8] Sin does not just affect us as individuals. The corruption of human beings leads to two other consequences of sin, which we will examine now.

The Effects of Sin on Our Relationships

Before the fall of mankind into sin, human relationship was characterized by joy, harmony, and love. The rebellion of man against God created enmity and strife in our relationships with other people, since the perversion of our most significant relationship inevitably impacts all of our other relationships as well. Paul explains this state of fallen people in Titus 3:3: "For we ourselves were once foolish, disobedient, led astray, slaves to various passions and pleasures, passing our days in malice and envy, hated by others and hating one another." Paul makes two devastating comments about the relationships of fallen people.

First, he says that in our sin, we pass our days in malice and envy. Malice has to do with a desire for wickedness to befall others, and envy is a desire to have the good things that others have. Because of sin, we want bad things to happen to those we know, and we desire that their good gifts be given to us instead.

Second, Paul says that we are hated by others, and we hate one another. The relationships of fallen people are characterized by

---

8. See Arthur W. Pink, *The Doctrine of Human Depravity* (Shallotte, NC: Sovereign Grace, 2001).

animosity. We spend our energy hating others, and they spend their energy hating us. This is a tragic reality in a world where God is defined by love and commands the same of us (cf. Matt. 22:37–40; 1 John 4:8).

The Effects of Sin on Our World

The consequences of sin radiate through every human being and out to the relationships we have with others. The consequences of sin affect the entire created order. It is an amazing demonstration of the consequences of sin that Adam's transgression not only impacted him but the entire existence of every other human being and their relationships, and even the world in which they live.

The Bible makes this clear in Romans 8:20–22:

For the creation was subjected to futility, not willingly, but because of him who subjected it, in hope that the creation itself will be set free from its bondage to corruption and obtain the freedom of the glory of the children of God. For we know that the whole creation has been groaning together in the pains of childbirth until now.

The Bible teaches that the entire creation, not just sinful human beings, is fallen because of the sin of Adam, who subjected it to a corrupt state. We now live in a broken world groaning with vicious animals, predatory viruses, violent windstorms and floods, and horrifying car accidents that create much of the pain we experience in our lives.

The Doctrine of Sin and Biblical Counseling

Biblical counselors, from the beginning of our movement, have articulated that all counseling is occasioned by a world that is broken by sin. Some have understood this to mean that biblical counseling will be limited to an examination of a counselee's responsibility for their individual sin. But the biblical counseling movement has never articulated such a view, which would actually reflect a very simplistic understanding of the doctrine of sin.[9]

The doctrine of sin informs three different contexts for counseling ministry. The first is when people seek counseling because they live life in a fallen world corrupted by sin. It is in this area that everything we saw above about our dying bodies and groaning world is relevant. In this counseling context, we are not talking about people seeking counsel for the purpose of addressing their own personal sin. The goal in this counseling context is not necessarily to assign blame to the counselee. The goal is to comfort them in the midst of the pain they are experiencing in a harsh world.

Even though this context for counseling does not emphasize responsibility for personal sin, this does not mean that sin is not involved in the person's problem, just that it is not the counselee's *personal* sin. In this case, problems occur because Adam sinned, ushering humanity into a world of pain. In such a world, people need help with the discouragement they face over a terminal cancer diagnosis, the pain of loss when their house is destroyed in a flood, the financial pressure that comes when a repair bill exceeds the amount of money they have in the bank, the exhaustion that comes from caring for a spouse with Alzheimer's disease, and many, many other things.

This is what initially led Sean and Sarah into trouble. They live life in a world that Adam corrupted, so now a car, limited knowledge, and a weak body combine in the tragic loss of a child. Sean, Sarah, and the police who investigated the event all concluded that nobody had done anything wrong, but a tragic confluence of events led to an excruciating loss. So much of the counseling we offer comes in this same context, and we will unpack this issue even further in the next chapter on suffering.

---

9. The person most famously accused of this simplistic understanding of sin is Jay Adams, who refuted the charge early in his ministry. See Jay E. Adams, *More Than Redemption: A Theology of Christian Counseling* (Grand Rapids, MI: Baker, 1980), 139–40. In another place I have tried to show that the focus of Jay Adams on personal sin in counseling traces not to a simplistic understanding of sin but rather to specific concerns he was addressing in his ministry context. See Heath Lambert, *The Biblical Counseling Movement after Adams* (Wheaton, IL: Crossway, 2012), 49–80.

A second context in which sin informs counseling deals with the personal sin of those we counsel. Much of the pain we experience in life that leads to our search for counseling help is indeed our fault. Everything outlined above about our inherited guilt, which corrupts our thinking, desires, emotions, and actions, comes into play here. As sinful people, we use our corrupt faculties to do sinful things. When we commit these sinful acts, we suffer the painful consequences sooner or later and need help. That is where counseling comes in.

We also see this counseling context in the lives of Sean and Sarah. Sean experienced a terrible tragedy that was not his fault and then responded with sin that was his fault. Nobody held Sean personally responsible for the accidental death of his son. Sean was truly innocent. Nobody held Sean responsible for being overwhelmed with sorrow in the loss of his son. A fallen world occasions the emotion of sorrow, but that does not mean it is sinful to experience sorrow. In fact, God himself responds to life in a fallen world with sorrow, so we are like him when we feel the same pain over the loss of something as precious as a son (cf. John 11:28–37). Where Sean became responsible is when he sinned in the aftermath of his suffering.

The same is true for Sarah. She is not responsible for the death of Coty, and she is not responsible for her husband's withdrawal from her and his enslavement to alcohol. She is responsible for choosing to respond to this pressure with sexual immorality. Biblical counselors are often called upon to help people respond to their sinful choices that create pain in their life. Below, we will see the biblical counseling response to sin in this counseling context.

A final context in which sin informs counseling ministry is when we experience the sins of others against us. Here, as before, we are not talking about a situation where someone is necessarily to blame for the problem requiring counseling. Instead, they are in pain because of wrongs committed against them by someone else who is guilty of sin.

We live in a world where people use their sinful intellects, emotions, desires, and actions to harm us and break our relationships. We see this with Sean and Sarah. Sean and Sarah have each sinned against the other, which means that they each have been sinned against by the other. Sarah received the sinfulness of Sean in their marriage as he made a sinful turn to alcohol to comfort himself in his pain. Sean received the sinfulness of Sarah in their marriage as she made a sinful turn to the comforts of another man to receive solace in her pain. In biblical counseling, we are constantly helping people know how to respond to these problems. We will examine what this looks like below.

Before turning to a biblical counseling response to these situations, it is important to make a crucial observation that Sean and Sarah's situation illustrates to us. These three separate counseling contexts of sin rarely occur independently of one another. It is unusual to counsel someone who needs counseling exclusively because they have been a victim of life in a fallen world or of the sins of another. It is also unusual for a person to come for counseling who is only guilty of personal sin without experiencing the difficulties of the sins of another or the sinfulness in a broken world. Very typically, counseling is a complex combination of each of these contexts. Effective biblical counseling requires an understanding of each context and a willingness to engage sin whenever it appears in counseling.

Counseling People Guilty of Sin

It is not enough to acknowledge the existence of a counselee's sin. It is the work of biblical counseling not only to identify the sin but to help people deal with it. We learned in the chapter on a theology of Christ that it is the work of our Savior to address sin in the lives of believers through his life, death, resurrection, and ascension. Christ's objective work of atonement secures our redemption, but we need to know how to lay hold of this work in counseling as people struggle against specific sin.

The Bible teaches that we lay hold of the grace of Jesus to address our specific sins through repentance. This reality is taught, among other places, in Proverbs 28:13: "Whoever conceals his transgressions will not prosper, but he who confesses and forsakes them will obtain mercy." This passage teaches two phases of repentance, and we must examine each of them.

Repentance Requires Confession

When we are guilty of transgressions, we often believe that the best way to address them is by covering them up. We want to keep our guilt a secret. We do not want anyone to know our struggles and shortcomings. We want to protect ourselves from consequences. The Bible teaches us that if we want to prosper, this is the wrong way to respond to our sins. The only way to obtain mercy for our transgressions is to, first, confess our sins. Biblical counsel requires counselees to confess any issues of personal sin. We do this because of our belief in the biblical doctrine of sin. We want to help our counselees address sin through confession. We can examine three biblical factors that should characterize a counselee's confession.

First, counselees must confess their sin to God. No matter what the sin is and regardless of whether that sin was an internal sin of desire, an external sin of behavior, or even if it involved another person, the primary person we sin against is always God (Ps. 51:4). It is his law that we are breaking. Because we have transgressed against him by breaking his law, we must confess that to him.

We can have confidence that when we come to God confessing our sin, he will forgive us because of the work of Christ.

> If we say we have no sin, we deceive ourselves, and the truth is not in us. If we confess our sins, he is faithful and just to forgive us our sins and to cleanse us from all unrighteousness. (1 John 1:8–9)

John says here that when we confess our sins, God will forgive us and cleanse us from all unrighteousness. God does this because, as the text says, he is faithful and just. God will never fail to forgive us when we confess our sins. The reason for this is that Jesus Christ paid the penalty for all sin (see chapter 5). It would be unjust for God to have punished Jesus Christ for our sins and then require a second payment from us. God the Father received the full payment from Jesus for all sin for all time. Because God will never be faithless or unjust, we can have confidence that he will forgive us of our sins whenever we ask him. This is an enormous encouragement for us to believe and share with our counselees, especially when they feel they have sinned so egregiously that God would never forgive them.

The need to confess our sins to God and the truth that he will forgive only those who believe and whose sin is covered by Christ demonstrate the importance of conversion in counseling. The only way for our counselees to deal with issues of their personal sinfulness is to confess that sin to God. Biblical counselors understand that the only people who confess their sins are those whose hearts have been changed by the Holy Spirit. This does not mean that we cannot have counseling conversations with people who are not converted. It means that such counseling will always be decidedly evangelistic.[10] For those who have been converted to Christ, we will urge them to live the Christian life by walking in repentance. For those who are unconverted, we will be calling on them to repent of their sins for the very first time, trusting in Jesus Christ to forgive them, and so be able to respond to sin in the only way God has provided.

A second reality that ought to characterize the confessions of counselees is that they confess their sin not only to God but to anyone else

---

10. I believe that many have misunderstood the teaching of Jay Adams on this matter. See discussion in chapter 10. Jay Adams taught that it was not possible to counsel unbelievers. Adams did not mean by this, however, that Christians should never have conversations with unbelievers. He was instead using a specifically biblical understanding of counseling, which "consists of the renewal of [God's] image. Anything less, any approach that doesn't involve the putting off of sin and the putting on of knowledge, righteousness and holiness that comes from God's truth, is unworthy of the label 'Christian,' misleads unbelievers and dishonors God." When Adams spoke in this context, he was intending to communicate that counseling had to do with change that honors God, which was possible only for Christians. He went on to describe the counseling conversations Christians have with unbelievers as a sort of evangelistic pre-counseling. See Jay E. Adams, *More Than Redemption: A Theology of Christian Counseling* (Grand Rapids, MI: Baker, 1980), 120–21. On page 19, Adams gives advice on how to do "counseling" with an unbeliever using the Scriptures.

they sinned against. This is hard for many people. They do not want to confront many of the difficulties that come from confessing their sin to others. Many problems can come from such a confession: the person who was sinned against may not have known of the sin and the confession would reveal it, leading to difficult consequences. Confessions of sin can create relational awkwardness in a culture that prefers superficiality to candor.

We need to remember that the cause of all of these problems is sin, not the honest confession of sin. Proverbs 28 says that it is the concealing of transgressions that leads us to fail to prosper. The path to mercy is the path through honest confession of our sin. After we have sinned, the only question is whether we will be honest about it to those we have wronged. When we are honest, we may need to bear some consequences for our sin, but the confession itself will ultimately lead to mercy in our life.

Humility is a third reality that should characterize our confessions. A confession cannot be humble unless it is candid. In our pride we sometimes want to "confess" our sin in a way that makes us sound as good as possible. We want to avoid saying, "I sinfully raised my voice and used language that was harsh and cruel," so we say, "I didn't mean to hurt your feelings." Such a statement really is not an honest confession. It makes our intentions sound good ("I did not *mean* to hurt your feelings.") instead of accepting the biblical reality that sinful words reflect sinful intentions of the heart (Matt. 12:33–35). A "confession" like that also does not identify the sinful behavior. It focuses on the effect of sin—the hurt feelings—rather than on the wrong behavior of sinful words. We help our counselees to have humble confessions when we help them to be forthright in their confessions.

To be humble, a confession must also be mournful. It is possible for a person to know they are wrong and confess their sin just to get things over with. All of us know people who confess sin with a note of such frustration that it complicates, rather than helps, the process of reconciliation. A humble confession is one that is clear that the person truly *feels* regret over the sin committed (2 Cor. 7:9–11). It is spiritually dangerous for a counselee to recognize his guilt but feel no anguish over it. When we encounter such a counselee, we must appeal to them to humble themselves and lead them to pray, seeking God's grace to grow in sorrow over their sin.

A confession that is humble is from someone who is ready to accept the consequences of sin. The Bible is clear that we can be forgiven our sin and still experience temporal consequences for our sin. After David seeks forgiveness for his adultery with Bathsheba and the murder of Uriah, Nathan assures him, "The LORD also has put away your sin; you shall not die. Nevertheless, because by this deed you have utterly scorned the LORD, the child who is born to you shall die" (2 Sam. 12:13–14). We are familiar with many contemporary examples of this: an employer may legitimately forgive an employee for stealing but still fire him, a wife may forgive her husband for hitting her but still report the crime to the police, a parent may forgive a disobedient son but still take away his driving privileges. The point here is that we should expect that our sin brings consequences and confess our sin expecting those consequences. It is evidence of arrogance for someone to confess sin and be frustrated with a person who holds them accountable for the consequences of his actions. Humility is marked by a willingness to embrace the consequences of our sin (2 Cor. 7:11).

Sean and Sarah each needed to confess their own sin against God and against each other. In Sean's case, this meant confessing his sin of selfishly withdrawing from Sarah and turning to alcohol for comfort in the dark days after Coty's death. In Sarah's case, this required her to confess her sin of committing adultery in response to her husband's sinful behavior in their marriage. Sean and Sarah were both unbelievers, which meant, by definition, that they needed to come to Christ, repenting of their life of sin for the very first time and trusting in Jesus' work on their behalf to forgive them of their sin.

It is important to be clear that there is no other Christian response to sin than this one. A counselor who would counsel Christianly must, regardless of whatever theoretical counseling system they adopt, call sinful people to repent of their sin. This is not a debatable issue for Christians, but is, rather, a matter of fundamental Christian faithfulness that we learn from our Savior (Luke 13:5). As we continue to consider the importance of repentance, we must remember that, in terms of Proverbs 28, confession is only part of what constitutes repentance. Genuine repentance requires a consideration of something else to which we now turn.[11]

Repentance Requires a Forsaking of Sin

Turning from sin requires more than a humble confession of sin—as important as confession is. Proverbs 28:13 requires that, in addition to confessing our sin, we also forsake it. In Christ, there must be a change in behavior corresponding to our confession of sin. The Bible describes this forsaking of sin using a two-part process.

The Bible refers to this two-phase process in a variety of ways. In Romans 6:13, Paul says, "Do not present your members to sin as instruments for unrighteousness, but present yourselves to God as those who have been brought from death to life, and your members to God as instruments for righteousness." Ephesians 4:21–24 says,

> The truth is in Jesus, to put off your old self, which belongs to your former manner of life and is corrupt through deceitful desires, and to be renewed in the spirit of your minds, and to put on the new self, created after the likeness of God in true righteousness and holiness.[12]

---

11. Resources often used in counseling about forsaking sin include Ken Sande, *The Peacemaker: A Biblical Guide to Resolving Personal Conflict* (Grand Rapids, MI: Baker, 2004); Ken Sande with Tom Raabe, *Peacemaking for Families: A Biblical Guide to Managing Conflict in Your Home* (Colorado Springs: Focus on the Family, 2002); Robert Jones, *Pursuing Peace: A Christian Guide to Handling Our Conflicts* (Wheaton, IL: Crossway, 2012).

12. There is some debate in this passage about whether Paul is talking about "putting off" and "putting on" as an event that happens at conversion or is a process that occurs after one is saved and is living the Christian life. I think it is likely that this text refers to an event at conversion. This language still has relevance for living the Christian life, because the passage immediately following teaches a two-part process of putting off and putting on as believers follow Christ (Eph. 4:25–32). See John Murray, *Principles of Conduct: Aspects of Biblical Ethics* (London: Tyndale, 1957), 208–15.

In Colossians 3:5–17 Paul uses still different language, speaking of putting sin to death (Col 3:5), or putting it away (Col. 3:8), and of putting on righteousness (Col. 3:12ff).

Whether we discuss the language of no longer presenting ourselves to sin, but to God; of putting off and putting on; or of putting to death or putting away, we are to think of forsaking sin as a two-part process. This two-part process consists not only of the sin we are to stop doing but of the righteousness we are to put on in its place.[13]

This is a very practical and positive teaching for biblical counselors. It keeps us from focusing exclusively on the negative aspects of human sinfulness that we must stop and keeps us placing positive righteousness before our counselees. This teaching also encourages us to slow down and consider how to employ this two-part process in the details of the specific situation of our counselee.

If you were counseling Sean, passages like this one encourage you to consider carefully practical strategies to help him stop retreating off by himself and turning to alcohol when he feels the pain and pressure of life weighing down on him. In this regard, we spent time talking about how to call out to Jesus for help in the midst of trouble as well as how close accountability could help him avoid this activity. These passages encourage us to think hard about what righteous thoughts and actions Sean will begin to have and do once he is working to stop drinking. We talked about how to turn to the Lord and about turning to his wife to minister to her, talk to her, listen to her, and serve her. Passages like this encourage us to work with Sarah to help her to take radical measures in breaking off her adulterous relationship and begin to positively pour into her relationship with her husband.[14]

---

13. This is an idea that Jay Adams covers very well and introduced as a crucial concept in the biblical counseling movement. See, for example, Jay E. Adams, *The Christian Counselor's Manual* (Grand Rapids, MI: Baker, 1973), 174–79. As helpful as Adams's treatment of this issue is, it is best for biblical counselors to avoid using the secular terms of *dehabituation* and *rehabituation*, using instead the biblical language noted above.

14. There is so much more to say here concerning the practicality of this two-part process. Such things more properly fall under the methodology of biblical counseling than the theology of biblical counseling, and so are beyond the scope of this book. For a helpful and accessible overview of this important issue, see Stuart Scott with Zondra Scott, *Killing Sin Habits: Conquering Sin with Radical Faith* (Bemidji, MN: Focus, 2013).

All of the preceding material concerns how we deal with the personal sin of the counselee in the context of biblical counseling. As I argued above, this is only one way that sin manifests itself in the counseling process. Before concluding this chapter, we need to deal with a second context for sin in counseling. That concerns the importance of addressing sin when the counselee has been a victim of the sins of another person.

Counseling People Afflicted by the Sins of Others

One of the most famous passages in the Bible is Romans 3:23 where Paul makes a simple but profound statement that "all have sinned and fall short of the glory of God." At least two implications flow from this statement. The first is the familiar implication for all who read it, namely, that we are all sinners. The second is what the passage teaches about the kind of people we interact with. This passage teaches that all who read it are sinful and that everyone we meet will be sinful as well. This ensures that not only will we have to address our own sins, but we will also need to respond to others when they sin against us. As counselors, we will have to help counselees who have been afflicted by the sins of others. The goal in counseling those who have been sinned against is to point them in the direction of forgiveness.

The Biblical Command to Forgive

Some of the most controversial teachings in the Bible have to do with the commands to forgive. These commands can be some of the hardest in Scripture to obey. Counselees can be sinned against in horrible ways that create tremendous personal agony. The call to forgive can seem overwhelming, even impossible. That is why we need to consider this issue as it relates to our counseling of those who have been sinned against. I will examine it here by looking at two of the most significant statements in Scripture about forgiveness.

The first is in Colossians 3:12–13:

Put on then, as God's chosen ones, holy and beloved, compassionate hearts, kindness, humility, meekness, and patience, bearing
with one another and, if one has a complaint against another,
forgiving each other; as the Lord has forgiven you, so you also
must forgive.

Paul makes forgiveness a command in this passage and says that the
standard for our forgiveness of others is God's forgiveness of us (cf. Eph.
4:32). If we want to know how we are to forgive others, we must look at
how God has forgiven us.

God makes very clear in Jeremiah 31:34 how he forgives his people.
In that passage God is predicting the New Covenant that will come
in Christ, and God promises, "I will forgive their iniquity, and I will
remember their sin no more." God is not promising a literal inability
to remember the sins of people who trust in Christ. Such a literal interpretation would compromise the omniscience of God that we saw in
chapter 4. The New Covenant does not create divine amnesia. Instead
God promises that in Christ he will not remember the sins of his people
against them. He will have knowledge of these sins, but when he sees
his people in Christ, he will not hold them responsible for their sin. It
is similar to what is said in Psalm 103:12: "As far as the east is from the
west, so far does he remove our transgressions from us." God separates
us from our sin as far as the east is from the west. We are removed from
our sin as far as possible.

God's separating us from our sin and not holding it against us is the
biblical standard we should help our counselees to consider when forgiving those who have wronged them. The goal of counseling those who
have been sinned against is to have them extend forgiveness to those
who have wronged them, and do it in such a way that they see the person and the sinful act as two separate realities. We want our counselees

to treat those who have sinned against them as though they did not sin against them.[15]

That statement is hard, controversial, and can even be painful. It is why I said above that the Bible's teaching on forgiveness is so hard. Our counselees can be sinned against in soul-crushing ways. When people sin against us, they wound and betray us. The pain makes us wonder how we could ever do what is required of us in forgiveness and begin to treat people in ways that disconnect them from their sin.[16]

When our counselees struggle in this way, we should point them to the mercy of Jesus Christ. This is what Jesus himself does when he gives the most extended instruction on forgiveness in the Bible in Matthew 18. In that passage, Jesus tells a story to demonstrate that his people should continually forgive those who wrong them (Matt. 18:21–35). The story is about a man who owes his master an incredibly large sum of money and is unable to pay it back. The master orders his entire family to be sold in order to pay back the debt. The servant begs for mercy, and the master mercifully decides to forgive him the debt.

After being forgiven, the servant leaves and finds one of his fellow servants who owes him a very small debt. The servant who had just been forgiven a massive debt is furious that the other servant is unable to pay him back and begins to choke him, demanding that the man pay the small debt he owes. He even has the man put in prison until he can pay the debt. Later on, the wealthy master hears of the attack and is furious at the servant he had forgiven. He poses a penetrating question to him that we must ask ourselves and every counselee who struggles to forgive: "Should not you have had mercy on your fellow servant, as I had mercy on you?" (Matt. 18:33).

The theme of Jesus' story about forgiveness is mercy. The servant in the story was mercifully forgiven a debt that was massively larger than

---

15. Not only is this the clear teaching of the passage we are considering, it also grows out of the most common New Testament word translated as forgiveness. That is *aphíēmi* and means to release from the legal and moral obligations associated with guilt.

16. This raises the question of consequences for sin, which will be addressed below.

the one he was owed.[17] When he attacked his fellow servant and sent him to prison, he was not thinking of all that he had been forgiven. He was thinking only about the comparatively little that was owed to him. Jesus points out through the character of the master that in thinking this way, the servant's mind-set was completely devoid of mercy.

People who will not forgive those who have wronged them are, likewise, devoid of mercy. Even when we are sinned against in horrifying ways, we are never asked to forgive others more than God forgave us when we trusted Christ with our salvation. Jesus is commending a very practical counseling strategy here. He is teaching us that when we encounter people who are struggling to forgive, we need to point them to the mercy of God they received in being forgiven of their own sin before him. We need to help them meditate on the rich and profound mercy of God that washes away all of their guilt and sin. They need to reflect on this mercy of God in their life until it overflows into the lives of those they need to forgive.

The Bible commands us to do a hard thing in forgiving others as we have been forgiven. As hard as this is, it leads to the infinitely greater joy of encountering the mercy of Jesus Christ in our own lives as we reflect on all that he has done for us. God calls us to forgive others so that we can experience the joy of being reminded of the amazing mercy of Jesus, who forgives us and makes us his own.

There is a second significant statement about forgiveness in the story about the unforgiving servant. As the story continues, the master is furious that his servant could have such a heartless lack of mercy, and for punishment throws him into prison until he pays the entire debt. At this point, Jesus warns his hearers, saying, "So also my heavenly Father will do to every one of you, if you do not forgive your brother from your heart" (Matt. 18:35). Jesus' command for forgiveness comes in the very

---

17. The unforgiving servant owed his master 10,000 talents. A talent was worth about twenty years of wages for a day laborer in the ancient world. That means the master was owed 200,000 years of his servant's wages. The other servant owed the unforgiving servant 100 denarii. A denarius was worth about one day of wages for a day laborer. That means the unforgiving servant was owed under four months of wages.

strongest of terms. He says that if we do not forgive others of their sins against us, then we will not be forgiven for our sins against God.

Jesus is not teaching a doctrine of salvation by forgiveness instead of a salvation by grace through faith.[18] He is elaborating on the point about mercy he had just made. He is teaching that those who have received the mercy of God in forgiveness need to extend that mercy to others by forgiving them. He is saying that the kind of person who refuses to extend mercy to others is the kind of person who has not grasped the overwhelming nature of God's mercy.

Jesus' command to forgive becomes even more radical when he says that believers must forgive others from the heart. This is a command to forgive those who have wronged us with the entirety of who we are. In chapter 7 on the doctrine of humanity, we saw that the word *heart* is one way of referring to the soul, or inner person, that directs all the affairs of human life. Based on the biblical anthropology in that chapter, we are able to conclude that forgiving someone from the heart means to forgive using all of the heart's functionality.

Forgiving from the heart means using the soul's conscience function to remind us of our own guilt before God and the forgiveness we have received through Christ. This reminder helps us to extend the mercy of our own forgiveness to others. Forgiveness also means using the soul's function of feeling to have genuine feelings of care for those who have wronged us. Forgiveness requires that we use the volitional function of our soul to seek to do good to those who have wronged us. When our counselees feel this is impossible, we can help them know how to begin this forgiveness in their thinking and conclude it with some very practical behaviors.

Before we can feel and act differently toward those who have wronged us, it is helpful to begin to think differently about them. Paul says, "We destroy arguments and every lofty opinion raised against the knowledge of God, and take every thought captive to obey Christ" (2 Cor. 10:5). When counselees find it challenging to forgive those who

---

18. The doctrine of salvation will be addressed in chapter 10.

have wronged them, we must help them take their thoughts captive by pointing them to the mercy of Christ who forgives them—including forgiving them of their failure to obey his commands to forgive. We must help them remember all that they have been forgiven. Perhaps we can help them to remember the good things that are true of the person Christ calls them to forgive. Perhaps we can help them to consider good effects that will come into their life as they follow Christ in this way. Perhaps we can point them to Scriptures (like the ones we are considering here) that they can memorize and meditate upon as they struggle to forgive. We can do all of these and more, but we must help them to take their thoughts captive. When they do, feelings and behaviors that are commensurate with forgiveness are more likely to follow.

As forgiveness flows out from the heart into behavior, it can be challenging for counselees (and even counselors!) to know what behaviors should take place that are in keeping with forgiveness. There are always at least two things we can do to point toward faithfulness in this regard. First, we can lead counselees to pray for those who have wronged them. Jesus says, "Love your enemies and pray for those who persecute you" (Matt. 5:44). Jesus' teaching here is straightforward. Even when we are unsure of what it means to love, we still can know what it means to pray. Jesus' instruction is directed toward how we are to treat our enemies. He asks us to consider the people who are completely opposed to us and have treated us in terrible ways. If we are urged to pray even for our enemies, then certainly we can pray for those who are seeking restoration in our relationship through forgiveness.

Second, we can work to help our counselees provide some comfort to those who have wronged them. Paul helps us to understand this in his correspondence to the Corinthians. In 1 Corinthians 5, the apostle Paul urges the church to take action against someone in the church who was apparently committing sexual immorality with his stepmother. By the time Paul writes 2 Corinthians, it seems that the church took Paul's recommended action and the man had sought forgiveness. In responding to this man, Paul tells the church, "This punishment by the majority is enough, so you should rather turn to forgive and comfort him, or he may be overwhelmed by excessive sorrow" (2 Cor. 2:6–7). Paul tells the church that their forgiveness of this sinful man should be paired with comfort to protect him from excessive sorrow. Paul does not go into the details about what this comfort would look like, so we have the freedom to explore different means of comfort with different counselees in different circumstances. Still, we can say that Paul is giving those in the church responsibility to minister care to one who had sinned against them. This man sinned against his father in ways some would find difficult even to consider. Yet the church is commanded to forgive and comfort him. We are not told that the man's father was a member of the church, but he may have been. If he was, this command to provide comfort would have gone to the father who was a recipient of his son's heinous sin.

In any case, we can know that the command to forgive here works through all of the functions of the heart and into behavior including, at least, praying for and comforting those who have wronged us. As we work with our counselees to take these—and many other—responses, we will want to do it slowly and carefully. We should understand that the change toward forgiveness often happens slowly and over time. As we monitor progress toward forgiveness, we must be on the lookout for evidence that a counselee is not forgiving those who have sinned against him. I want to consider four common indicators that this kind of forgiveness has not taken place.

One indicator that counselees are not forgiving those who have wronged them is when they allow themselves to think about the person or what they did in a way that leads to a sinful emotion like anger.[19] This is evidence that they have not taken their thoughts captive in the way referenced above. Thoughts like this are the first evidence of our need to ask Jesus for help in forgiving our brothers and sisters. It is crucial to deal with the problem at this earliest level because these thoughts will eventually lead to sinful actions.

---

19. I do not mean to indicate by this that all anger is sinful. It is not (see Eph. 4:26).

Another indication that our counselees have not engaged in biblical forgiveness is when they bring up the sin to the person who wronged them in order to attack that person with it. This would be a clear example of remembering the sin against the person and harming them with it. Once a person commits a sinful action against someone, there is no mechanism available in God's world to make it so the sin never happened. Even though sinners can often wish it were otherwise, they cannot undo their sin. They can only confess the sin and pursue forsaking it. When we attack the person by bringing up sin they are attempting to forsake, we are treating them in a way that God himself does not treat them.

We also see evidence that our counselees are not engaging in forgiveness when they reveal the person's sin to others in order to harm them. There are ways to bring up someone's sin to others and to them in a way that is not a harmful attack. We may, for example, describe the ways God has changed the person as a way to encourage the person and others about how they have grown in Christ. But when we share information about a person's sin for the purpose of damaging their reputation or even just venting our frustrations, we need to be ready to repent for our sin.

We should also be concerned about a lack of forgiveness when we see counselees adding unnecessary penalties to the consequences of sin. It is important to be clear here: there are appropriate consequences for sin that are not at odds with the granting of forgiveness. We saw this earlier as we discussed God's forgiveness of us. We must see it now in our forgiveness of others. In a fallen world, we will often balance the tension between genuine forgiveness and meaningful consequences: an adulterous pastor can be forgiven by his congregation but still lose his job; a murderer can be forgiven by the family of his victim but still go to jail; a former pedophile can be embraced by his church but kept away from children during Sunday services. Forgiveness and consequences are not at odds with one another.

In most cases, consequences should be natural extensions of the sin itself, as seen in the examples above. Typically, when those who have been sinned against begin to create unnatural and arbitrary penalties, it is an example of a lack of forgiveness. We can look at Sean and Sarah as an example. Sarah was terribly wounded by Sean's drunken distance in their relationship. It would be entirely natural for Sarah to forgive Sean but still find relational intimacy with him to be a challenge for some time since they have been emotionally distant for so long. For her to say, however, that she can never speak to him again is an unnecessary penalty going beyond what is the natural consequence. It would indicate a failure to forgive.

The same goes for Sean. We could imagine Sean forgiving Sarah but saying, for example, that they cannot have sexual relations together until an appropriate time has passed to demonstrate that Sarah does not have a sexually transmitted disease. Such a decision is wise and a natural extension of Sarah's sin. If Sean said he could never have sex with Sarah again, it would be an unnatural penalty indicative of a lack of forgiveness. Such matters can be challenging to sort through and require much wisdom and prayer. These guidelines, however, can serve as helpful rules of thumb.

Does Forgiveness Require Repentance?

Before concluding our discussion on forgiveness, we need to address one more very important issue: Should we forgive someone who has not confessed their sin and forsaken it? Some believe that the biblical commands on forgiveness apply even if a person has not sought forgiveness. Others contend that the Bible endorses a sort of conditional forgiveness that occurs only after someone requests forgiveness.[20] This issue is an important one, as it impacts how we help counselees who have been wronged by someone who will not admit it or does not care that they have sinned. We can make at least three observations to help us in the counseling task.

---

20. See Chris Brauns, *Unpacking Forgiveness: Biblical Answers for Complex Questions and Deep Wounds* (Wheaton, IL: Crossway, 2008) and Robert D. Jones, *Pursuing Peace: A Christian Guide to Handling Our Conflicts* (Wheaton, IL: Crossway, 2012).

First, we have already observed that we are to forgive others as God has forgiven us. One implication of this—beyond what we saw above—is that God forgives only those who have sought his forgiveness through a humble confession of sin. If the model of our own forgiveness is the kind we have received from God, then this rules out extending forgiveness to someone who will not admit guilt or does not seem interested in pursuing reconciliation.

Second, even when someone is not interested in confessing sin, we are not allowed to become embittered. Ephesians 4:31 says, "Let all bitterness and wrath and anger and clamor and slander be put away from you, along with all malice." A lack of contrition on the part of those who have sinned against us does not constitute divine permission for us to nurture anger and bitterness. We want our counselees to think, feel, and pray about those with unconfessed sin in much the same way we want them to think, feel, and pray for those who have wronged them and have confessed. In this light, it is helpful to think about helping counselees to develop the *attitude* of forgiveness even when the offender's lack of confession will not allow the *act* of forgiveness to take place.

Finally, we should extend forgiveness when the person who sinned against us confesses sin. The biblical teaching that we examined above is relevant at this point. When someone confesses sin to a Christian, that Christian is required to forgive as a person who has been forgiven.

Dealing with Sin in Counseling: Confession and Forgiveness

We have covered two of the counseling contexts for sin in this chapter—what to do when a counselee is guilty of sin and what to do when they have been sinned against. The next chapter covers the issue of the third counseling context for sin, namely, responding to the sin of Adam as we live life in a fallen world. What we can observe now is that the issue of human sinfulness in counseling is not an anomaly. It actually provides the context for *all* counseling. The only issue concerns the context in which we will be addressing it. Counselors who are not equipped to address the issue of human sinfulness in counseling are not equipped to do their work.

The matters we have addressed in this chapter of sinning and being sinned against do not constitute strange and abnormal situations in counseling. They concern the people who come to us for help every day. Not everyone will look exactly like Sean and Sarah, but the same themes of human sinfulness will be there with a million different specifics. The only way to address these matters is through the Christ-centered understanding of confession and forgiveness we have seen in this chapter. If we do not address these matters with Sean and Sarah, we will not help them even if we make them feel better.

The only people who know this are Christians using their Bibles in counseling. This means we are not lacking anything essential in the counseling task. We have the assets to deal with the problems that everyone faces. Secular resources that lack God's instruction about sin, confession, and forgiveness have to operate at a deficit concerning counseling resources. Christians have the benefit of the overflowing wisdom of God's Word to guide us in this work. Using the Bible, we can point Sean and Sarah to the only solution to their problems.

But Sean and Sarah can choose not to listen to God's Word when we counsel them. In fact, Sarah ultimately refused to honor God in her response to Sean's sin and her own sin. While Sean ultimately came to faith in Christ in the context of our meetings, Sarah rejected Christ and nearly everything I said to her. She came to counseling for a few weeks but never got on board. She never confessed that her adultery with Tom was sinful, and she certainly never forsook her relationship with him. She also said that she forgave Sean, but she never turned from her anger over his behavior, and she never changed her thinking about how to respond to it. She continued to remember it against him. She divorced Sean and married Tom fairly quickly.

In the course of a few years, Sean had lost his entire family. Though he was responsible for his sinful behavior that contributed to the end of his marriage, he was not responsible for the death of his son. Sean was in tremendous personal pain. The things he had done and the things that had happened to him proved to him every day that he was living in a sinful world that was in desperate need of the full redemption of Jesus Christ. Sean did what the Word of God required of him in confessing his sin. He had worked hard to attain forgiveness with Sarah. But now he was still in pain. We have talked about personal sin in the life of Sean and Sarah. Now we need to talk about how to live as a Christian in a world of pain. That is the topic we will address in the next chapter.

CHAPTER 9

BIBLICAL COUNSELING

and a

THEOLOGY OF SUFFERING

I n the last chapter we were introduced to a man I know named Sean.
Sean experienced the tragic loss of his young son in a car accident and
responded to that painful loss with sinful withdrawal from his wife and
with alcohol abuse. Sean repented of this and was working to change
when his wife left him for another man. Through a combination of tragedy and transgression, Sean lost his entire family in a matter of a few
years. As I argued in the last chapter, all of Sean's trouble came about
because he lives in a world stained by sin, but not all of that trouble
traces back to sin in the same way.

We saw that Sean's drunken withdrawal from his wife traces back to
his own sin, which he is personally responsible to confess and forsake in
repentance. We also saw that Sean's pain over his wife's infidelity traces
back to her sin, which he must forgive when she repents. We have not
yet unpacked a third category of sin in counseling Sean. That third category is the tragic suffering he has confronted in his life in general and
in the loss of his son, Coty, in particular. This pain traces back to sin as
much as the other areas of Sean's difficulty, but not to Sean and Sarah as
individuals. This pain traces back to the sin of Adam, which corrupted

the world in which we live. Because of Adam's sin against God in the garden, all people now live in a world of profound pain.

This is pain that we must address in our counseling with Sean. It is pain that we must address in the lives of many of our counselees. I noted in the last chapter that most counselees come for help with a combination of difficulties tracing back to sin. Very few need counseling exclusively because of their own sin or the sin of someone else. Every counselee is also experiencing the pain of living in a broken world. Biblical counseling does not only address a counselee's personal sin and the sins of those who have wronged them. Biblical counseling also addresses the pain of living in a fallen world. In this chapter we will examine how to understand this crucial element of counseling so that we can be effective in offering care to Sean and others who are so troubled by the existence of sin in the world.

Categories of Suffering

The Bible allows us to do more than assert that the presence of sin in the world creates human suffering. It allows us to be fairly specific about various kinds of suffering we experience in a world plagued by sin. In this section we will examine six different categories of suffering that the Bible discusses.[1] After that we will examine what the Bible has to say about helping counselees who encounter these various troubles.

Suffering and Human Sinfulness

The first category of suffering we can examine is the one we considered in the last chapter. That category concerns the suffering brought into our life by our own sin and by the sin of others. We saw in the last chapter that Adam's sin makes us guilty, corrupt, and responsible. We

---

1. For a survey on how the biblical counseling movement has developed in its articulation of the experience of human suffering, see Heath Lambert, *The Biblical Counseling Movement after Adams* (Wheaton, IL: Crossway, 2012), 49–67.

can say here that Adam's sin not only leads to our own sin, but that sin leads to suffering.

When we sin, and when we experience the sin of others, it brings pain into our lives sooner or later. Even when we deal with this sinfulness in a way that is biblical, it does not take away the pain. Sean addressed his sin through a biblical process of repentance. Though he addressed his sin, there is still an ache over the death of his son, the way he compounded his wife's pain, and his contribution to his failed marriage. Additionally, Sean still feels the pain of his wife's betrayal in leaving him for another man. Even if she were to one day seek forgiveness from him for her sin, and even when he overflows with gratitude for the good things God worked in that situation, he will still feel an ache for what happened. As it is, there has not been reconciliation in his relationship with his former spouse, and there is a painful longing for that to take place.

Our own sin and the sins of others are not something we can merely address and leave off. Our sin not only is wrong, it causes pain. The memory of its consequences stays with us. We remember and wince. This is not a failure to forgive or failure to trust in the providence of God. This is a recognition that sin is sin. It is bad. It poisons what it touches. This pain is a longing for things to be different than they are in the fullness of Christ's coming kingdom.

Suffering and the World

Another kind of suffering is the pain caused by the world. When the Bible talks about "the world," it often does not mean the physical planet populated with people and spinning around the sun. There are times when the Bible talks about the world in this way. John 3:16 is one example: "For God so loved the world, that he gave his only Son, that whoever believes in him should not perish but have eternal life." Here God means to communicate that he has love for every person who populates the entire earth. This is only one way the Bible talks about the world.

249

Another way the Bible talks about the world is to describe those who inhabit it as possessing a sinful disposition, orienting the entire human race away from God and his law. In this sense the world is a mind-set of the human race that is opposed to Christ and his kingdom. This is the sense in 1 John 2:15–17:

> Do not love the world or the things in the world. If anyone loves the world, the love of the Father is not in him. For all that is in the world—the desires of the flesh and the desires of the eyes and pride of life—is not from the Father but is from the world. And the world is passing away along with its desires, but whoever does the will of God abides forever.

We know that John does not use the term *world* in the same sense here as he quoted Jesus as using it in John 3:16. In John's gospel, God loves the world. In John's first letter, the love of the world is opposed to the love of the Father. What is the difference? In John, Jesus is talking about the world as filled with people God desires to save. In 1 John, the apostle is talking about the sinful desires that people need to reject. In 1 John the world is the system of sinful desires of sinful people, which separates them as a group from the living God.

This world system brings about suffering in many ways. One massive example is the anything-goes sexual libertarianism that is advanced by our society. We live in a world where you are free to embrace almost any sexual sin you desire. Pornography is accessible to anyone young enough to know how to surf the Web; advertisements on television, billboards, and store windows promote immodesty to the entire culture; any expression of concern about the impact on young children of homosexual marriage is treated as hate speech. We live in a world that beckons us toward sexual sin instead of righteousness. These worldly temptations do not remove responsibility from the people who choose to sin, but they do create a context of suffering. Many struggling for sexual purity in this sexualized culture long for the day when modesty and chastity are the societal norms.

Another example of worldliness has to do with the direct attacks on Christians in the midst of a world that hates the Christ we serve.

> If the world hates you, know that it has hated me before it hated you. If you were of the world, the world would love you as its own; but because you are not of the world, but I chose you out of the world, therefore the world hates you. (John 15:18–19)

The world persecutes Christians because the world is opposed to the commitments of the Christ we serve. We know on the authority of Jesus that Christians will suffer because they are Christians.

Suffering and the Devil

Another category of suffering in a sinful world is the Devil. First Peter 5:8 says, "Your adversary the devil prowls around like a roaring lion, seeking someone to devour." The Devil is a real enemy for believers and unbelievers alike. Peter tells us that the Devil is a dangerous enemy who is actively seeking out people to destroy. Peter describes what happens to those who succumb to the Devil, using the graphic imagery of being attacked and eaten by a lion. The Devil brings much agony into the lives of those he seeks to destroy.[2]

---

2. Faithful Christians agree that demons are real and do much harm to people inside and outside the church. There is not as much agreement when it comes to acknowledging the presence of demons and responding to them in ministry. The Devil is portrayed in the New Testament utilizing a number of different operations, including direct and open temptation (Matt. 4:1ff; Mark 1:12–13; Luke 4:1ff); manifestations of the supernatural (Luke 8:26ff); manifestations of strange or bizarre behavior (1 Sam. 16:14–16, 23; 18:10–11; Mark 5:1ff; Luke 8:26ff); manifestations of sickness or physical impairment (Matt. 9:32–34; 12:22; 17:14–18; Mark 9:14ff; Luke 11:14ff, 13:10–17; 2 Cor. 12:7), the Devil disguises himself, making his explicit presence unknown (Gen. 3:1–2; 2 Sam. 24:1; 1 Chron. 21; Luke 6:17–18; John 13:27; Acts 5:3–11; 2 Cor. 11:14; 2 Tim. 2:25–26); the use of "magic" (Acts 8:9ff; 6:16ff; 19:19); the use of occult practices (1 Sam 28:1ff); there are times when the explicit operations of the Devil are unidentifiable by us at all (Matt. 4:24; 8:16; 15:21ff; Mark 1:32–34; 7:24; Acts 5:16; 8:7; Eph. 6:11); sometimes when the work of sinful people is ascribed to him (Matt. 16:23; John 8:44; Acts 13:8–10; James 3:15; 1 John 3:8); and other times when even the work of righteous persons is ascribed to him (Matt. 10:25; 11:18; 12:22ff; Mark 3:22ff; Luke 11:14ff; John 7:20; 8:48ff; 10:19). Knowing such information can, at times, make it easier to identify the operations of the Devil and demons. When we identify the demonic, we can sometimes be confused about how to respond. Part of this confusion stems from the examples in the New Testament of demon

Suffering and the Pain of Others

In the last chapter we saw that in a sinful world, painful emotions, like sorrow, exist. We looked at Romans 9:2–3 where Paul says, "I have great sorrow and unceasing anguish in my heart. For I could wish that I myself were accursed and cut off from Christ for the sake of my brothers, my kinsmen according to the flesh." This passage not only shows us that Paul was sad but shows us what was causing that painful emotion, namely, the terrible plight of his fellow Israelites.

Paul observed the separation of Israel from God, and he ached for them with "unceasing anguish." Paul's pain for his people was like ours should be. The sufferings of others led to Paul's suffering. This example is noteworthy because the Israelites were not even aware of the suffering that caused Paul pain. The lesson of this passage is that a sinful world, which occasions the suffering of so many, ought to cause us pain as we have compassion on them.

Suffering and Confusion

In chapter 4 we examined the divine attribute of omniscience and saw that God possesses knowledge of all things. That is an attribute of God that is not shared with any created thing. All creatures have, by definition, limited knowledge. In heaven, when we exist forever in moral perfection with Christ, we will still have limited knowledge. There will never be any point in our eternal existence when we share the unlimited knowledge of God. Limited knowledge is not part of our fallen existence but is part of what it means to be a human creature.

---

exorcisms. Some have argued that believers today should engage in exorcisms as a mechanism to deal with the demonic. The problem is that, in the New Testament, the people who actually cast out demons are limited to a small group who were directly commissioned for the work, including Jesus, the apostles, and the seventy-two (Matt. 10:1, 8; Mark 3:14–15, 6:7, 13; Luke 10:17–20; Acts 5:12–16). Others in the New Testament who attempted exorcisms do not serve as models for Christians in this way (unbelievers doing this: Matt. 7:22; Mark 9:38–40; Luke 9:49–50; and the situation in Acts 19:11ff that goes terribly wrong). The Bible emphasizes that Christians respond to the demonic not by exorcism, but by faith in the Lord Jesus Christ (Acts 26:18; Eph. 6:16; James 4:7; 1 Peter 5:9). For more information, see David Powlison, *Power Encounters: Reclaiming Spiritual Warfare* (Grand Rapids, MI: Baker, 1994).

Our limited knowledge would not be a problem on its own, but sin brings a separation between our knowledge and the God on whom we were made to depend. This means our knowledge, in addition to being limited, has now been corrupted by sin, as we saw in the last chapter. Our limited knowledge is separated from the life-giving wisdom of God, so our thinking processes are not only limited but faulty.

This guarantees that we will struggle to make the right decision even when we have a desire to do what is right. This confusion is the context for much suffering. We wonder whether we should stay married or get divorced; whether we should work harder to earn more money or make less and spend more time at home; we are perplexed about how best to invest our money; we agonize over what to say to a dear friend who is going astray; we wonder if we should try to buy time with an experimental new drug or decide that it is time to die; and on, and on. So much of counseling is about helping people make these kinds of decisions in a world where sin causes us to feel puzzled about which path is the wise one.

Romans 14 provides wisdom for decisions that are not described in the Bible as always right or always wrong for all Christians at all times. While many aspects of such decisions are addressed, at the core is the motive. In such situations, we are to do what we believe best honors God for us, knowing that may be the opposite of what accomplishes that purpose for another believer. "The one who eats, eats in honor of the Lord, since he gives thanks to God, while the one who abstains, abstains in honor of the Lord and gives thanks to God" (Rom. 14.6).

Suffering and Death

A final category of sin is the physical weakness of our bodies that leads eventually to death. I am being careful to say physical weakness that leads to death because I am not just referring to the final moment of life when our soul is separated from our body. I am talking about all of the physical weaknesses we face that cause us trouble. We do not just die, we lose our eyesight, we have physical handicaps, we are born with Down syndrome, we develop hypothyroidism or diabetes, we get gangrene in a wound and lose a limb. Even a mild case of the flu brings its own kind of suffering that is possible only in a world stained by sin.

These physical issues are frequently the topic of counseling conversations. As we discussed in chapter 7, this does not mean that the Bible is sufficient for medical treatments. It does mean that medical treatments will never be enough to resolve the pain our counselees go through when they experience their pain. Even the finest medical care will need to be paired with counsel that points to hope beyond the ultimate failure of every single medical intervention this side of heaven.

It is important to understand the categories of suffering recounted here. They prepare us for the diversity of struggles we will face in counseling ministry. Not only is a biblical view of sin multifaceted, our view of the kind of suffering generated by sin is multifaceted. When we understand these categories, it shows us that the biblical view of suffering is just as revolutionary as the biblical view of sin that causes the pain.

A review of this list shows that a biblical grasp of the kinds of trouble we can face is very different from what any secular counseling system would create. The world has a category for death and dying, and they have a category for confusion. They also make room for a sense of compassion when others are in difficulty. Even with those similarities, a biblical understanding of trouble is unique. Secular counseling has no category for human sinfulness, which generates its own category of pain and generates every other item on the list. They have no category for a world system opposed to Christ ("Who is Christ, after all? And why should we not be opposed to him?"). They definitely have no category for a spiritual foe called the Devil and are likely to look at us curiously when they learn we do. The Bible is unique in its understanding of human pain. And what makes that so relevant for counseling is that the Bible's unique perspective is *God's* perspective. That it is God's perspective means it reflects the way things *truly are* in a way that nothing else does.

God's perspective on our pain is the one that conforms to the reality of the struggles we face. It is the one that actually stands the test when people come for answers, solutions, and help. God's Word not only describes the difficulties we have, it also shows us how to address them. It is to a consideration of how we help people with these problems that we now turn.

Trusting God's Character

Living in a sinful world brings pain. Whether we suffer because of our own sin, the direct sin of others, the sins of the world, the pain of others, the operations of the Devil, our own confusion, or the slow decline of our bodies toward death, we suffer. This brings many people to seek help from biblical counselors. We need to know how to help them respond. We have seen that the biblical response to the personal sin of the counselee is repentance, and the biblical response when a counselee is sinned against is forgiveness. In this chapter we will learn that the biblical counseling response to experiencing the sin of Adam in a fallen world is to trust God.

One passage that lays a biblical foundation for the trust we are to have in God is Psalm 119:68: "You are good and do good; teach me your statutes." This passage makes an assertion and an appeal. The assertion is twofold and says first that God is good. The good character of God is the foundation for all the help we have to offer as we counsel those in pain.

God's Good Character

We examined God's character in chapter 4 as we looked at his attributes of strength and care. God's attributes of strength—his self-sufficiency, infinity, omnipresence, omniscience, omnisapience, and omnipotence—are on display as he controls every event that happens in his world. His attributes of care—his holiness, faithfulness, goodness, love, mercy, grace, and wrath—are highlighted as he directs those events, ultimately, toward the good.

When we face trials of various kinds, as noted in the previous section, we need to trust that these trials occur underneath the sovereignty of a good and powerful God who will never do anything that is wrong and will never do anything to his people that is not for their ultimate good.

That statement is biblical and true, and yet is the very thing that causes many people trouble when they experience pain. They wonder, if God is good, how could he allow the kinds of suffering we experience in this world? This is a very personal question for people like Sean. How do we help someone like him trust in the good power of God after such a tragic loss?

One thing we can say is that the alternatives are not good. If we do not trust the God of the Bible who has revealed himself to be good and strong, then whom will we trust? The overwhelming forces of suffering do not permit us to trust ourselves since we cannot control them. Neither can we trust fate—that there is some abstract force in the universe driving things to an unalterable conclusion. We cannot trust our loved ones since, sooner or later, they will face the same overwhelming forces as we do. Whom will we trust if not God? The reality is that without God, we are all alone and without help. That is more fearful than facing hard questions we might not understand how to answer.

There are some hard teachings in the Bible, and the issue of human suffering is one of them. However, we must not allow our inability to comprehend every issue to drive us away from simple trust in the God of the Bible. In John 6, Jesus taught about some very controversial things, and many who had been following him turned back. Jesus asked the disciples if they would leave as well. Simon Peter answered, "Lord, to whom shall we go? You have the words of eternal life" (v. 68). There is no evidence that Peter had a more profound understanding of Jesus' controversial teaching than any of those who walked away. What he did have was a profound trust in Jesus as he lived his life. This kind of trust in the midst of incomplete understanding is what we are called to have as well.

God's Good Character Preserved
in First and Second Causes

One way Christians have responded to concerns about the good power of God in a world of suffering is through what theologians call first and second causes. The Bible teaches that God is the primary cause of every event that happens in the world because of his sovereign omnipotence that we examined earlier. Nothing comes to pass in this world apart from the sovereign will of God. This means that God is sovereign even over evil since he "works all things according to the counsel of his will" (Eph. 1:11). As soon as we assert that God is sovereign over evil, we must also confess that God is good, as 1 John 1:5 says, "God is light, and in him is no darkness at all." This means that, though God is sovereign over evil, he never *does* evil.

This is where secondary causes come in. Secondary causes are the other actors in God's world who operate according to his sovereignty but are responsible for their own actions. God oversees the world as the sovereign first cause of all that happens and is never charged with wrongdoing. Secondary causes, such as sinful people and demons, are the ones who are held responsible for the evil in the world.

We saw the truth of first and second causation in chapter 4 on the doctrine of God when we examined the compatibility of human responsibility and divine omnipotence. In the narrative of Joseph, we saw that God works together with human actors in every human event. God was the first cause in this action as he reigned as sovereign king over Joseph's relocation to Egypt so that God could preserve his people. The secondary cause was Joseph's brothers, who sinfully sold Joseph into slavery and were rightly held responsible for the sinful action growing out of a wicked intention. In the one action, there were two different actors with two different intentions. We see the same idea in Acts 4:27–28 in a prayer of the early disciples:

> Truly in this city there were gathered together against your holy
> servant Jesus, whom you anointed, both Herod and Pontius Pilate,

along with the Gentiles and the peoples of Israel, to do whatever your hand and your plan had predestined to take place.

Similar to the Joseph narrative, this text is a description of compatibilism. The text is clear that God was the first cause of the crucifixion of Jesus as he predestined that Jesus would be executed in Jerusalem. And yet Herod, Pilate, Gentiles, and Israelites are crucial second causes who are held responsible for that wicked act. There are two sets of actors and a set of different intentions in one act. While God superintends the act for the salvation of mankind, human actors had various sinful motives that informed their involvement in the death of Jesus.

An understanding of first and second causes allows us to identify the various actors in the doctrine of compatibilism. The primary actor is always the sovereign God. The secondary actor is always the other created agents who are sinful and charged with wrongdoing.[3]

Preserving God's Good Character with His Active and Passive Will

We can say one more thing regarding the sovereign goodness of God in a world plagued with evil. Some theologians have referred to the asymmetry in the sovereignty of God. Something is asymmetrical when it has two sides, but those sides are not identical. What theologians mean when they refer to asymmetry in God's sovereignty is that God has an active will where he positively wills good in the world and a passive will where he allows sinful people to do wicked acts that he could prevent.[4] This explanation demonstrates how the sovereignty of God relates in different ways to secondary causes.

---

3. For more information, see D. A. Carson, *How Long, O Lord: Reflections on Suffering and Evil* (Grand Rapids, MI: Baker, 2006), 177–204; Bruce A. Ware, *God's Greater Glory: The Exalted God of Scripture and the Christian Faith* (Wheaton, IL: Crossway, 2004), 97–130.

4. Paul Helm, *The Providence of God: Contours of Christian Theology* (Leicester, England: InterVarsity 1993), 190. Helm says, "According to Scripture, there is an important asymmetry between acts of moral evil and acts of goodness. In the case of evil, whatever the difficulties may be of accounting for the fact, God ordains evil but he does not intend evil as evil, as the human agent intends it. In God's case there is some other description of the morally evil action which he intends the evil action to fill. There are other ends or purposes which God has in view."

Jonathan Edwards makes this point brilliantly with an analogy about the sun:

There is a vast difference between the sun's being the cause of the lightsomeness and warmth of the atmosphere, and brightness of gold and diamonds, by its presence and positive influence; and its being the occasion of darkness and frost, in the night, by its motion, whereby it descends below the horizon. The motion of the sun is the occasion of the latter kind of events; but it is not the proper cause, efficient or producer of them; though they are necessarily consequent on that motion under such circumstances; no more is any action of the Divine Being the cause of the evil of men's Wills. If the sun were the proper cause of cold and darkness, it would be the fountain of these things, as it is the fountain of light or heat; and then something might be argued from the nature of cold and darkness, to a likeness of nature in the sun; and it might be justly inferred, that the sun itself is dark and cold, and that its beams are black and frosty. But from its being the cause no otherwise than by its departure, no such thing can be inferred, but the contrary; it may justly be argued, that the sun is a bright and hot body, if cold and darkness are found to be the consequences of its with-drawment; and the more constantly and necessarily these effects are connected with, and confined to its absence, the more strongly does it argue the sun to be the fountain of light and heat. So, inas-much as sin is not the fruit of any positive agency or influence of the Most High, but, on the contrary, arises from the withholding of his action and energy, and, under certain circumstances, neces-sarily follows on the want of his influence; this is no argument that he is sinful, or his operation evil, or has any thing of the nature of evil, but, on the contrary, that He and his agency are altogether good and holy, and that He is the fountain of all holiness.[5]

---

5. Jonathan Edwards, "Inquiry into the Freedom of the Will," in *The Works of President Edwards*, reprint of the Worcester edition, 4 vols. (New York: Leavitt and Trow, 1843), 2:160, https://books.google.com/books?id=wTIaAAAAYAAJ&pg=PA160&dq=sun%27s+being+the+cause+of+lightsomeness&hl=en&sa=X&ved=0CBwQ6AEwAGoVChMI2M6KlZ_tyAIVSuwmCh0 tTAw7#v=onepage&q=sun%27s%20being%20the%20cause%20of%20lightsomeness&f=false.

Edwards makes several important points. First, he makes clear the distinction between God's active will, which is a positive demonstration of his good attributes, and his passive will, which is the withdrawal of these attributes. Edwards draws an analogy to the sun. The sun's positive effect is to bring light and heat. The sun occasions darkness and cold by the withdrawal of its positive effects through the motion of the earth. Second, Edwards makes the point that the darkness and the cold, which come about from the absence of the sun, actually work to prove the true nature of the sun if there is no light and heat without it.

In the same way, the asymmetry in the active and passive will of God works to prove his righteousness rather than disprove it. If goodness goes away when God withdraws his active will, and wickedness happens as a result of God passively allowing what he could forbid with his active will, then it proves he is indeed the source of all goodness. This is yet another way of demonstrating the goodness of God in a world of evil.

The Character of God and the Counseling Task

These explanations are biblical. Christians should believe them and know them. I think they form the foundation of our commitment to trusting God, and yet most of the time, these are not the kind of answers that our counselees are looking for when their pain is most acute. In fact, I do not remember a time when I have explained the difference between primary and secondary causes at the funeral home to comfort a grieving parent like Sean.

When suffering strikes, we need to be reminded in the simplest terms of the character of the God we serve. In the Bible, God shows us how to combine an understanding of his strength and his care in ways that are profound, accessible, and decidedly untechnical. Psalm 23 is one famous example of combining God's strength and care in a way that ministers tender mercy to people in trouble:

The LORD is my shepherd; I shall not want. He makes me lie down in green pastures. He leads me beside still waters. He restores my soul. He leads me in paths of righteousness for his name's sake.

Even though I walk through the valley of the shadow of death, I will fear no evil, for you are with me; your rod and your staff, they comfort me.

You prepare a table before me in the presence of my enemies; you anoint my head with oil; my cup overflows. Surely goodness and mercy shall follow me all the days of my life, and I shall dwell in the house of the LORD forever.

This passage is full of strength and care. The Lord exerts his power for our good to keep us from want, to make us lie down in green pastures, to restore our souls, to make us righteous, to protect us from evil, and to ensure that goodness and mercy follow us all the days of our life. Psalm 23 is like the rest of the Bible in talking about God's character in a way that assumes he is trustworthy and so beckons us simply to trust him.

That is what we do in counseling. We point counselees to the strong and loving character of God and plead with them to trust him. We appeal to them to believe that when bad things happen, we can trust that he loves us in his care and is able to use his power in good ways that may not be understandable to us.

Several years ago I had a very resistant strain of strep throat for over three months. I had several courses of antibiotics, and it never went away. Finally, my physicians decided they needed to take my tonsils out, since strep throat becomes very dangerous when it lingers for so long. They warned that since I was an adult, the recovery from the procedure would be extraordinarily painful. The surgeon even described that it was likely to be the most intense pain I would experience in my life. He said that for two weeks, it would feel like I had a hot poker in my throat. He believed, though, that the pain would be worth it as it was very likely to address my persistent strep throat.

I was nervous about the pain he warned of, but I decided to have the procedure, and the physician was right. There was pain, but the procedure cured my strep throat. I had strep throat every year of my life growing up—a total of twenty-five times. In the last five years I have not had it once, even when the rest of my family has. I tell that story to illustrate that we trust people like medical doctors all the time to lead us through painful experiences toward a good result. If we can trust people with fallen characters and limited knowledge to do this, how much more should we trust the God of heaven and earth who exemplifies wisdom, power, and love.

Trusting God's Plan

The Bible encourages us not only to trust God's character but also to trust his plan. This is the second assertion in Psalm 119:68: "[Lord] you are good and *do* good" (emphasis added). The Lord not only is good, but he does good things. In fact, the goodness of his plans are based on the goodness of his character—we are able to trust what he does precisely because of who he is.

We live in a world of suffering, but that suffering happens within the providence of a loving and wise God. The evil of secondary actors is not chargeable to him, but he superintends those actions with his good and loving purposes. For every instance of suffering that happens in this wicked world, we can say with Joseph that though sinful men intended it for evil, God intends it for good. In what follows, I want to look at the biblical teaching that God uses the suffering we experience for our good. Suffering benefits us. In a world where humanity has rebelled against God, he uses those actions and overrules the evil intentions of sinners to accomplish good.

Romans 8:28 has brought comfort to untold numbers of God's people. "We know that for those who love God all things work together for good, for those who are called according to his purpose." The straightforward meaning of this passage is that God will use all the suffering of his people to produce good things in their lives. It can be hard for us to understand how God can use pain for our good, but just as a skilled surgeon uses a scalpel to cut us for our benefit, so we must believe that God can do this. Here we will see three different categories of benefits of suffering in a sinful world.

Suffering Is Good for Us

The Bible teaches that God uses suffering to good benefit in our lives. One way that suffering benefits us is by bringing about spiritual fruit in our lives. One of these fruits is joy. Romans 5:3–5:

> We rejoice in our sufferings, knowing that suffering produces endurance, and endurance produces character, and character produces hope, and hope does not put us to shame, because love has been poured into our hearts through the Holy Spirit who has been given to us.

Suffering causes Christians to rejoice not because we love pain, but because we love what the pain produces. In Romans 5 suffering leads to heavenly hope. As many have observed, hope in the Bible is not tantamount to a wish or a dream. In the Bible, hope is a confident expectation.[6] Hope is something that belongs to us, but that we do not have yet (cf. 1 Peter 1:13). Suffering causes us to depend on the Lord, remember that this world is not our home, and long for the hope of heaven. Suffering pushes us toward the joy of the eternal things of Christ rather than the fading comforts of earth.

It is at this point that we can address what theologians call the doctrine of last things. In a systematic theology textbook, this issue would be addressed toward the end of the book and cover all manner of topics, including the return of Jesus Christ and its relationship to his millennial reign. Such topics can become very technical and are highly debated. I

---

6. Jay Adams underlined this reality on hope. For one example, see Jay E. Adams, *More Than Redemption: A Theology of Christian Counseling* (Grand Rapids, MI: Baker, 1980), 45.

think such discussions are important, and I have my own commitments about these matters. In this book, however, I feel no pressure to deal with matters in that typical way.[7]

Very often when the Bible addresses the topic of last things, it does so for the purpose of giving us hope and joy in the midst of our struggles in our life on earth (John 14:1; Rom. 8:18–30; 1 Thess. 4:18; Rev. 21:4). Since the Bible addresses last things in this way, it is appropriate to cover this material in a chapter on a theology of suffering. Although Christians often debate the finer points of the doctrine of last things, I will emphasize the five realities that are agreed upon by all faithful Christians and which provide the most hope for struggling believers.

First, most Christians agree that the Bible teaches that believers go immediately into the presence of Christ when they die (2 Cor. 5:8; Phil. 1:23). Second, all Christians confess that Jesus Christ will physically return from heaven at the end of history to gather his church (1 Thess. 4:14–17; 2 Thess. 1:7). Third, the Bible clearly teaches that all of humanity will be exposed to God's judgment on the last day (Matt. 25:31–40; Rev. 20:11–15). Fourth, Christians confess that all those who have not trusted in Jesus Christ will be exposed to the punishment of hell (Matt. 25:41; 2 Thess. 1:8). Finally, those who trust in Jesus Christ will be ushered into the presence of Christ, living with him in the new heaven and new earth forever (1 Thess. 4:17; Rev. 21).

These five realities form the core of Christian confession and hope when it comes to the doctrine of last things. They encourage us that though this life can be unspeakably painful, God means to judge all actions by the righteous standard of Christ, to punish all who oppose Christ and his people, and to ultimately honor and reward all who trust in him. Such teaching is meant to give us joy in the midst of trial. Christians are called to long for these precious realities as we face much suffering in this fallen world.

---

7. For more information about such things, see Anthony A. Hoekema, *The Bible and the Future* (Grand Rapids, MI: Eerdmans, 1994). Also see the helpful summary of millennial positions in Wayne Grudem, *Systematic Theology: An Introduction to Biblical Doctrine* (Grand Rapids, MI: Zondervan, 1994), 1,109–39.

As we long for heaven, another way that suffering benefits us is by proving that we belong to Jesus, and this inheritance he has promised belongs to us. First Peter 1:6–7 says,

> You have been grieved by various trials, so that the tested genuineness of your faith—more precious than gold that perishes though it is tested by fire—may be found to result in praise and glory and honor at the revelation of Jesus Christ.

The crucial point that Peter is making is that our faith stands in need of testing to be genuine. In the preceding verses, he has held out the hope of our heavenly inheritance, and he raises a crucial issue we must consider. How are we to know that the promised inheritance will be ours? How are we to know whether we love the good God or God's good gifts?

Peter's point is that we can know we love God, rather than his gifts, when God takes those gifts away. If we still love God in our suffering, then it is God we love. If we hate God amidst the removal of those blessings, then we never really loved him at all. In a fallen world, we need suffering to demonstrate whether we are faithful followers of Christ or whether we idolatrously follow the things of the world.

In Hebrews 12 the author is addressing the discipline of God as he says, "It is for discipline that you have to endure. God is treating you as sons. For what son is there whom his father does not discipline?" (v. 7). He draws an analogy between the discipline of God and the discipline of human fathers. He says that when we receive the discipline of our earthly parents, it demonstrates that we are their children. The same is true with God. The point here is similar to the one considered above in proving that we belong to Christ.

The author of Hebrews also says that discipline is essential for something else. He says, "For the moment all discipline seems painful rather than pleasant, but later it yields the peaceful fruit of righteousness to those who have been trained by it" (Heb. 12:11). The discipline of the

Lord is a kind of suffering that comes to us as a result of our own sinfulness. This kind of suffering is painful like any other kind we would experience, but it proves that we belong to God as his children and are no longer children of wrath (cf. Eph. 2:3).

This allows us to make an important distinction. The suffering of discipline that believers endure when they sin is very different from the suffering of wrath that unbelievers receive when they sin. God will never be wrathful toward believers since Jesus has already received the wrath they deserve (Rom. 8:1). The discipline is a kind of displeasure, but it is the displeasure of love that a kind father shows to his children because they are his.

Another benefit of this kind of suffering is that it makes us holy. Hebrews 12:11 says that discipline yields the peaceful fruit of righteousness to those who have been trained by it. The suffering of discipline makes us more godly. In the same way that the discipline of an earthly father shows us the error of misbehavior and urges us toward obedience, so God's discipline demonstrates the folly of sin and leads us into Christlikeness. This kind of suffering is essential as we grow in godliness.

Suffering Is Good for Others

It is a biblical reality that suffering benefits us, but it is also true that suffering benefits others. Suffering helps people to see the glory of God. This is the point that Jesus made in John 9:1–3 with the man born blind. The disciples saw this suffering man and wondered why he was experiencing such difficulty. They made the mistake of assuming that it might have been caused by his own sin or the sin of someone else (this is tantamount to the error of a counselor assuming that someone needs help only because of their personal sin or the sin of someone else). Jesus pointed out that neither was the case. He explained that the man suffered in order that "the works of God might be displayed in him" (John 9:3).

God wants to show his glory in this fallen world as he overcomes our pain and our suffering. Sometimes we are afflicted with pain so that God can be seen to overcome the darkness of this world of suffering with the bright light of his glory. The man in John 9 would have had many days of struggle and pain. There must have been memories from childhood that caused heartache. It had to be difficult to be alone on the side of the road with no wife and no family. He would have been broke, hungry, and stigmatized in a culture with no welfare state. This man's experience would have been full of suffering that few of us can fathom.

Then one day he heard the voice of a man who mixed his spit with dirt and spread the mud on the blind man's eyes. A few minutes later, as he was rinsing off the mud with water, he would have been astounded to see sunlight for the very first time. Can you imagine what it must have been like to finally know what a bird looks like? What another person looks like? To see a tree? This man is our brother in Christ (John 9:38), and he has been in heaven now with Jesus for thousands of years. His story has been told all over the world and in hundreds of languages. There is no chance that he is anything other than absolutely grateful for those years of suffering leading to his healing that has caused countless millions to give glory to God through his story.

Closely related to this is the fact that our suffering spreads the gospel to people who do not know Christ. Paul went through an incredible amount of suffering for no other purpose than to see more and more people come to know Jesus Christ as Savior and Lord. One particular kind of suffering he endured was imprisonment for the sake of the gospel. In Philippians 1:12–13, Paul shares his heart with us about his suffering:

> I want you to know, brothers, that what has happened to me has really served to advance the gospel, so that it has become known throughout the whole imperial guard and to all the rest that my imprisonment is for Christ.

Paul had to dislike prison as much as you or I would, and yet when he talks about it, he makes it clear that what he is focusing on is that his suffering led to many unbelievers hearing about Jesus Christ. Does Paul perhaps feel frustrated that he was imprisoned in order for others to hear about Jesus? He does not. He says his concern is only that Jesus Christ is proclaimed (Phil. 1:18).

Suffering also allows us to be a blessing to others. Second Corinthians 1:3–4 says,

> Blessed be the God and Father of our Lord Jesus Christ, the Father of mercies and God of all comfort, who comforts us in all our affliction, so that we may be able to comfort those who are in any affliction, with the comfort with which we ourselves are comforted by God.

One of the purposes of suffering is that we would learn God's comfort in our own trials and share that comfort with our brothers and sisters in their difficulties. When we receive God's comfort in our sufferings, it allows us to be a blessing to others. God sends suffering into our life so that we can grow in our ability to be a blessing to others. When we suffer well, it serves to unify believers as they grow in comforting one another.

If we are not careful, suffering can make us selfish. One of the main lessons of the Bible about suffering is that God uses it in our lives to be a blessing to others. Of course, the fundamental lesson of the Bible is that suffering is ultimately about the glory of God, and so it is to that topic that we will now turn.

Suffering Glorifies God

The primary benefit of suffering stated in the Bible is that it glorifies God by maximizing our need for him. Paul describes his own difficulties, showing they are designed to point to the glory of God. One place where he does this is 2 Corinthians 1:8–9:

For we do not want you to be unaware, brothers, of the affliction we experienced in Asia. For we were so utterly burdened beyond our strength that we despaired of life itself. Indeed, we felt that we had received the sentence of death. But that was to make us rely not on ourselves but on God who raises the dead.

Paul describes a very acute experience of suffering. He was despairing of his very own life. But Paul immediately puts that suffering in perspective, explaining what its purpose was. He was suffering to show that he needed God more than he needed comfort.

Paul develops this idea further later in the same book. He describes his experience of the thorn in his flesh and his repeated appeals for the Lord to take it away. We know that Paul loved God, and God loved Paul. It would seem so easy for God to demonstrate his love by taking away the painful experience of suffering. In his wisdom, however, God wanted to accomplish a good blessing in Paul's life that required a thorn. God himself explains to Paul why he does not take the thorn away: "My grace is sufficient for you, for my power is made perfect in weakness" (2 Cor. 12:9). Paul describes his response to the divine message in verses 9 and 10:

Therefore I will boast all the more gladly of my weaknesses, so that the power of Christ may rest upon me. For the sake of Christ, then, I am content with weaknesses, insults, hardships, persecutions, and calamities. For when I am weak, then I am strong.

Paul is able to embrace his suffering, and to help us embrace ours, because he sees the higher purpose in it of pointing to the glory of God. Suffering demonstrates his weaknesses and ours and highlights our need for God.

We need to remember that sinful human beings are responsible for the fact that suffering is required to learn of our dependence on God. The human race fell in the garden because of our rebellious attempt

269

to live on our own without dependence on God. Mankind rejected his proper role of depending on God by failing to obey his Word ("Of the tree of the knowledge of good and evil you shall not eat" [Gen. 2:17]) and instead attempted to be autonomous. Misery followed. Suffering is the natural consequence of living life without dependence on God. It is God who knows how life works best and who graciously encourages us to live that way. In our sinful autonomy, we rebelled against God's Word and have needed to learn the hard way that life can only be lived fruitfully when we live it dependently for God's honor and glory. Suffering is a hard teacher, but we need it, and it is the one we have chosen in our sin.

The irony of the pain of suffering is that it points us to the higher joy found in Christ alone, in the midst of a supermarket of temptations to delight in other lesser realities. We sinful people tend to judge the degree of blessedness by the degree to which comfort and ease are afforded to us. When we learn to judge the degree of our blessedness by the degree to which Christlikeness is being formed in us, we will be able to make more room in our hearts to embrace suffering as Paul did.

Suffering and Biblical Counseling

Earlier in this chapter I pointed out Psalm 119:68: "You are good and do good; teach me your statutes." We observed that this passage makes a twofold assertion and an appeal. We examined the twofold assertion by seeing how we need to trust God and his plan when we suffer. Now we need to look at the appeal to be taught the statutes of this God who is good and does good things.

Psalm 119:68 is easy to read in times of joy and comfort. It is easy for us to believe that the Lord is good and does good things in times of happiness. We want to know the statutes of this good God in those times of obvious blessing. Times of suffering test our ability to embrace this passage. The immediate context of this verse provides some evidence that it is not a passage reserved only for times when we feel good. Indeed, the verses surrounding Psalm 119:68 all speak of suffering and our need to depend on the Word of God in times of trial (cf. Ps. 119:67, 69–71). If we are to read this verse the same way as we read the sur-rounding verses, then that means it is a passage that helps us respond to suffering.

The psalmist intends for the passage to lead us to trust in God in times of suffering. The psalmist intends for us to trust God's plans when life hurts. The psalmist means to point us to our need for the Word of God in suffering. Suffering highlights our need to be taught the Word of God. That means suffering requires biblical counseling.

James 1:2–4 describes various trials as a weight. In our physical bodies, we know that the longer we lift a heavy object above our head, the more likely it is that we will drop it on our head. James describes a different outcome for the suffering Christian who asks for help (v. 5) and who does what the Word says (vv. 22–25). For us, to be steadfast results in *increasing* strength (v. 4). When our counselees remain reso-lute in trusting God's promises and living out the Scriptures, they are blessed by God. They grow to become more mature and complete, lack-ing nothing (v. 4), despite ongoing life problems. It is a great joy for the biblical counselor to observe this outcome in counselees. It is a joy for the counselor to experience this outcome in their own life.

It is the Bible that teaches us the kind of suffering we experience in this life. It is the Bible that teaches us where that suffering came from. It is the Bible that teaches us how to respond to that suffering. And it is the Bible that teaches us how that suffering will ultimately be put away from God's people forever. When people are struggling with pain, we need to be committed to biblical counseling, because it is the Bible alone that provides us with words to say that matter.

Christians simply do not have the prerogative to decide to have a counseling conversation with suffering people that is based on any other foundation than the Bible. Even if we did have the right, we should not have the desire. We should know that when people are in pain, they need to be taught the Word of God because they need to see God and his good purposes. There is no other source that provides this. A decision to counsel people who are in pain without using the sufficient resources of the Bible is ultimately a decision by the counselor to be irrelevant in counseling. We do not need other resources. We do not need to integrate. God has told us what he wants to say to people in pain. The Bible addresses that issue. Suffering requires biblical counseling.

Sean knew this. Sean came to counseling suffering because of human sinfulness—his own and that of his wife. He came suffering because of the tragic death of his son. He came suffering because he was confused about how to save his marriage and be a better husband. Counseling did not take any of the problems away. In fact, with the departure of his wife into the arms of another man, things got worse before they got better.

Sean suffered a great deal, but that doesn't mean that there was no blessing in the pain. Sean lost his son and his wife, but he came to know Jesus Christ. If he could tell you his story, he would tell you about the tremendous pain. This pain can still make him cry. But in the loss, he gained Christ. After coming to Christ, he grew in grace as he learned through the Lord's mercy to trust God with his life. God's grace trained him to fight bitterness and pursue love with Sarah. He knows that his loss of Sarah is permanent, but he longs for the day when she would confess her sin and he could call her his sister in Christ, which is better than calling her his wife. He also learned that he could minister to others out of the overflow of his pain and is now actively involved in his church as he ministers to those going through grief through loss of life or the loss of a marriage.

One of the most encouraging concepts for Sean about suffering, which still gives him strength, was a long discussion we had about the lessons of the cross of Christ for suffering. We talked about the good sovereignty of God in the death of Jesus Christ (Isa. 53:4–6, 10). We talked about the sinful involvement of the human actors and the Devil (John 13:27; Acts 2:23). We discussed how the death of the innocent Son of God is the single most horrifying example of moral evil that has ever occurred or will ever occur. Then we talked about the fact that, as believers, we will spend an endless eternity praising God for all the blessings that flowed from this one wicked act that God uses for our eternal good.

The crucifixion of Jesus is the ultimate example of the good sovereignty of God in the midst of sinful tragedy. If God can cause the highest possible good to come from the worst imaginable tragedy, then God can bring good out of our lesser tragedies as well. This reality allows us as counselors—as it allowed Sean—to have a Christ-centered view of suffering. Ultimately the comfort we offer to those in pain is the comfort of Jesus Christ himself, who said, "In this world you will have trouble. But take heart! I have overcome the world" (John 16:33 NIV). In suffering, Jesus is with us. And we need to look no further than his person and his work to trust God's character and God's plan in the midst of our pain.[8]

8. For resources to use in counseling people struggling through suffering, consider Jerry Bridges, *Trusting God: Even When Life Hurts* (Colorado Springs: NavPress, 2008); Joni Eareckson Tada and Steve Estes, *When God Weeps: Why Our Sufferings Matter to the Almighty* (Grand Rapids, MI: Zondervan, 1997); Randy Alcorn, *If God Is Good: Faith in the Midst of Suffering and Evil* (Sisters, OR: Multnomah, 2009); Paul David Tripp, *Suffering: Eternity Makes a Difference* (Phillipsburg, NJ: P&R, 2001).

CHAPTER 10

BIBLICAL COUNSELING

and a

THEOLOGY OF SALVATION

Lorie apologized as she sat down in my office. She indicated that she knew I was very busy and said she hated using up my time on such a small problem. As she began to explain her trouble, she described experiencing nagging anxiety in almost every area of her life. When her husband was out of town, she worried that he would get hurt. She was nervous about how much money their family had. She felt compelled to check on her kids when they slept too late for fear they had died. During holidays she was anxious and upset that she would not make enough food for everyone.

As Lorie continued, she wanted to make clear that it was not as though her life was ending. In fact, she lived a very happy life. She had a wonderful marriage, great kids, dear friends, and she was meaningfully involved in the life of our church. Even though her life was not falling apart, she wanted to seek counseling help because she hated the tight feeling of panicked nervousness that she carried with her nearly all of the time. She also knew that it was sometimes draining on her family, who felt increased tension when she was nervous and who often felt pestered by her consistent need to check in on them to make sure they were

OK. Lorie thought it might be good to seek biblical counseling for help with this problem.

In that first meeting with Lorie, I spent a lot of time getting to know her as I listened carefully to her experience of difficulty. As part of that process, I spent a good deal of time trying to discover whether Lorie was a Christian. She had a very clear testimony of how she became a Christian at a church camp in her late teens. Her testimony was confirmed by many of her friends and family that I knew who were aware of Lorie's reputation for being a devoted follower of Christ.

Why is it important for a biblical counselor to know if a counselee, like Lorie, is a believer before counseling begins? What difference does it make to counseling whether Lorie is a Christian or not? After all, the problem of anxiety is a common problem, and Lorie's was not even that serious by some comparisons. Does Lorie's salvation really matter on such a small problem? I would argue that whether or not Lorie is a Christian has *everything* to do with the change process in counseling. In this chapter I want to show you why that is true.

I want to explain the importance of a theology of salvation to counseling by examining what theologians refer to as the "order of salvation." When theologians discuss the order of salvation, they are trying to understand each element of the process of salvation in its proper order. When a person experiences salvation, they experience a multifaceted event with many wonderful blessings. Though we often think of salvation as a single event, when you examine the biblical teaching on salvation, you see that it is actually many different, interrelated events, each with several significant benefits. In this chapter, we will look at each element of salvation to see how the various aspects of salvation have many benefits for counselees like Lorie.

Election

The first element in the order of salvation is the doctrine of divine election. Election is the biblical teaching that God chose from the very beginning of time those people who would ultimately come to faith in Jesus Christ. That choice was not based on any advance knowledge that God had regarding which sinners would choose to become Christians and which ones would not. On the contrary, God's choice was the determining factor in saving them. They came to trust in Christ solely *because* of God's sovereign will in choosing them.[1]

The doctrine of election is taught in several places in the Bible. One is Romans 9:10–21:

When Rebekah had conceived children by one man, our forefather Isaac, though they were not yet born and had done nothing either good or bad—in order that God's purpose of election might continue, not because of works but because of him who calls—she was told, "The older will serve the younger." As it is written, "Jacob I loved, but Esau I hated."

What shall we say then? Is there injustice on God's part? By no means! For he says to Moses, "I will have mercy on whom I have mercy, and I will have compassion on whom I have compassion." So then it depends not on human will or exertion, but on God, who has mercy. For the Scripture says to Pharaoh, "For this very purpose I have raised you up, that I might show my power in you, and that my name might be proclaimed in all the earth." So then he has mercy on whomever he wills, and he hardens whomever he wills.

You will say to me then, "Why does he still find fault? For who can resist his will?" But who are you, O man, to answer back to God? Will what is molded say to its molder, "Why have you

---

1. Every Christian must embrace the doctrine of election in some way because the truth is repeatedly taught throughout the Scriptures. Not everyone understands election in the same way I have articulated it here. For information about a view of election that is different from the understanding I have adopted, see Jack Cottrell, *What the Bible Says about God the Ruler* (Eugene, OR: Wipf and Stock, 2000).

made me like this?" Has the potter no right over the clay, to make out of the same lump one vessel for honorable use and another for dishonorable use?

Here we learn that God makes a choice that determines those who will belong to his people. We are told that he chose to love Jacob and hate Esau. Paul uses the example of Jacob and Esau in his letter to the Roman church because God's choice of Jacob over Esau is an individual case study for how God treats all people. Elsewhere Paul writes, referring to all of God's people, that "[God] chose us in [Jesus Christ] before the foundation of the world, that we should be holy and blameless before him" (Eph. 1:4). What was true about Jacob as a specific example is true in general of all who believe. God chooses those who will be his people.

Romans 9 teaches us the basis for God's choice of Jacob. Paul says the basis of God's choice was *not* Jacob's behavior: "though they were not yet born and had done nothing either good or bad" (v. 11). God did not look down the portals of time and see what kind of person Jacob would be or what kind of decisions he would make to demonstrate his faith and then "choose" him on that basis. Instead, God's choice of Jacob was based on God's own desire to reveal himself as a God who elects "in order that God's purpose of election might continue, not because of works but because of him who calls" (v. 11).

God's choice of lost people is not based on the wise choices they make or the good things they do. Election is based on God's desire to exalt himself as the fountain of all mercy. "I will have mercy on whom I have mercy, and I will have compassion on whom I have compassion" (Rom. 9:15). Our eyes are drawn to God, not to our works or efforts at moral improvement. The doctrine of election ensures that there is no ground for our boasting in our salvation. If salvation were based on a decision we made or in a work we performed, we would be able to take some level of credit for it. Election ensures that human beings do not get the glory for their salvation. All glory in salvation goes to the God of mercy, who elects lost people, saving them from certain destruction.

Election is the doctrine of God's omnipotence applied to salvation. We examined in chapter 4 that God exerts comprehensive sovereignty over the world he has made. This omnipotence includes his sovereignty over those who come to Jesus for salvation. If the doctrine of election were not true, then the decisions of people to be saved would be a crucial area outside of the sovereign power of the infinitely wise God.

Among evangelical Christians, the doctrine of election is one of the most controversial in the order of salvation. Some evangelicals have been concerned that a focus on the doctrine of election might dampen evangelistic zeal. I am sensitive to these concerns. Most of my vocational ministry has been concentrated in pastoral ministry. I am devoting my life to the Great Commission with a passionate desire to see the kingdom of Christ expand as lost people are saved and saved people are built up in the faith. I never want to do anything that would hinder the full conviction of every Christian to call all people to repentant faith in the Lord Jesus Christ.

There is no reason to believe that the doctrine of election threatens evangelism, because the same authors God inspired to teach the church about election also teach the church about the importance of evangelism. As an example of this, we can discuss the apostle Paul. In Romans 9 we examined the teaching of Paul on election. Just a few verses later, in Romans 10:1–17, Paul issues an urgent appeal to preach the gospel, promising that all who confess and believe in the Lord Jesus Christ will be saved. So for Paul, election does not impede evangelism, it fuels it. We spend our lives preaching the gospel to lost people with all of our strength, confident that all who confess Jesus will be saved. Our confidence comes in the fact that God's electing grace guarantees that people will hear and believe.[2]

The doctrine of election is the first element in the order of salvation. Every other element we will see in the flow of the doctrine of salvation

---

2. For more information on this topic, see Thomas R. Schreiner and Bruce A. Ware, *Still Sovereign: Contemporary Perspectives on Election, Foreknowledge, and Grace* (Grand Rapids, MI: Baker, 2000); John Piper, *The Justification of God: An Exegetical and Theological Study of Romans 9:1–23* (Grand Rapids, MI: Baker, 1993).

comes from this one. It is the doctrine of divine election that connects the other elements of salvation to the individuals who enjoy them.

Calling

When theologians speak of calling, they are referring to two biblical realities. The first is what is often referred to as the "general call." The general call is the proclamation of the gospel, which goes out to everyone who hears, that Jesus Christ is Lord and Savior who has accomplished redemption for all who believe. Every instance of faithful gospel preaching is an example of the general call. We see Jesus doing this as he beckons people to find their rest in him (cf. Matt. 11:28). We also see the apostles engaging in the general call as they urge people to repent of sin and trust in Jesus Christ (cf. Acts 2:38; 17:30–31).

This general call is an incredible blessing to all who receive it, but it does not lead to salvation in everyone who hears it. Those who receive the blessing of the general call do not necessarily come to faith in Christ. This is why theologians draw a distinction between the general call and the "effective call." The effective call is the work of God to summon the elect to follow Christ through the preaching of the gospel. The effective call refers to the proclamation of the gospel that leads to salvation in the life of the person who hears it preached. Many passages teach the effective call (Rom. 1:6–7; 11:29; 1 Cor. 1:9, 24; 7:18; Gal. 5:13; Eph. 4:4; Phil. 3:14; 1 Thess. 5:23–24; 1 Tim. 6:12; 2 Tim. 1:9; Heb. 3:1–2; 9:15; 1 Peter 2:9, 21; 5:10; 2 Peter 1:10).

First Peter 2:9 is a passage that summarizes many of the elements of the effective call. It says,

But you are a chosen race, a royal priesthood, a holy nation, a people for his own possession, that you may proclaim the excellencies of him who called you out of darkness into his marvelous light.

Notice that the effective call comes from God (i.e., "*him* who called you," emphasis added). The general call is a sincere offer for sinners to repent, and it comes in good faith from the one who extends it, but it is not always attended with the power of God. The effective call applies God's special grace to save in the heart of the sinner so that the words of the human minister effectively bring about fruitfulness in the preaching of the gospel. Without this calling of God, no preaching of the gospel would ever be effective, and no person would ever believe.

Another factor of the effective call is that it comes to individuals at a specific time. God calls persons to himself in a particular time. Many passages in the New Testament make a connection between election and calling while also making clear that there is a distinction in these two elements of salvation (1 Cor. 1:26ff; Gal. 1:15–16; 2 Thess. 2:13–14). The doctrine of election teaches that God determined to save people before the foundation of the world. In this sense, it differs from the doctrine of effective calling that teaches that God begins to call out his elect individuals at a specific period of time and during a particular ministry of preaching.

The effective call includes specific blessings. First Peter mentions being called out of darkness into [God's] marvelous light. Other blessings of our calling are eternal life (2 Thess. 2:14), holiness (1 Cor. 1:2), and hope (Eph. 1:18)—to name just a few. Often, when the Bible uses the language of calling, it serves as a summary of all the blessings believers are called unto as they live the Christian life.

The salvation of an individual begins in eternity past with the doctrine of election. An individual begins to actually *experience* salvation when God adds his sovereign power to the preaching of the gospel, rendering it effective in the lives of individuals.

Regeneration

Regeneration is the sovereign and invisible work of God the Holy Spirit transforming us from people who are opposed to him to people who love him. This is the work of God that changes a general call into an effective call. A person who hears the gospel preached and whose heart is not changed to love Christ has received the general call. A person who hears the gospel and whose heart is changed to love Christ has received the effective call.

The Old Testament describes the changes of regeneration that occur in the New Covenant in Ezekiel 36:26–27:

> I will give you a new heart, and a new spirit I will put within you.
> And I will remove the heart of stone from your flesh and give you
> a heart of flesh. And I will put my Spirit within you, and cause you
> to walk in my statutes and be careful to obey my rules.

Under the New Covenant, God changes his people by giving them a new heart and his Spirit, and the change flows outward into their lives from there. This is very good news, considering what we covered in chapter 8 about the complete corruption that sin has brought into our lives. Because we have been completely corrupted by sin, this regeneration must be God-wrought. As we see in Ezekiel, this change of heart is something that God himself does. In John 3:8, Jesus speaks of being "born of the Spirit." Because a person is passive during their own birth, to say that regeneration is to be born of the Spirit means the Spirit does this work without the cooperation of the sinful person in their change of heart. Regeneration is, therefore, the work of God, where one who had been dead in their trespasses and sins is rendered to be a completely new creation (2 Cor. 5:17; Titus 3:5–6; James 1:17–18; 1 Peter 1:3, 23, 25).

Christians can misunderstand the doctrine of regeneration in several ways. One common misunderstanding is to undervalue the magnitude of the heart change that has taken place in believers. The Puritans were often guilty of this. I have several Puritan paperbacks on my shelf that have helped me immensely in my walk with Christ, and one of the most well worn is *The Valley of Vision*. I prayed prayers from this book almost every day when I was in college. This book gave voice to my desire to be more like Christ and helped me articulate my brokenness over sin. The opening line of "Yet I Sin," the prayer I have prayed most frequently, says this:

> Eternal Father,
> Thou art good beyond all thought,
> But I am vile, wretched, miserable, blind . . .[3]

Another prayer, "Heart Corruptions," had me praying,

> I am full of infirmities, wants, sin; thou art full of grace.
> I confess my sin, my frequent sin, my willful sin;
> All of my powers of body and soul are defiled:
> A fountain of pollution is deep within my nature.[4]

As meaningful to me as these prayers from *The Valley of Vision* were at times in my life, words like these improperly confess the nature of a regenerate person. These words are written out of a well-intentioned brokenness over sin, but they express things that are no longer true of believers. Let me explain.

Believers retain indwelling sin and are, therefore, still able to sin, but they are dramatically new people. The Bible says, "We know that our old self was crucified with him in order that the body of sin might be brought to nothing, so that we would no longer be enslaved to sin" (Rom. 6:6) and "If anyone is in Christ, he is a new creation. The old has passed away; behold, the new has come" (2 Cor. 5:17). These passages

---

3. Arthur Bennett, *The Valley of Vision: A Collection of Puritan Prayers and Devotions* (Carlisle, PA: Banner of Truth Trust, 1975), 70.

4. Bennett, *Valley of Vision*, 73.

teach that Christians, having been regenerated by God, are new creatures no longer enslaved to sin.

Prayers like those I've quoted from *The Valley of Vision* constitute an unintentional denial of the doctrine of regeneration. Christians are not vile, wretched, miserable, and blind. Though Christians do sin frequently, it cannot be said *of believers in Christ* that "all of their powers of body and soul are defiled." Christians are new, and if we deny this fact, we deny the biblical truth of regeneration. It is harmful and confusing to believe doctrines, pray prayers, or live lives that minimize that truth.

Another misunderstanding Christians sometimes make regarding the doctrine of regeneration is to overstate the positive blessings of regeneration and our experience of this truth this side of heaven. Charles Leiter is guilty of such overstatement in his book *Justification and Regeneration*. The central argument of Leiter's book is that Christians are truly new creations, but Leiter makes the error that theologians have referred to as an over-realized eschatology. That is, he fails to rightly acknowledge the effects of indwelling sin in his understanding of regeneration. Leiter writes,

> The deepest and ultimate truth about the Christian is that he is a new man. This is his essential identity. The new man represents who he "really" is at the present time and who he will be a thousand years from now.[5]

Leiter states that Christians have realized the fullness of their newness in Christ. While I am grateful that he affirms the newness of being a Christian, in doing so he dramatically overstates what is true of Christians as they live this present life and await the fullness of their redemption in Christ. Leiter forgets that in this life, as we await the fullness of our redemption, Christians "are being transformed . . . from

---

5. Charles Leiter, *Justification and Regeneration* (Hannibal, MO: Granted Ministries, 2009), 173.

one degree of glory to another" (2 Cor. 3:18). Christians are new, yet we are also "being renewed day by day" (2 Cor. 4:16).

Each of these extremes misses the balanced middle of biblical truth on this issue. The doctrine of regeneration teaches that believers in Jesus Christ really are new creations (Rom. 6:4). Believers are not a mixture of old man and new man (2 Cor. 5:17). Tremendous blessings come from the work of regeneration that renders Christians new people. Christians, as new people, are no longer enslaved to sin and so can truly obey the command not to let sin reign in their lives (Rom. 6:6, 12). Because believers have been made new by the process of regeneration, they can now engage in the change process that is possible only for those who have put off the old and put on the new (Eph. 4:20–32).

And yet Christians are not yet new in every aspect of their life and experience. Colossians 3:10 teaches that the new self must still be *renewed*. Second Corinthians 4:16 teaches that the new heart of a believer is being renewed every day. Christians are legitimately new creatures. We are not the same people who were dead in trespasses and sins. But it is not true to say we are as new now as we will be a thousand years from now. This is actually good news for us, because it means that we have God's power to live the Christian life as we grow through a process called "sanctification." That we are not yet as renewed as we will be someday fills us with heavenly hope as we long for that day when we will see Christ as he is, face-to-face, and be fully renewed and exactly like him in his moral character.

Conversion

To this point in the order of salvation, the person who comes to Christ has been passive. The changes wrought in that person have been the work of God alone, not dependent on human effort or human will. God the Father elected to save that person before the foundation of the earth. A human being preached the gospel, and God's Spirit made that preaching effective. God reached into the soul, turning that person from a rebel to a friend in regeneration. These events all happened as the labor of another and not anything that person did.

Conversion, the next aspect of salvation, is the first work that requires activity on the part of the elect person.[6] In order to experience conversion, a person must know something of his own sinfulness before a holy God who demands perfection. He must know something of the righteousness of Christ, who lived a perfect life to earn our righteousness, who died an agonizing death to pay our penalty, and who arose from the grave as evidence of his victory over death. A potential convert must know something of God's holy character, his own sinful breaking of God's law, and about Jesus' work as Savior. These elements will typically be heard in the general call, the preaching of the gospel message.

Conversion requires more than knowledge of and agreement with these facts. Assent to information is essential but not enough. In order for a person to be converted, they must possess repentant faith. Repentance and faith have been called the twin pillars of the Christian life because they are each required in order to convert.[7] When the apostle Paul summarizes his ministry to the Ephesian elders, he says it was one of "testifying both to Jews and to Greeks of repentance toward God and of faith in our Lord Jesus Christ" (Acts 20:21). Sometimes the biblical witness emphasizes the necessity of repentance in this partnership (Luke 15:7; Acts 2:38; 3:19; 17:30; Rom. 2:4; 2 Tim. 2:25; 2 Peter 3:9), while at other times it emphasizes faith (John 20:31; Acts 8:12; 10:43; 13:39; Rom. 4:3; Gal. 2:16). Both are essential.

Hebrews 11 begins with a description of what faith is: "Now faith

---

6. I am placing regeneration before conversion in the order of salvation. There is a long tradition of theologians and theological statements that does the same thing, including my own denomination, the Southern Baptist Convention. Their statement on regeneration says, "Regeneration, or the new birth, is a work of God's grace whereby believers become new creatures in Christ Jesus. It is a change of heart wrought by the Holy Spirit through conviction of sin, to which the sinner responds in repentance toward God and faith in the Lord Jesus Christ," "Current Baptist Faith and Message Statement," Southern Baptist Convention, http://www.sbc .net/bfm2000/bfmcomparison.asp. Some, like Millard Erickson, place conversion before regeneration. For a discussion on this, see Millard J. Erickson, *Christian Theology* (Grand Rapids, MI: Baker, 1998), 941–59.

7. Sinclair B. Ferguson, *The Christian Life: A Doctrinal Introduction* (Carlisle, PA: Banner of Truth, 2013), 62, 70.

is the assurance of things hoped for, the conviction of things not seen" (v. 1). The rest of chapter 11 teaches us that faith is trusting in God and his Word in the face of realities that are unforeseen. Faith is trusting that God made the world even though we can see the creation but not the Creator (v. 3). Noah had faith to listen to God and build an ark even though the cataclysmic flood was unforeseen (v. 7). Abel, Enoch, Noah, Abraham, Isaac, Jacob, Sarah, and many others all had faith though they never received the things they were promised, but greeted them from afar (vv. 13, 39). Faith is a confident trust in the character of God to believe what he says. The kind of faith that is necessary for conversion is trust in God's verdict about our sin and trust in his promise about what Christ has done for us because of that sin.

A classic illustration of repentance is found in Jesus' parable of the prodigal son. The Prodigal Son left his father, took his inheritance, and spent it all in wild and sinful living. After squandering his inheritance, the man became convicted that he had sinned and repentance followed. The parable illustrates the steps of his repentance. First, the Prodigal was broken over his sin (Luke 15:17–19; cf. 2 Cor. 7:10–11). Repentance requires a sense of pain that God's law has been broken and God himself has been offended. Second, the Prodigal engaged in a change of behavior. He turned from his sin and went back to his father (Luke 15:20). Repentance has not happened when a person feels bad about his sin but continues to persist in that sin. Repentance requires a change in behavior, from sin to righteousness.[8] Finally, the Prodigal Son confessed his sin (Luke 15:21). We have seen previously that confession of sin is a crucial part of repentance because of the importance of humbly admitting our wrongs.

We are talking about faith and repentance in the context of conversion, but it is important to note that while faith and repentance are required at the beginning of the Christian life, they are also essential

---

8. The Greek term *metanoia* is often translated repentance, which literally means "to change one's mind."

elements throughout the Christian life. Paul can say, "I have been crucified with Christ. It is no longer I who live, but Christ who lives in me. And the life I now live in the flesh I live by faith in the Son of God" (Gal. 2:20). The resurrected Christ can say to believers in Ephesus, "Remember therefore from where you have fallen; repent, and do the works you did at first. If not, I will come to you and remove your lampstand from its place, unless you repent" (Rev. 2:5). The Christian life is a life of continual faith and repentance because it is a life of continual turning from sin to depend on Christ. Conversion does not mark the only instance of faith and repentance in the life of the believer, but the first.

Justification

Justification is based on the work of Jesus Christ and is the response of God to repentant faith, where he makes a legal declaration that his elect are forgiven of sin and possess his own righteousness. The doctrine of justification has been hotly debated among Protestants and Catholics. My purpose here is not to cover those debates but to offer four observations about this area of theology and how it applies to the task of counseling.

First, justification deals with our moral standing before God. As we saw in chapter 8 on the doctrine of sin, one of the effects of sin is that it renders us guilty. As guilty sinners we are condemned before a holy God and are destined to bear the punishment for that sin forever. When God justifies a sinner, he pronounces that the sinner is forgiven of their sin and that they possess positive righteousness in God's sight. Romans 4:4–8 says,

> Now to the one who works, his wages are not counted as a gift but as his due. And to the one who does not work but believes in him who justifies the ungodly, his faith is counted as righteousness, just

as David also speaks of the blessing of the one to whom God counts righteousness apart from works: "Blessed are those whose lawless deeds are forgiven, and whose sins are covered; blessed is the man against whom the Lord will not count his sin."

In this passage it is clear that justification involves the forgiveness of sin: "Blessed are those whose lawless deeds are forgiven, and whose sins are covered" (Rom. 4:7). Paul also deals with the positive application of righteousness in this text: "His faith is counted as righteousness" (Rom. 4:5). Justification is God's gracious provision to reverse the moral guilt we possess after the fall.

Second, justification deals with this moral guilt through a legal declaration of righteousness. Theologians have used the language of a legal declaration regarding justification for a few important reasons. The Greek term from which we get the word *justification* often means "to declare to be righteous."[9] When God justifies a human being, he states that someone is righteous who is still a sinner, as we saw above: "him who justifies the ungodly" (Rom. 4:5). When God justifies a sinner, he declares him innocent of moral crimes for which he is objectively guilty. The courtroom language of a legal declaration has been a helpful analogy the church has used to explain that someone can be both guilty of sin and yet declared by God to be forgiven and righteous in spite of the objective existence of their sin.

Third, this legal declaration of forgiveness and righteousness is based on the merit of Christ to earn righteousness for his people that we saw in chapter 5. But how can God declare people to be righteous when they have obviously sinned? This is where the courtroom analogy breaks down. In our legal system, there are times when guilty criminals are declared "not guilty" by a court of law. But when this happens,

---

9. The Greek term is *dikaioō* and is used in places like Luke 7:29: "When all the people heard this, and the tax collectors too, they declared God just, having been baptized with the baptism of John." The people did not make God righteous in their statement, since such a thing would be impossible for anyone to do. When they declared that God is righteous, they were stating that it is true that he is righteous.

we acknowledge that it is a miscarriage of justice. God's verdict of "not guilty" and "righteous" for sinners is not unjust because of the work of Christ to earn the righteousness of his people and to pay their penalty. When God looks at a sinner and justifies that person, he does it on the basis of all Christ is and all he has done for his people. This is why theologians talk about the necessity of the *imputation* of Christ's righteousness on the sinner. Imputation means that God applies the morality of one person to someone who did not earn it. We have previously seen imputation applied when we talked about Adam's representation of the human race (chapter 8). It also was in the context of Jesus carrying the sin burden of his people (chapter 5). Now we see imputation in the matter of moral righteousness, in that believers are considered to possess Christ's own righteousness.

Finally, justification happens through faith. The apostle Paul was quoted above, saying, "To the one who does not work but believes in him who justifies the ungodly, his faith is counted as righteousness" (Rom. 4:5; cf. Rom. 3:22, 25–26; 5:1; Gal. 2:16; 3:24; Phil. 3:9). God does not justify sinners because they do good things. Indeed, they are sinners and cannot do good things! God justifies his people through their faith. Faith is the instrument of justification because it is the attitude of the heart that does not rely on any work that we can perform. Faith must necessarily rely on the merits of another. And so God exalts the righteousness of his Son when he justifies sinners who look exclusively to that righteous Son, trusting in his merits as the only ground of our salvation (Rom. 4:16).[10]

---

10. For more resources on justification, see Thomas Schreiner, *Faith Alone—The Doctrine of Justification: What the Reformers Taught . . . and Why It Still Matters* (Grand Rapids, MI: Zondervan, 2015); John Piper, *Counted Righteous in Christ: Should We Abandon the Imputation of Christ's Righteousness?* (Wheaton, IL: Crossway, 2002); Brian Vickers, *Jesus' Blood and Righteousness: Paul's Theology of Imputation* (Wheaton, IL: Crossway, 2006).

Adoption

Adoption, the next aspect of salvation we will consider, means that those who possess repentant faith in Jesus Christ are brought into God's family as his own sons and daughters. Apart from Christ, all human beings are "the sons of disobedience" (Eph. 2:2; 5:6), described as "children of wrath" (Eph. 2:3). Adoption means that this status completely changes for Christians. "But to all who did receive him, who believed in his name, he gave the right to become children of God" (John 1:12).

This blessing of salvation is overwhelming. As sinful people, we are completely undeserving of any blessing that we could ever receive from God. Even though we deserve no blessings, God still showers us with many. One blessing we saw in a previous chapter is the blessing of common grace. Even when we do not know Christ, we can still have a life on this earth full of blessing and joy through common grace. We are discovering in this chapter that God gives us the blessing of election, which guarantees our coming to know him. He gives us the blessing of regeneration, which changes our hard, sinful heart to a soft heart able to obey. He also gives us the blessing of justification, removing our legal guilt. The doctrine of adoption teaches us that God gives us even more blessings. He makes us his own sons and daughters (Rom. 8:14). Our status as God's sons and daughters gives us boldness to come to him in prayer as a child runs to their Father; we do not have to cower in fear (Rom. 8:15). Because we are children of God, we can have confidence that the eternal inheritance on the last day will be ours (Rom. 8:17). We can also be confident that, as we await this inheritance, our status as sons and daughters ensures we will never know God's wrath, even as we experience pain (Heb. 12:7–11).

Sanctification

Sanctification is the lifelong process in which Christians strive by divine grace to grow in Christlikeness in their entire person. The doctrine of regeneration shows us that God gave us a new heart, which still needs renewal. The doctrine of justification teaches that God declares us to possess the righteousness of Christ. The doctrine of sanctification is the biblical teaching of how this renewal takes place and how we come to be like Christ in both attitude and action.

Several observations are necessary regarding the doctrine of sanctification. First, we should understand that sanctification is a lifelong process: "And we all, with unveiled face, beholding the glory of the Lord, are being transformed into the same image from one degree of glory to another" (2 Cor. 3:18; cf. Col. 3:10; Heb. 12:14). Paul indicates here that we grow in holiness over time and by degrees and that we do it as we look to Christ (cf. Heb. 12:1–2). This process of becoming like Jesus by beholding him will continue until we die or Christ returns and we are made fully like him because we shall see him in his fullness (1 John 3:2). Though the Bible teaches this process of sanctification, it also teaches that sanctification is something that happened to us when we first believed (Acts 20:32; 1 Cor. 6:11). Christians undergo a process of sanctification as those who have been sanctified in a certain definitive way at the time of their regeneration. This process is, essentially, growth in putting off of sin and putting on righteousness. Sanctification is the process of growing in our trust and dependence on God, especially in our suffering.

Sanctification involves Christian effort and striving. Christians are called to work out their salvation with fear and trembling (Phil. 2:12; 1 John 3:3). This human element of sanctification separates sanctification from some other elements in the order of salvation that we have examined. Sanctification is a synergistic process, meaning that God and man cooperate in the work.[11] Human effort is involved. Other aspects of salvation, like regeneration and justification, which we discussed previously, are monergistic. The word *monergism* means that God alone does the work to bring about these results.[12]

Some Christians today are uncomfortable talking about human

---

11. The word *synergistic* comes from Greek and refers to a work (*erg*) that happens together (*syn*).

12. The word *monergism* is from Greek and refers to a single (*mono*) work (*erg*).

effort in the doctrine of salvation.[13] Such discomfort comes from an understandable desire to avoid an exaltation of human effort in the doctrine of salvation that would obscure the work of Christ. It is important to affirm that the Bible greatly honors human work, but we must place this work in the proper context.

Moral effort is of no value in the doctrine of salvation when it comes to the initiation of the Christian life in regeneration and justification. As sinners, human beings have no ability to change their status before God and be acceptable to him. But this does not mean there is no place for moral effort at all. When it comes to our continuation in the Christian life, we are called to make effort that is in keeping with our profession of faith (2 Cor. 10:5; Eph. 2:10; Col. 1:10; 2 Thess. 1:8; Heb. 5:9; 1 Peter 1:2). In fact, when James says, "Faith apart from works is dead" (James 2:26), he is talking about the effort of those who have been justified by faith. His point is that justification that flows from faith in the merit of Christ will always produce moral effort in sanctification.

But even this moral effort does not happen apart from God's help. As I said earlier, sanctification is a synergistic work. It involves our effort, but this effort is made possible by divine enablement. That is why the definition above is clear that our striving is made possible by divine grace. I referenced Philippians 2:12 as biblical evidence of our need for moral effort. Paul commands justified sinners in that passage to "work out your own salvation with fear and trembling." But Paul's teaching

---

13. One contemporary person who has been very vocal on this matter is Tullian Tchividjian, who has been critical of talking about moral effort with regard to sanctification. During one conference talk I attended, Tchividjian was addressing what he called "gospel sanctification" and said, "Let me tell you how you get better. You get better as you increasingly realize that if you never get better, God will still love you. That's how you get better. The only people who get better are those people who increasingly realize that their standing with God is based on what Jesus has done for you and not what you have done for him. God's love for me and approval of me, if I am united to Christ, does not get bigger when I obey or smaller when I disobey. And guess what? This makes me want to obey him more and not less." See Tullian Tchividjian, "Evangelical, Missional, Christ-Centered" talk given at "Our Fathers & Our Future" conference March 2011, Orlando, FL, http://resurgencecdn.com/resurgence/2011/02/23/tullian-tchividjian-evangelical-missional-christ-centered. Tchividjian demonstrates here some real confusion about the distinction between justification (which bases God's acceptance of sinners exclusively on the work of Christ rather than on their own merit) and sanctification (which calls Christians to effort in pursuing Christlikeness).

does not end with that passage. He continues, "For it is God who works in you, both to will and to work for his good pleasure" (Phil. 2:13). Paul grounds his command for the moral effort of sanctification in the divine grace that works in Christians to make it possible (1 Cor. 12:6; 15:10; 1 Thess. 5:23; Heb. 13:20–21; Jude 24).

Finally, sanctification has the goal of developing Christlikeness in the entirety of who we are. As we saw above, we are sanctified as we look to Christ, who is the aim of our sanctification (2 Cor. 3:18; Eph. 5:2; Heb. 12:2). This Christlikeness happens in our whole person as we are changed from our inner person in thoughts, feelings, desires, and consciences as these flow out to the outer person in our physical behaviors. Biblical sanctification, which reflects Christlikeness, is not about mere behavior change, but about a completely new person changing from the inside out (Col. 3:1–4:1).[14]

Perseverance

The next aspect of salvation, the doctrine of perseverance, teaches that every person who has been truly saved by God will be kept by the grace of God in that salvation forever. The Bible teaches that those who have truly trusted in Christ cannot lose the salvation that God has given to them. Jesus teaches this in John 10:27–29:

> "My sheep hear my voice, and I know them, and they follow me. I give them eternal life, and they will never perish, and no one will snatch them out of my hand. My Father, who has given them to me, is greater than all, and no one is able to snatch them out of the Father's hand."

Jesus makes clear that he gives his sheep who hear his voice the gift of eternal life. He promises that they will *never* perish. He guarantees

---

14. See Kevin DeYoung, *The Hole in Our Holiness: Filling the Gap between Gospel Passion and the Pursuit of Holiness* (Wheaton, IL: Crossway, 2004); J. I. Packer, *Rediscovering Holiness: Know the Fullness of Life with God* (Grand Rapids, MI: Baker, 2009).

that no one will snatch them out of his hand. He further promises that no one will snatch them from the Father's hand. You might say that Jesus teaches here that we are in the double grip of God! We are in the hands of both the Father and the Son, and in those mighty hands the Christian is safe. We can have confidence that we will endure to the end (John 6:38–40; Eph. 1:14; Phil. 1:6; 1 Peter 1:5).

Our perseverance is based on the faithfulness of God (1 Cor. 1:7–9; Col. 1:22; 1 Thess. 3:13). God demonstrates his own glory and faithfulness in preserving for eternity those whom Christ has bought with his blood. When a person insists that Christians could lose their salvation, they may intend to be making a statement about the seriousness of sin, but they are actually making a statement about the faithfulness of God. The doctrine of perseverance teaches that God is a faithful and loving Father who does not permit his children to be lost.

The doctrine of perseverance does not teach that people remain in the Christian faith regardless of any sinful attitudes and actions on their part. In fact, the biblical teaching on perseverance requires that Christians must continue in the faith in order to demonstrate the authenticity of their faith. Hebrews 3:14 says, "For we have come to share in Christ, if indeed we hold our original confidence firm to the end" (see Col. 1:23; Heb. 3:12). The evidence that Christians have been saved is that they demonstrate God's faithfulness to them in their own faithfulness over time. The doctrine of perseverance teaches that those who have been truly saved have been truly changed so that they desire to follow Christ in lifelong obedience. Those who appear to "fall away" from Christ demonstrate that they were never in Christ to begin with: "They went out from us, but they were not of us; for if they had been of us, they would have continued with us. But they went out, that it might become plain that they all are not of us" (1 John 2:19).

This teaching may raise questions for some Christians who struggle with doubts about their salvation, wondering if they will ultimately persevere in the faith or "fall away." This is a key issue in counseling. Doubts like these can bring serious pain in the lives of people who experience them. We can respond to such doubts in two ways. The first is by help-ing struggling ones to grow in their faith in God. Doubts about the loss of one's salvation almost always trace back to an unhelpful focus on individual experience. Our experience of salvation is important, but our faith is not founded on our experience but on the work of God. We need to remind people of the grace of God in electing them, in effec-tively calling them, in giving them new hearts, in justifying them, and in adopting them as his own sons and daughters. These are God's works, and his faithfulness is at stake in whether he upholds his word and his works. We must point people to confidence in God's ability to keep them as his children despite their doubts and difficulties.

Having laid a foundation about salvation, we should examine the experiences of those who are struggling with doubts. They may have doubts because their experience of salvation is not genuine. They may have made a profession of faith, yet failed to actually possess faith in Christ alone for salvation. If that is true, then faithfulness would require us to point them to the importance of repentant faith in Christ that truly saves. Perhaps they have doubts because, though they are truly saved, they are struggling with a serious sin. In this case, we must help them to grow in grace through the process of sanctification, becoming more like Christ.

Glorification

The final aspect of salvation is the doctrine of glorification, which refers to the complete perfection of believers in body and soul at the return of Jesus Christ. The Bible teaches that when believers die, their souls depart to be with Christ even as their bodies remain on earth to decay (2 Cor. 5:8; Phil. 1:23). It is a precious truth to think of being spiri-tually present with the Lord immediately following our death. But the splendor of glorification is more precious than even that. Glorification happens when Christ returns and reunites the souls of those who have died with their bodies and, together with all believers, gives them their new resurrection bodies, which are no longer subject to weakness or decay.

Paul talks about this glorification in Philippians 3:20–21:

> But our citizenship is in heaven, and from it we await a Savior, the Lord Jesus Christ, who will transform our lowly body to be like his glorious body, by the power that enables him even to subject all things to himself.

In this passage, Paul ties glorification to the return of Christ, just as other passages do (John 5:28–29; 6:39–40, 44, 54; 1 Cor. 15:23). He says that glorification will involve the transformation of our "lowly" bodies to be like Jesus' "glorious" body. Jesus Christ, in his resurrection body, is the firstborn of the resurrection (Col. 1:18) and the prototype for our resurrection bodies. In his most extended teaching on the glorified bodies believers will receive at the resurrection, Paul characterizes them as imperishable, glorious, powerful, and spiritual (1 Cor. 15:35–49).

We know a great deal about our glorification. We know we will be made perfect, we know we will be with Christ, and we know it will last forever. We must be honest, however, that even with descriptions like this, it is impossible to imagine what it will be like to experience such wonderful realities. Glorification is the last stage in the order of our salvation, and it will be wonderful. For endless ages, we will be together with other Christians and with the triune God himself, reveling in what God began in eternity past with our divine election. We will enjoy forever the blessings of regeneration, of justification, of full sanctification and holiness with a glorified body fully restored from the effects of the fall and without the weakness we currently know. It will be more wonderful and glorious than we could ever understand right now.

Lorie, Biblical Counseling, and the Doctrine of Salvation

We began this chapter with Lorie's story and her experience of what she described as a "small" problem with anxiety. Lorie lived a happy life in front of the backdrop of constant anxiety. I asked whether we should be concerned whether Lorie is a believer when we counsel her with such a problem. After all, the problem was relatively mild by comparison to the difficulties some experience with anxiety. Additionally, there are plenty of secular resources available for people with anxiety. Do we really need to be overly concerned about whether Lorie is saved when counseling a garden-variety problem like this one?

It matters. Whether our counselees are Christians matters. Nothing is more significant in our lives than God's work of salvation. Salvation has to do with our eternal relationship with the infinite God and the powerful resources he provides for us to exist in that relationship. Salvation has to do with everything about our lives. It addresses every part of who we are. It informs every joy we experience. Our salvation impacts every problem we confront. The doctrine of salvation teaches that Christians have genuine and tangible resources to deal with the problems that confront us in counseling. Regardless of where those problems are on the continuum of mild to extreme, God intends for us to have his real power to confront what is wrong with us.

By using Lorie as an example, we can see that all the individual doctrines in the larger process of salvation speak relevantly, concretely, and powerfully into her life and struggle. Lorie is a Christian and her life is functional, but worry has spread into every area of her life and is robbing her life of joy. That Lorie has a saving relationship with the God of heaven and earth has everything to do with whether she can experience meaningful change in this area of her life.

Because Lorie has come to Christ in repentant faith, she is assured of unfailing love for her that stretches back into eternity past when God set his electing love on her. That Lorie has been elected before the foundations of the earth means that a wise, loving, and sovereign God has determined to devote himself to her into eternity future, ensuring that she will ultimately be glorified with him in heaven forever. Worry is shattered when believers come to know that God has been planning their good since before he made the world and guarantees their good forever after this current world is renewed. Worry is actually a very rational response to trouble when these things are not true for a person or when they do not know they are true for them. When believers are convinced about these doctrines of salvation, worry stops making sense.[15]

God's love for Lorie is bounded by nothing less than his eternal plan to do her good in him, and he manifests this care to her in concrete ways during her existence on earth. The doctrine of the effective call is the first evidence that Lorie would have remembered and understood of God's visible care for her.[16] His eternal electing love took concrete form in raising up someone to share the gospel with her in a way that began to make sense. God then showed even more care for her by dramatically and unilaterally changing her heart in regeneration to awaken her love for him. God, on his own initiative, showed care to Lorie by fixing her heart so that she could see and know him, the most beautiful and desirable Being in all of existence.

Then God showed care for Lorie by declaring her innocent of every sin she had ever committed or ever would commit. Even more than this, God did not just forgive her, leaving her in a state of moral neutrality similar to Adam; she received positive righteousness that gives her complete moral acceptance. This declaration that is true of her requires us to see another element of God's care for Lorie that makes that declaration possible. Jesus was born thousands of years before Lorie. He lived his life for her. He died on the cross for her. He rose from the dead for her.

---

15. Wayne A. Mack and Joshua Mack, *Courage: Fighting Fear with Fear* (Phillipsburg, NJ: P&R, 2014). Edward T. Welch, *Running Scared: Fear, Worry, and the God of Rest* (Greensboro, NC: New Growth, 2007).

16. Lorie would, of course, have experienced God's care for her in his common grace before he called her to faith in Christ, but—as we have examined—this common grace is not part of his saving grace. Also, as a sinner, she would not have been able to acknowledge and thank God for this good care.

The triune God lavished his eternal care on Lorie in the precious gift of Jesus, who lived in order to die and rise for her. This truth is revolutionary for worriers who, by definition, do not believe that all will be well. Justification destroys the logic of worry, reminding us that the God who gave us his Son will give us everything else along with him (Rom. 8:32).

God gives Lorie even more resources in her battle against worry. God has brought Lorie into his family. She is his daughter. We know by common grace that daddies are to love their daughters and care for them. God teaches us in the Bible that he has infinite care and regard for his precious children, adopted through the work of Jesus Christ. In particular, Lorie can know that the doctrine of adoption means that she has access to her loving Father to call to him for help in the midst of any struggle (Rom. 8:15). Because she is a precious daughter of God, the Holy Spirit testifies of God's eternal purpose to do good to her all the days of her life (Rom. 8:16–17). There is no room for worry in a child's heart filled up with the loving care of an omnipotent Father.

If all of that were not enough, God gives still more blessings to Lorie. His work of regeneration makes possible the change process of sanctification. Because of God's work for her and in her, Lorie is able to change. She is able to put off the disposition of a heart geared toward worry and replace it with a disposition of trust and joy in God's good and eternal care for her. God has not just made the process of sanctification possible in her life, he has shown her how it can take place in his revelation, the Bible. God wrote the Bible precisely to show us how to live a life full of joy that is honoring to him. This means the Bible is as relevant to show us how to fight worry as it is to chart the path forward in any other difficulty (2 Tim. 3:16–17; 2 Peter 1:3–4).

The doctrine of salvation matters in counseling. What is true by way of example with Lorie and her struggle with anxiety is true in principle with any other problem. The Bible is a glorious book about salvation, the ultimate deliverance from all of our difficulties. That means the Bible is about counseling. Each of these doctrines has *everything* to do with Lorie, her problem, and what we would say to her to help bring about change in her life. Rich resources exist for counseling in the doctrine of salvation because salvation is about real power that God gives us in our lifetime to confront our real problems. When we admit that the Bible is a book about salvation, we do not limit its applicability to a few "religious" issues. When we understand the doctrine of salvation, it actually maximizes the relevance of the Bible for all of life and counseling. The resources revealed in Scripture about the doctrine of salvation are so incredibly profound that Christians should never dream of trading them—not for the entire corpus of secular knowledge about worry.

All of this raises a crucial question. Does the biblical teaching about the powerful resources in Scripture to those who have been saved mean that biblical counselors cannot counsel unbelievers? This is a powerfully relevant question. If God has given his resources to change only to those who have trusted in Christ, then perhaps biblical counselors have nothing meaningful to say to those who are not Christians. I do not think this is true for two important reasons, but before I discuss them, I want to correct a common misunderstanding some have about biblical counseling.

Many incorrectly believe that biblical counselors cannot counsel unbelievers. I often find that this belief can be traced to the convictions of Jay Adams about counseling because Adams taught that it was not possible to counsel unbelievers. In saying this, Adams did not mean that Christians should never have conversations with unbelievers. He was speaking about counseling in a very specific and biblical way that is different from the more general understanding of counseling that many use today. For Adams, counseling

> consists of the renewal of [God's] image. Anything less, any approach that doesn't involve the putting off of sin and the putting on of knowledge, righteousness and holiness that comes from God's truth, is unworthy of the label "Christian," misleads unbelievers and dishonors God.[17]

---

17. See Jay E. Adams, *More Than Redemption: A Theology of Christian Counseling* (Grand Rapids, MI: Baker, 1980), 120–21. See also page 19 where Adams gives advice on how to do "counseling" with an unbeliever using the Scriptures.

When Adams spoke in this context, he was intending to communicate that counseling had to do with change that honors God, which is possible only for Christians. He went on to describe the counseling conversations Christians have with unbelievers as a form of evangelistic pre-counseling.

Whether we can do biblical counseling with unbelievers depends on how we define counseling. The understanding of counseling that I have adopted in this book is a bit different from the one Adams used that I quoted above. In this book I refer to counseling as providing answers, solutions, and help to the questions, problems, and trouble that people face. Adams's very specific understanding of counseling bases the *possibility* of counseling on whether one is a Christian or not. My more general understanding of counseling bases the counselee's *response* to counseling on whether they are a Christian or not. We are in agreement that one must be a believer in order to change in the way God desires. We are also in agreement that biblical counselors should engage believers and unbelievers in the difficulties they face and try to minister the Scriptures to them so that they experience change that honors Jesus Christ. Any disagreement on this issue is semantic, having to do with how we are using the language of counseling.

I believe it is accurate to say that biblical counselors can offer counsel to believers and unbelievers alike. Yet you might still wonder, how this can be true when it is only believers who have God's powerful blessings of salvation that enable change. I have two responses to this issue.

First, biblical counselors can offer effective counsel to unbelievers because biblical counseling is Christ-centered, pointing people to faith in Christ to address all of their problems in living. Biblical counselors are constantly talking about the power of Jesus Christ to change and comfort. Biblical counselors are constantly pointing counselees to rest in Christ's power and fight for change by faith in him. This does not change regardless of whether one is a believer or not. I pointed out in the discussion of conversion that repentant faith happens for the first time immediately following regeneration, but it continues throughout the entire Christian life. Christians live a life of faith. When we call people to respond to their difficulties by faith in Jesus, we are saying the same thing to those who already trust him and to those who have not yet done so. The summons to faith is a bit different in each case. We are calling the unbeliever to faith unto salvation. We are calling the believer to faith unto sanctification. But we want believers and unbelievers to respond in faith regardless of their problem and regardless of whether they currently have faith in Christ. For lost people, that call to faith is of an evangelistic nature. For those who are saved, that call to faith is of a discipleship nature.

A second reason we must confess that biblical counseling is for unbelievers is because when counseling begins, we often do not know whether our counselee is a believer or not. When Lorie first came to me for counseling, I had strong reason to believe she was a Christian. I was her pastor and knew of her profession of repentant faith in Christ. I had also seen the fruit of sanctification in many areas of her life. As counseling continued, I became increasingly certain of the authenticity of her faith in Jesus as she learned by grace how to put off worry and put on trust.

Not every counselee is like Lorie. I have had counselees I thought were saved when counseling began, but who turned out not to be; counselees I thought were unsaved who turned out to be saved; and counselees I was uncertain about, but for whom my clarity about them grew as counseling progressed. If we have to be absolutely certain that a person is a Christian in order to have biblical conversations, then we will not do much counseling at all. In fact, one of the things for which the Word of God is sufficient is the issue of charting the choppy waters of a conversation with someone when some of the invisible realities of salvation are not altogether clear to us. This sufficiency of the Word of God for lost and saved alike is why everyone, from Moses to Jesus to Paul, could have conversations with people who were outside of God's grace. The sufficient Word gives us meaningful words to say to all kinds of people and shows us how to evaluate their profession of faith and their experience to determine whether they are trusting in Christ.

Good counselors know that when a person comes for counseling help, they often have more problems than they are even aware of. A biblical theology of salvation teaches us that the primary problem people have is their relationship to a sovereign God, who has made it possible for him to be reconciled to them through the work of Jesus as that is applied to individuals in salvation. Counselors do not have the right to know this and fail to make salvation of pressing importance in counseling. When we understand the doctrine of salvation, we understand the primary problem that people have. We understand that the resources God gives to his people are powerful tools to address their problems in counseling. We as biblical counselors are able to talk about God's love and his power that releases people from their trouble. In other words, we are able to talk about the things that matter more than anything else in the entire world. No other counseling approach is sufficient for such high and holy work.

CHAPTER 11

BIBLICAL COUNSELING

and a

THEOLOGY OF THE CHURCH

✝

W e have considered several theological realities and have looked at their implications for counseling. One final doctrinal issue that we have not considered is our theology of the church. Understanding the doctrine of the church in a theology of biblical counseling is important because the church is the place where counseling ministry will most meaningfully happen. While it is important to understand theology and doctrine, we need to apply what we learn in a community of believers—in the church. The church is the location—even the organism—where the truths we have studied in this book find their home. Paul describes the church as the "household of God" and a "pillar and buttress of the truth" (1 Tim. 3:15). By the plan of God, every issue in Christian doctrine requires the church to uphold it. It is not enough to know the truth or even to value the truth. The truth must take root in the church. If counseling is grounded in our understanding of the truth, and the truth is rightly upheld in the context of the church, then counseling finds a real home in the church.

Every area of Christian doctrine about the church is important in the ministry of counseling. When theologians write about the doctrine of the church, they discuss matters related to church government, the ordinances of the church, the marks of a true church, and many other things. As important as each one of these issues is, it would be unwise for me to attempt to deal with all of them in this book. As I have done in other chapters, I will frame the doctrines of the church around a dear friend, Randy, I met in counseling. I will highlight the truths about the local church that were the most helpful in ministering to him.

Randy

Randy is a precious friend of mine. Our friendship began years ago when he was a member of my church. I had been getting to know him for a while when he confessed to me that he had a significant problem with pornography. As I sat with him, I learned that Randy's problem was characterized by daily viewing of pornography, sometimes spending as much as five hours watching pornographic images into the early morning. He knew viewing pornography was at odds with the call of Christ on his life. He also knew that his problem was extreme. In spite of his awareness, he had not wanted to seek help, ashamed to explain what his problem was.

That decision not to talk changed one night when he connected with a woman online and the two agreed to meet for a sexual encounter. Before the meeting, he came under tremendous conviction and reached out to me for help. I met with Randy regularly for the next several months and irregularly for several years. In that time, I saw Randy change from a man enslaved to pornography to a man captivated by Christ. Randy is now walking closely with the Lord, is not struggling with pornography, and is a ministry leader in his current church home. If you have followed my argument so far in this book, you will know that this change in Randy happened through the ministry of the Word and the powerful ministry of the Spirit, who applied the grace of Jesus Christ to his heart.

The point I want to make is that all of the Christ-centered, Spirit-empowered, and Word-based change happened in the context of the local church. When we say that the church is a pillar and buttress of truth, what we mean is that the church is the location for counsel to be heard and applied. God gave us truth for the purpose of changing our lives. The church is the pillar and buttress of truth. It is designed to support and uphold the truth that changes our lives when we are in trouble. In what follows, I want to highlight just a few ways that counseling in the context of the local church was instrumental in the change Randy experienced.

Biblical Counseling and the Office of Elder

One area that theologians talk about in a theology of the church concerns the officers in the church. The Bible teaches that a biblical church will have the offices of elder and deacon (1 Tim. 3:1–13; Titus 1:5–16). Both of these offices are essential in the life of the church, but I want to focus here on the office of elder.

The Bible is clear that in the life of the local church, elders are responsible to fill the roles of teaching and leading (1 Tim. 3:2, 5; 5:17). In the context of a book about the theology of biblical counseling, I want to explore the relationship of these to the role of counseling in the local church.

I will begin with the work of teaching. Typically, when Christians think of the task of preaching, they think of the public manifestation of this role as pastors preach to the congregation on Sunday. It is unbiblical and simplistic, however, to constrain the ministry of teaching to its public manifestation. In fact, the Bible is clear that teaching happens in a public context of preaching and in a personal context of conversation. Jesus is an example of a biblical teacher who spent far more time counseling than he ever did preaching. The apostle Paul is another example of a Bible teacher who exercised his teaching ministry in the settings of preaching and conversation, "I did not shrink from declaring to you anything that was profitable, and teaching you in public and from house to house" (Acts 20:20). Pastors err when they fail to follow in the footsteps of Jesus and Paul, who gave themselves to the teaching work of counseling and preaching.

I have spent a great deal of time in this book arguing for the sufficiency of Scripture for counseling. My argument has been that the contents of Scripture are intrinsically related to the kinds of conversations that counselors have. Counseling is ministry of the Word in every way that preaching is ministry of the Word. Pastors must not think of their labor in the Word as being exclusively bound up in preaching. They must also be deployed in the ministry of counseling. Pastors are ministers of the Word in whatever form that ministry takes. Pastors must labor in the kind of ministry of the Word that heralds God's message to the gathered flock of saints in corporate worship. They must also labor in the kind of ministry of the Word that heralds God's message to individual Christians struggling with all manner of temptations, sins, and sufferings.

Such an idea can serve to expand our understanding of who is qualified for the work of pastor. The Bible is clear that in order to be an elder, a man must be able to teach (1 Tim. 3:2; Titus 1:9). Often when we apply this qualification to men we are considering for elder, we think only of the public kind of teaching that happens in preaching. An understanding, however, that counseling is ministry of the Word reminds us that there are many gifted teachers in our churches who are not skilled in public oratory but are quite gifted to discuss the truth of God over coffee with a person in pain. I have had the privilege of serving with many men in ministry whose service in the office of elder never requires them to preach but has them regularly using the gift of teaching in counseling.

Elders are also called to lead. We often think of the work of leadership as setting goals for church, taking action steps to reach those goals, managing staff, supervising the budget, and other similar and important work. The Bible makes clear that one important job of the pastor or elder is to lead the people in his church to grow in the task of counseling. Paul teaches that the pastoral work of shepherds and teachers is a gift from Jesus Christ to his church to help them learn to do the work of ministry. He says that the work of this ministry is essential so that the whole body can grow up into the maturity of Christ (Eph. 4:11–14). Paul also makes clear that one of the significant ways that this growth in maturity happens is as the church members have conversations among themselves that are wise and loving (Eph. 4:15). The church members grow in maturity as they grow in their ability to have counseling conversations that are wise and loving. This passage clearly instructs pastors to exercise their leadership for the purpose of raising up people in their church to be equipped to counsel others. A biblical church leader is one who uses his influence to grow the ability of his members to minister to one another in counseling.

I mentioned above that there are a variety of ways that a pastor might demonstrate the gift of teaching. The teaching gift is not limited to preaching but also includes counseling. I mentioned that I have served with many who are not skilled preachers, but who excel in the kind of one-on-one teaching that happens in counseling. The reverse is also true. It is possible for someone to be very skilled in public proclamation and be weaker when it comes to teaching individuals the truth of God in counseling. I offer two responses for such weaknesses. First, such ministers should try to strengthen their areas of weakness and grow in the ability to do the more personal ministry of the Word—counseling. The second is the kind of pastoral leadership taught in Ephesians 4—to speak the truth in love to build up the body of Christ.

Pastors need to be committed to creating a group of ministers in the local church who are equipped to build the body up in Christ in the context of conversations. It is unbiblical for a pastor to exclude counseling from the ministry of the local church simply because that mode of ministry of the Word is not the one in which he excels. He must submit to the teaching of Ephesians and use his leadership role in the church to equip his flock to grow in the kind of conversational wisdom so crucial to help people like Randy grow up into Christ.

When it came to counseling Randy, the pastors in our church took the lead in his counseling care. We did this because we believed that our training in theology equipped us with relevant truth to point Randy in the direction of change. We did this because we believed God had called us to teach people like Randy in deeply personal ways, not just to proclaim general truth to a general audience from behind a pulpit. The content of our counsel with Randy was much of the same content that we have already examined in this book. It sprang to life in his trouble as it did in the lives of the other people I have introduced you to in this book. Jesus powerfully changed Randy through that same truth, in the context of wise and loving relationships with his pastors.

Biblical Counseling and Christian Community

The church has people who are not called to be elders, yet they have a role to play in the counseling process. In fact, most of the people in our local churches are members who are not called to the roles of leadership and authoritative teaching. The flock has a significant role in ministry to people like Randy as well. Here I will examine four crucial ways that the church came together to help Randy.

First, the church created a context for Randy to worship. In our counseling together, I spent a lot of time with Randy, showing him how to worship on his own and even how to live his life as a form of worship (Rom. 12:1). As crucial as it is to think of worship in this way, it is also deeply comforting to engage in corporate worship with other believers. It is a powerful experience to share in the singing, preaching, and ordinances that happen on Sunday with other believers. This is a normal means of grace that all Christians need—Randy included.

Second, the church provided fellowship for Randy. One of the reasons that Randy's sin struggle was so significant was because he had isolated himself from the body of believers. Randy needed to reengage with other Christians. This reengagement did not need to constitute anything "special," like some sort of support group or a gathering that focused uniquely on Randy. Randy just needed to be with other believers. This was accomplished as Randy attended regular worship. He got connected with a fellowship group in our church. Involvement in this group had Randy meeting with other believers at least once a week, studying the Bible and praying. Involvement in this group also had Randy spending fun time in growing friendships, attending cookouts, hiking, going to the beach, and talking into the night over coffee about everything from Jesus to soccer.

Third, members of our church taught Randy in the context of counseling. Randy had a severe problem with pornography. A problem with his level of difficulty required a lot of counseling attention. In fact, it was more attention than I could give by myself, as I had many other responsibilities in our church. I was able to connect Randy with several people in our church to meet with him regularly about numerous issues, including helping him with his use of time, helping him to know how to pray, working on budgeting priorities, and several other things. Each of these issues was important, but they were more than I could deal with on my own because of time constraints. At one point in the early stages of counseling, Randy was having four different counseling appointments a week with four different people in order to deal with urgent issues in his life.

Finally, the church was able to provide accountability for Randy. I have been emphasizing that Randy's problem with pornography was severe. In fact, it was so severe that it required a great deal of oversight in his life to help him to turn the corner. Randy had grown accustomed to viewing pornography whenever he wanted. The path toward pornography in his life was one that was well worn. It was going to take intense effort for Randy to learn to walk new paths. In order to succeed in this effort, Randy needed oversight. Everyone involved in Randy's care (including Randy) came to the conclusion that he would never be able to succeed without someone living with him to hold him accountable. Randy received that accountability for a time after a member of our church moved in with him as his roommate.

The church held Randy accountable despite his significant season of failure partway through his counseling. Randy returned to pornography, began avoiding those who were trying to help him, and ultimately quit coming to counseling for a time. In response to this long season of persistent sin and after much pleading for restoration from his brothers and sisters in Christ, the church publicly removed Randy as a member (Matt. 18:15–20). This process was deeply painful for Randy and the rest of the church, who loved him a great deal. Randy now says that it was facing that consequence from people he knew loved him that caused him to understand how serious was his need for genuine repentance. Shortly after being disciplined from membership, Randy began a process of repentance. A little less than a year later, he was restored as a member with many happy tears. Randy is now a growing member of the church. He has the ministry of the church to thank for it.

When you step back and look at what was happening in our church's intervention with Randy, you see an astounding amount of care. Randy was having numerous weekly counseling conversations about his problems with people who were expert in the issues they were addressing with him. He was folded into personal fellowship with dozens of people in a community group and was regularly welcomed into their homes and families. He had a beloved brother in Christ move in with him to provide close accountability right where he lived. Several people in our church were available for him to call at any hour of the day or night to help with any temptations.

This kind of close and comprehensive care would be impossible to find in any other secular or religious venue outside of a local church. No other outlet has anything that even approaches the resources to invest in this way over the long term. If such a place did exist, that kind of involvement would cost hundreds—probably thousands—of dollars a week. This kind of care came to Randy at no charge. It was his by virtue of his involvement in our local church. This kind of close involvement and expertise is the stuff secular practitioners dream of. Christians have it right at their fingertips, just waiting to be used. This is just one more demonstration that Christians are not operating at any deficit when it comes to counseling resources. When God wrote the Bible and created the church, he thought of everything! We have an overflowing abundance of resources that would be the envy of any other counseling outlet.

Such resources encourage Christians to make ample use of our churches as the centers of counseling care that God intended them to be. And yet the profound abundance of resources that Christians have in the church does raise a question. Is it ever appropriate for Christians to create freestanding counseling centers staffed by biblical counselors? This is an important question in light of the tension created by several factors: The church has abundant resources to do counseling, but many churches do not take advantage of these resources. Because of that, many Christians have created counseling centers disconnected from local churches to augment the lack of resources. What is a faithful response to such a situation? A few responses are appropriate.

This issue concerns the larger issue of the appropriateness of parachurch ministry in general. I have contributed to a chapter-length discussion of this issue in another book and will not repeat that work here.[1] I will point out that if parachurch ministry is acceptable in general, then there is nothing about biblical counseling ministries in particular that is unacceptable. Many vibrant biblical counseling ministries that provide excellent care to troubled people exist outside the local church. There is nothing about a biblical counselor's commitment to the local church that would lead them to decide such ministries outside the church are inappropriate. Given the fact that so many churches do not provide the counseling services that they should, we would actually conclude that such parachurch counseling ministries are essential for people to get the biblical care they need. Our belief in the centrality of the church for counseling care would, however, urge us to keep counseling centers as connected to the local church as possible in several key areas.

First, counseling centers should, as much as possible, be under the

---

1. See Heath Lambert and David Powlison, "Biblical Counseling, the Church, and the Para-Church" in Bob Kellemen and Kevin Carson, eds., *Biblical Counseling and the Church: God's Care through God's People* (Grand Rapids, MI: Zondervan, 2015).

authority of a local church. There are numerous ways to do this. Larger churches can create counseling centers that are intrinsically connected to the church's mission in a community. In such a scenario, employees of the counseling center would ultimately be employees of the church and accountable to the pastoral authority in the church. Another way to do this would be for the center's board to be made up of pastors from a local church. Being intrinsically connected to a local church in these or other ways can help the counseling center be accountable to faithful Christian theology and faithful counseling practice. Such accountability would apply not just to the overall direction of the center but even to the hiring of counselors. One of the greatest assets a counselor can have is accountability to theological and methodological faithfulness in counseling. Being under the authority of a church can help greatly with this.

Second, counseling centers should be as connected as much as possible to the life of the church. A close relationship with a faithful church is indispensable in the kind of work we do in counseling. Counselors need to be able to send their counselees to a faithful church where they know the counselees will get faithful teaching that does not conflict with the counseling instruction they are receiving. Counselors also need to connect their counselees with solid and helpful relationships with other people who will not work against the goals of counseling. Locating counselees in community groups in faithful local churches is a tremendously effective way to do this.

Third, counseling centers should be connected with a local church for the potential help they can offer with regard to funding. *Someone* has to pay for counseling services. Counseling is never free. Counselors have utility bills and mortgage payments like everyone else. Facilities cost money to keep up. The question is, who is paying for it. One of the most uncomfortable situations we face is that often the people most in need of counseling services are the people least equipped to pay for them. Counseling is one of those necessities of life that people do without if they cannot afford it. As Christians we must be committed to providing personal counseling care to anyone who needs it, whether or not they can pay for it. Some counseling centers arrange their fee schedule in such a way that they have budget dollars reserved to cover the expenses of anyone unable to pay. Another approach is to have the counseling center be a part of the budget of a local church. If the counseling center is part of the church, then that local body would underwrite the expenses of the ministry. It is also possible to have the church fund a portion of the expenses of the center. In any scenario, a close connection with a local church that provides funding can dramatically decrease the strain on a counseling ministry and will dramatically increase the likelihood that people will seek help even when they cannot afford it.

Biblical Counseling and the Church

The people in the church, whether leaders or members, demonstrate that the church is indispensable in the ministry of counseling. All of the truth we have talked about in this book was counseled, implemented, and located in the context of the local church. In Randy's case, there is no other place he could have gone to receive the level of community, the kind of counseling instruction, and the amount of loving fellowship he received in our church. These are powerful resources that nobody else in the world has. These are powerful resources that God used to change Randy's life. He will use the same resources to change those he sends to you.[2]

---

2. For more resources, see Dietrich Bonhoeffer, *Life Together: The Classic Exploration of Christian Community* (New York: HarperOne, 2009); Mark Dever, *Nine Marks of a Healthy Church* (Wheaton, IL: Crossway, 2013); Colin Marshall and Tony Payne, *The Trellis and the Vine: The Ministry Mind-Shift That Changes Everything* (Kingsford, Australia: Matthias, 2009); T. L. Dagg, *Manual of Church Order*, original edition "A Treatise on Church Order" in *Manual of Theology*, 1858, Southern Baptist Publication Society (na: Gano, 1990).

CHAPTER 12

BIBLICAL COUNSELING

and the

GOAL OF THEOLOGY

The task of this book has been to summarize certain key doctrines and show their relevance to counseling ministry. I have tried to show that the foundation for counseling ministry is expressly theological. This theological foundation for counseling exists whether individual practitioners know it exists and whether their theological foundation is right or wrong, helpful or unhelpful. I have tried to show that there is an inseparable connection between theology and counseling by demonstrating how particular doctrines uphold the counseling task. If the inherent relationship between theology and counseling exists in the way I have argued, then talking about theology as the foundation of counseling is only one way to describe this relationship. There is another way to explain this relationship. As I conclude this book, I want to explain this relationship with a story about my son Carson.

Carson is our oldest son, and as I write these words, he is about to turn ten years old. My wife, Lauren, and I first learned that we were pregnant in January 2005, about a year and a half after we got married. We were ecstatic. We both stared at the pregnancy test, literally screaming with joy, hugging and kissing one another, and crying because we were so happy. We began gleaning as much information as we could about this precious life growing in my wife's body. We made doctor appointments, asked friends for advice, and read a lot of books—books about parenting, about what to eat when you're pregnant, and not a few books on baby names. One ritual we engaged in every week involved a book full of stunning pictures that provided a week-by-week explanation of the details of child development before birth. This book became our pregnancy prayer guide. Every week we would pull this book off the bookcase by our bed and read about how "our little peanut" was developing that week, and every week we would pray for the details of that development. I have great memories from those days as Lauren and I huddled over that book in our little apartment. I held on to my wife and we prayed for our son's liver, for his vertebrae, his brain, and for every other part we read about.

As the pregnancy progressed, we got much more personal knowledge of this developing person. We heard his heartbeat, saw his form on a 3D ultrasound (we could not see his face because he always covered it with both hands, the shy little guy), we discovered he was a boy, we started calling him Carson, and we ultimately felt him kicking in Lauren's tummy. We were thrilled to be getting all of this information and to be growing in our understanding of all God was doing to knit together a life in his mother's body. But we also were discontented with this information. It was not enough to stare at pictures in a book or even to stare at *his* picture on our fridge. We wanted more.

The very process of pregnancy requires you to recognize that every new and exciting discovery points to the longing of all loving parents to see their baby in person. Lauren and I craved an unmediated look at our child. We wanted to hold him in our arms, feel his skin against ours, kiss him, and rock him to sleep. Every piece of knowledge we gleaned about prenatal development in general, and about Carson in particular, only stoked our anticipation to experience life with this precious boy.

Then one day Lauren went to the hospital. In just a matter of hours, I was standing agape as this remarkable life rushed into my life. I watched and cried as the doctor helped remove him from my wife's body. Before

I cut the umbilical cord, I reached over and touched his face and chest. I bent over and kissed him on the lips, nose, and forehead (I always joke with my kids that I started kissing them when they were still blue and gooey!). A nurse laid him on my wife's chest, and we had our first of many family snuggles. A few days later we brought him home, I laid him on my chest, and as I felt him breathing and smelled his hair, we both fell asleep. All of that knowledge, prayer, and anticipation had finally reached its culmination in our experience of life together with this little boy. I was thrilled as I realized the fulfillment of all our anticipation. It would be wrong to have lived content with knowledge about my son but desiring no experience of him. My growing knowledge of my unborn son created an insatiable desire to see that knowledge culminate in actually holding that boy in my arms and sharing my life with him.

In the same way, it should never be enough for Christians to merely know theology. The pursuit of theological knowledge is precious and enjoyable. Some of the most fulfilling moments of my life have been the fruitful reading of a helpful book or hours bent over my Bible trying to think through some puzzling text. But our knowledge of the truth of theology does not terminate with the knowledge itself. The culmination of our study of theology is superior to the mere knowledge of the information. I want to close this book by asking, What serves as the culmination of our theological knowledge? I offer two answers.

First, in our pursuit of God through the study of theology, the central reality we are striving to behold is God himself. We do not study theology for the sole purpose of possessing theological knowledge. We study theology to know Christ. And we pursue a relationship with Christ now so that we can experience that relationship in its undiluted fullness in the new heavens and new earth.

This is the point that Paul makes in Philippians 3. Paul had massive amounts of theological knowledge about Christ. His goal was not merely to know information but to know *Christ*. "*I count everything as loss because of the surpassing worth of knowing Christ Jesus my Lord*" (Phil. 3:8, emphasis added). The goal of Paul's life was to use everything, including his powers of knowledge, to have a measure of knowledge of Christ in this life and to experience the fullness of relationship with him in eternity: *"That I may know him and the power of his resurrection, and may share his sufferings, becoming like him in his death, that by any means possible I may attain the resurrection from the dead"* (Phil. 3:10–11, emphasis added; cf. 3:13–14).

For Paul, the goal of theological knowledge was knowing Jesus Christ. That should be our goal as well. We should take our efforts at understanding the truth of Christian doctrine and do more than commit such matters to memory. We should use them to propel our striving to know Jesus Christ himself. We should strive to know him as much as possible in this life and then know him fully in the next when we see him face-to-face. I spent more than a decade of my life earning three degrees in theology and have taught at a theological seminary for nearly that long. I have seen and even fought against the temptation to have the pursuit of theology be merely about our own storehouse of information. These are deadly temptations that fuel pride rather than worship (1 Cor. 8:1). Theological knowledge finds its ultimate culmination in our knowing Christ.

But there is another goal of theological knowledge. This goal is ministry. God desires that we take the things we know of him and pour that knowledge into others for their benefit. This is what we see Paul doing in Philippians 3, even as he articulates his ultimate goal of knowing Christ. Paul's work in the letter to the Philippians is a labor of ministry.

It took a massive amount of theological knowledge for Paul to compose this letter. In Philippians 3 alone, Paul makes statements that require knowledge about justification, the doctrine of God, the doctrine of Christ, a theology of sin and suffering, the doctrine of perseverance, and many others. Paul takes all of that theological information and uses it in ministry to point people to the beauty of Christ and the delight of spending eternity with him (Phil. 3:20–21). Paul took all of the truth he gleaned from theology, and his own desire to know Christ fully, and used it in ministry to point others to Christ.

This is what we do in counseling. We take what we know from the truths of theology, and we apply it to people who are suffering under the weight of all the kinds of pain this world has to offer. We apply biblical truth to struggling people for the purpose of building their hope and increasing their joy in truly knowing Christ in this life and ultimately in the life to come.

The relationship between counseling and theology is not merely that theology serves as the foundation of counseling. When we think as Paul does, one of the most significant aspirations of theology is counseling. It is not the goal of Christian thinkers merely to know theology. It is our goal to know Christ. And as we live this life, waiting to see him face-to-face, one of our goals is to take what we know and help others make the journey to also know him. The goal of this book is not merely that counselors care about theology, but that theologians care about counseling.

And so this book ends where it began—with theology. We counsel with the words we do because of theological commitments. We counsel in the setting that we do because of theological commitments. What you choose to counsel and where you choose to counsel are immanently theological. The only issue is whether your theology is faithful or faithless. As Christians, when we understand the rich theology of the Christian faith, we are driven to offer uniquely biblical counsel to hurting and struggling people. This is a theology for the church that honors Jesus and is grounded in the Word.

Statement from the Association of Certified Biblical Counselors Regarding Mental Disorders, Medicine, and Counseling

In 2014 the Association of Certified Biblical Counselors approved a formal statement expressing theological convictions about the problem of mental illness. I was on the committee that drafted this statement with the help of counseling professionals, medical doctors, and legal experts. I include it here as a helpful summary of how Christians should think about pressing cultural and counseling issues in a way marked by theological faithfulness.

I. Mental Disorders and Biblical Counseling

We live in a broken world full of people suffering with profound trouble and intense pain. One manifestation of that brokenness is the problem that our culture recognizes as mental disorder. Increasing numbers of people are diagnosed with these complex difficulties, which require wisdom and multifaceted care. We confess that, too often, the church of Jesus Christ has not been recognized as a source for profound hope and meaningful help for such difficult problems. We further acknowledge that many Christians have contributed to a negative stigma attached to such diagnoses through simplistic understandings of these problems, and have offered solutions grounded in ignorance.

As an organization committed to pursuing excellence in biblical counseling, the Association of Certified Biblical Counselors has, for decades, been calling upon faithful Christians to grow in the twin tasks of understanding complex problems and learning skills to address them in the context of counseling. As an organization committed to the sufficiency of Scripture for counseling, we believe that the Bible provides profound wisdom to guide us in caring for people diagnosed with mental disorders.

One example of this wisdom is the biblical teaching on dichotomy. The Bible is clear that God created human beings to consist of both a body and soul. To be a human being is to exist in these two constituent parts, which are separable only at death. Even after death, Christians confess that the bodies and souls of human beings will be restored at the Last Day. This biblical truth points to the high honor and regard that God gives to both the physical and spiritual realities of humanity (Gen. 2:7; Matt. 10:28; 1 Cor. 7:34; 2 Cor. 5:1; 1 Tim. 4:8ff).

A theological reality like this one requires Christians to honor both body and soul as crucial to human existence. Christians, therefore, should respect medical interventions as a fully legitimate form of care for those struggling in this fallen world. Examinations by medical professionals are crucial adjuncts to a biblical counseling ministry as they discover and treat, or rule out, physical problems that lead many to seek counseling help.

Another example of this biblical wisdom is the teaching in Scripture on the dynamic nature of problems that we experience in a fallen world. Human beings have difficulties, which always carry physical and spiritual implications. Both aspects need to be addressed in an appropriate fashion. Human beings experience problems with spiritual implications for which they are morally culpable and must repent. Human beings experience other physical and spiritual problems that are not a consequence of their sins, are not their fault, but which are painful realities that attend life in a fallen world (Matt. 5:8; 26:38; 2 Cor. 7:9–11; 1 Thess. 5:14).

This theological reality requires Christians to approach problems in a complex way, rather than a simplistic one. Christians understand that some spiritual realities will require a rebuke, but others will require encouragement in the midst of pain. Still others will require help in the midst of weakness.

II. Mental Disorders in Contemporary Culture

Christians today live in a secular and therapeutic culture, which lacks the sophistication of the Scriptures in understanding these matters. This culture attributes physical causation to many problems, ignoring their spiritual roots and implications. This practice is confusing and unhelpful since the Bible teaches that not all serious problems are medical problems. The Bible's teaching on humanity leads us to conclude that many problems are physical in nature, many others are spiritual in nature, and each of these affects the other. God's revelation in the Scriptures about the complexity of humanity forbids the secular reductionism that makes all problems merely physical.

The contemporary language of mental illness is one example of this reductionism. The compendium for mental illnesses that our culture recognizes as authoritative is *The Diagnostic and Statistical Manual for Mental Disorders* (DSM). This manual makes many accurate observations about the manifold problems that afflict people. For biblical counselors, the DSM paints an inadequate and misleading picture. It fails to express, recognize, or understand the spiritual aspect of problems that afflict people. Because of that failing it cannot offer clear help and hope for people diagnosed with its labels. While some of the disorders listed in DSM are medical in nature, many others are not. Even when the problems in DSM have a physical component, the spiritual and Godward elements of humanity are not addressed by the DSM, which biblical counseling must take into account. Christians must be committed to a way of understanding and speaking about complex problems that is more likely to lead to real and lasting change than that recorded in the various editions of DSM.

III. Counseling Practice

In light of these realities, ACBC endorses the following standards of belief and practice for its certified counselors and counseling centers that would care for people diagnosed with the complicated problems identified as mental disorders.

1. Biblical counselors must acknowledge that human beings struggle with physical and spiritual problems.

2. Biblical counselors shall encourage the use of physical examinations and testing by physicians for diagnosis of medical problems, the treatment of these problems, and the relief of symptoms, which might cause, contribute to, or complicate counseling issues.

3. Biblical counselors shall help their counselees respond biblically to physical problems, but deny that spiritual interventions are the only proper response to problems with a medical element. They reject any teaching that excludes the importance of the body and the goodness of God, which leads to the blessing of medical care.

4. Biblical counselors reject the notion that medical interventions solve spiritual problems. They embrace the use of medicine for cure and symptom relief but deny that medical care is sufficient for spiritual problems, which require Christ and his gospel for ultimate relief and lasting change.

5. Biblical counselors shall be committed to counseling those with medical problems, but should not attempt to practice medicine without the formal qualifications and licensing to do so. When they have questions or concerns of a medical nature, they should refer their counselee to a competent medical professional for diagnosis and treatment.

6. Biblical counselors shall nurture a spirit of humility, understanding that many issues at the nexus of body and soul defy simplicity. They recognize that many problems are combinations of physical and spiritual issues. Others are problems which are not easily identified as one, the other, or both.

7. Biblical counselors do not reject the true observations found in *The Diagnostic and Statistical Manual of Mental Disorders*, but do reject that DSM is an authoritative guide for understanding the cause and treatment of complex problems of human behavior, thinking, and emotions. They affirm that God's Word in Scripture serves as this authoritative guide. Biblical counselors move toward using biblical language to refer to the counseling problems that people face. They are committed to applying the Bible to an understanding of the causes of and treatments for these problems.

8. Biblical counselors are committed to biblical discernment in understanding the nature of spiritual issues and to dealing with sin through gentle, Christ-centered correction.

9. Biblical counselors are committed to biblical discernment in understanding the nature of spiritual issues and to dealing with suffering through Christ-centered encouragement.

10. Biblical counselors are committed to biblical discernment in understanding the nature of spiritual issues and to dealing with weakness through loving care in the context of the body of Christ.

Biblical Counseling, General Revelation, and Common Grace

Theological confusion has sometimes been present in the history of the debates between biblical and Christian counselors about the difference between common grace and general revelation. Integrationists, in particular, have demonstrated some level of theological confusion concerning the nature of general revelation. One example of this confusion is articulated by Larry Crabb:

> All truth is certainly God's truth. The doctrine of general revelation provided warrant for going beyond the propositional revelation of Scripture into the secular world of scientific study expecting to find true and usable concepts.[1]

Crabb grounds the examination of science and the expectation of finding true and usable concepts for counseling in the doctrine of general revelation. But Crabb's statement demonstrates a misunderstanding of what general revelation is.

In Christian theology, general revelation is the reality that God shows himself to the world in the things he has made so that the world

---

1. Larry Crabb, *Effective Biblical Counseling: A Model for Helping Caring Christians Become Capable Counselors* (Grand Rapids, MI: Zondervan, 1977), 36. See also John D. Carter and Bruce Narramore, *The Integration of Psychology and Theology: An Introduction* (Grand Rapids, MI: Zondervan, 1979); Gary R. Collins, *The Rebuilding of Psychology: An Integration of Psychology and Christianity* (Carol Stream, IL: Tyndale, 1977).

is without excuse in their rejection of him. General revelation, therefore, condemns mankind by an obvious declaration of the existence and goodness of God, which they reject in their sin. The Bible teaches this in Romans 1:18–20:

> For the wrath of God is revealed from heaven against all ungodliness and unrighteousness of men, who by their unrighteousness suppress the truth. For what can be known about God is plain to them, because God has shown it to them. For his invisible attributes, namely, his eternal power and divine nature, have been clearly perceived, ever since the creation of the world, in the things that have been made. So they are without excuse.

Paul tells us several things about general revelation here. First, he makes clear that general revelation is *revealed*. It *is* revelation. It is not something that people discover. It is something that "God has shown," and if God does not show it to us, we will never know it.

Second, general revelation is about God. The object of general revelation is God himself. What makes this kind of revelation general is not the kind of information it conveys. (It is not, as Crabb indicates, concerned with the world of scientific study *per se*.) What makes this kind of revelation general is the audience, namely, every person who has ever lived. The subject matter of general revelation is the character of God, "his eternal power and divine nature." General revelation is not general truth in the world. It is specific truth about God to a general human audience.

Third, the truth about God conveyed in general revelation is suppressed by unbelievers. Romans 1 is clear: God has made his existence and character known to the world in the things he has made, but people reject that revelation. In our sin, we simply cannot admit the truth that all that exists points to God who made it. We cannot admit it because such an admission would reveal our accountability to God. Because sinful people cannot bear to confront their own guilt, they suppress the truth of God revealed in general revelation.

Finally, general revelation leads to condemnation. God has plainly disclosed himself to people in the world, but sinful people reject that revelation, and so God reveals his wrath against them. In the immediate term, God demonstrates his wrath by giving people up to more and more sin (Rom. 1:24–32). In the long term, people are judged forever in hell for their rejection (Rom. 2:5). General revelation renders God righteous in the condemnation of the wicked who reject him.

General revelation is not what your cardiologist knows about how to do heart surgery, it is not what your electrician knows about how to fix the lights in your house, and it is not what dog breeders know about how to run a kennel. More relevant for our discussion is that general revelation is not what a psychologist knows about human functionality.

God reveals his existence and his glory in the beating of a human heart, in the wonder and joy of animals, and in all the ways that human beings function. Unbelievers are likely to know a great deal about these things, often knowing far more than Christians. The ability of people to know these things is not due to the theological reality of general revelation, but rather to the doctrine of common grace. The doctrine of common grace allows unbelievers to know true things about the world even as they reject the God who creates those truths and reveals himself in them.

It is not an abstract theological point of order to insist that we place the findings of psychology under the category of common grace rather than general revelation. General revelation is an authoritative display of the character of God in the things that have been made. It is binding on all people. Its authority is not held in check by another reality. If we were to place the findings of psychology under the doctrine of general revelation, we would imbue it with a sense of authority that it does not deserve.[2] We must be clear that secular psychologists can know accurate information because of God's common grace, but we also insist that their thinking can be corrupted because of the noetic effects of sin.

---

2. Douglas Bookman, "The Scriptures and Biblical Counseling" in John F. MacArthur Jr. and Wayne A. Mack, *Introduction to Biblical Counseling: A Basic Guide to the Principles and Practice of Counseling* (Nashville: Thomas Nelson, 1994), 63–97.

Both of these assertions allow us to approach secular psychology with biblical realism. We can expect that psychologists will make many accurate and fascinating observations. We also expect them to have error in their thinking and to be confused about the ultimate nature of many of the realities they most want to understand.

The Standards of Doctrine of the Association of Certified Biblical Counselors

The Preamble. We are an association of Christians who have been called together by God to help the Church of Jesus Christ excel in the ministry of biblical counseling. We do this with the firm resolve that counseling is fundamentally a theological task. The work of understanding the problems which require counseling and of helping people with those problems is theological work requiring theological faithfulness in order to accomplish that effectiveness which honors the triune God. Because theological faithfulness is a necessity in counseling, it is required of this association to articulate our convictions in this regard. We lay down this summary of Christian doctrine, which we believe represents the biblical standards of doctrine that biblical counselors must embrace to do their work faithfully.

I. The Doctrine of Scripture. The sixty-six books of the Bible in the Old and New Testaments constitute the completed and inscripturated Word of God. God the Holy Spirit carried along the human authors of Scripture so that they wrote the exact words that he desired them to write. The words in Scripture penned by human authors are thus the very words of God himself. As inspired by God the Bible is completely free from error, and serves as the inerrant, infallible, and final rule for life and faith. The Bible speaks with complete authority about every matter it addresses. The words of Scripture concern issues of life and faith before God, and because counseling issues are matters of life and faith, the Bible is a sufficient resource to define and direct all counseling ministry.

Acts 1:16; 2 Timothy 3:1–17; 2 Peter 1:3–21; 2 Peter 3:15–16

II. The Doctrine of God. God is eternal and infinite in all of his perfections. This one God exists eternally in three distinct, fully divine persons: Father, Son, and Holy Spirit. God is creator of all that exists. He made the heavens and the earth out of nothing. He exerts comprehensive sovereignty over all of his creation. He possesses exhaustive and perfect knowledge of all events: past, present, and future. He is present everywhere at all times. He is infinitely good with no shadow of sin in any part of his being.

Genesis 1–3; Psalm 139:1–16; Isaiah 46:8–11; Acts 5:1–4; Romans 9:5; Ephesians 1:11

III. The Doctrine of Jesus Christ. Jesus Christ is the eternal Son of God, the second member of the Trinity. He exists as one person with two distinct natures, fully divine and fully human, without any mixture of the two. He was born of a virgin. He lived his entire life on earth without transgressing the law of God, thus earning righteousness for his people. He suffered a violent death on the cross to pay for the sins of his people. He rose miraculously from the grave on the third day as Lord and Savior, demonstrating his victory over sin, death, and the Devil. He ascended bodily into heaven, where he reigns over all creation and actively upholds and intercedes for his people, as his bride, the church, awaits his glorious return.

Matthew 1:18–25; John 17:6; 1 Corinthians 15:1–8; Ephesians 1:21–23; 1 Thessalonians 4:13–18; Titus 2:11–15; Hebrews 4:14–15; 7:25

IV. The Doctrine of the Holy Spirit. The Holy Spirit is the eternal third member of the Trinity. He is the person who convicts of sin and who indwells Christians. He regenerates believers and empowers them to live the Christian life, to understand the Scriptures, and to worship Jesus Christ. He is thus essential to the change sought in biblical counseling. He is the sovereign God who equips believers with gifts of service to do ministry in the church. He is the promised Counselor who continues the work of the Wonderful Counselor, Jesus Christ.

John 16:4–15; Romans 8:9–11; 1 Corinthians 12:12–30; Ephesians 1:13–18

V. The Doctrine of Divine Grace. Salvation is thoroughly a work of divine grace from beginning to end. Before the foundation of the world, the Father elected to save a people who would compose the church. Jesus Christ purchased the salvation of those individuals through his life, death, and resurrection. The Holy Spirit applies the work of Christ to all who believe, creating the gift of faith in their hearts, and he keeps them in that faith forever.

Romans 3:21–23; Ephesians 1:3–14; 2:1–10; Philippians 1:6

VI. The Doctrine of Man. God created man out of the dust and breathed life into him so that he became a living person. Human beings are made in the image of God and were created by him to be the pinnacle of creation. God made mankind in two complementary genders of male and female who are equal in dignity and worth. Men are called to roles of spiritual leadership particularly in the home and in the church. Women are called to respond to and affirm godly servant leadership particularly in the church and home. God created the human person with a physical body and an immaterial soul, each possessing equal honor and essential to humanity. The Bible depicts the soul as that which motivates the physical body to action. These constituent aspects are separable only at death. The great hope of Christians is the restoration of body and soul in a glorified existence in the new heavens and new earth. Man is by design a dependent creature standing in need of divine counsel to serve God and to be conformed into the image of Christ.

Genesis 1:26–27; 2:7; Proverbs 4:23; Romans 8:29; 1 Timothy 2:8–15; Ephesians 5:22–33; 2 Corinthians 4:16–5:10

VII. The Doctrine of Sin. God created mankind in a state of sinless perfection, but the human race fell from this state when Adam willfully chose to rebel against God and ate of the tree of the knowledge of good and evil. Since that time every human being, except Jesus Christ, has been born in sin and separated from God. Every element of human nature is inherently corrupted by sin so that mankind stands in desperate need of the grace of God to be cleansed from sin by the Holy Spirit through repentance and faith in Jesus Christ. Sin increases the need for all counseling as people seek ministry to resolve problems in living caused by their own sin, the sin of others, and the consequences of sin in the world.

Genesis 3:1–7; Psalm 51:5; Romans 3:1–21; 5:12–21

VIII. The Doctrine of the Church. The church is the bride of Christ called to proclaim the Word of God, administer baptism and the Lord's Supper, and exercise church discipline. The church is the organism through which God accomplishes his mission in the world. It is the main agent for all ministry of the Word, including the ministry of counseling and discipleship.

Matthew 16:18–20; 18:15–20; Romans 15:14; 1 Peter 2:1–12; Revelation 19:6–10

IX. The Doctrine of Regeneration. Regeneration is the sovereign work of the Holy Spirit where he transforms the hardened heart of a sinner into the soft heart of a believer who loves God and obeys his Word. It is what makes the new life in Christ possible. Regeneration, along with the God-given gifts of repentance and faith, is granted solely by grace, resulting in all the attendant evidences of our great salvation in Christ.

Ezekiel 36:25–27; Acts 20:21; John 3:1–9; Titus 3:4–6; James 1:18

X. The Doctrine of Justification. Justification is the sovereign declaration of God that the righteousness of Jesus Christ has been imputed to those who have trusted in his sinless obedience and his substitutionary atonement on the cross for their salvation. When God justifies a person, he no longer treats him as a sinner but reckons him to possess that righteousness which Jesus Christ earned on his behalf. The declaration of justification does not come through any past, present, or future merit in the sinner. Justification is based exclusively on the merits of Jesus Christ and is received through faith alone.

Luke 18:9–14; Romans 4:1–12; Philippians 3:1–11

XI. The Doctrine of Sanctification. Sanctification is a joint work between God and man, where God supplies grace for Christians to grow in obedience to Christ. While Christians are made holy in a definitive sense at conversion, it still remains for them to grow in holiness. This work of grace requires believers to utilize, by faith, the normal means of grace such as Bible reading, prayer, thought renewal, and fellowship in the context of the local church. Christians will experience real progress in growing more like Christ, yet this work will be incomplete in this life. The work of counseling is fundamentally the work of helping Christians to grow in this grace of sanctification.

Acts 26:17–18; Romans 6:1–14; 2 Corinthians 3:18; Philippians 2:12–13; Colossians 3:1–17

XII. The Doctrine of Revelation. God discloses himself to humanity in two ways. Special revelation is God's disclosure of himself to his people in the pages of Scripture. General revelation is God's disclosure of himself to the entirety of humanity in the things that have been made. General revelation and special revelation each come from God and so are of equivalent authority, though they differ in content. Special revelation discloses detailed information about the character of God and how to live all of life in a way that honors him. General revelation is a disclosure of the beauty and power of God, which leads to judgment. The subject matter of general revelation is the character of God and not mere facts about the created order. General revelation requires special revelation to be properly understood and applied.

Psalm 19:1–6; Romans 1:18–23

XIII. The Doctrine of Common Grace. God extends his goodness to all people by making provision for their physical needs and granting them intellectual gifts. This goodness, also known as common grace, is what grants unbelievers the ability to apprehend facts in science, for example, and is why believers can affirm the true information that unbelievers come to understand. The chief manifestation of God's grace is his salvation of sinners by the blood of Jesus Christ to all who believe. Common grace cannot overcome the corrosive effects of sin upon human thinking without this special, saving grace of Jesus. This reality guarantees that, though unbelievers can know many facts, they will misunderstand information that is most central to human life, which includes information about God, the human problem, and its solution in Christ. Because the central elements of counseling include God, the nature of the human problem, and God's solution in Christ, the counseling methods of secular people are ultimately at odds with a uniquely biblical approach to counseling.

Matthew 5:44–45; John 1:9; Romans 1:18–23; Colossians 1:21

XIV. The Doctrine of the Great Commission. The church has been called to go into the world with the task of evangelism and discipleship. In giving this commission, Jesus requires his people to use their conversations to point people to Christ in evangelism, and to build people up in Christ in discipleship. The Great Commission necessitates that all faithful counseling conversations must have Jesus Christ as their ultimate goal. Our Lord and Savior does not give believers the option to avoid counseling conversations, or to avoid directing those conversations toward Jesus. The commitment of Christians to the Great Commission and to faithful biblical counseling is therefore one and the same.

Matthew 28:16–20; Romans 10:1–17; 2 Corinthians 5:11–21; Colossians 1:24–29

XV. The Doctrine of Last Things. Jesus Christ will return for his church at a moment known only to God. At Jesus' coming, he will sit in judgment on the entirety of the human race. At the conclusion of this judgment, he will usher all humanity into the eternal state. All those who have spent their lives persisting in unbelief will go away into everlasting torment. The righteous in Christ will go away into everlasting joy in the presence of Jesus Christ. Christians can therefore have hope that all wrongs will be punished, that all righteous acts will be rewarded, and that God's people will ultimately abide with him forever. The hope of the new creation is the foundation of all counseling.

Matthew 25:31–46; Romans 2:6–11; 1 Thessalonians 4:13–18; Revelation 21

SCRIPTURE INDEX

Finally Free

Fighting for Purity with the Power of Grace

Heath Lambert

If you have struggled personally against the powerful draw of pornography, or if you have ever tried to help someone fighting this battle, you know how hard it is to break free. But real freedom isn't found by trying harder to change. Nor is it found in a particular method or program. Only Jesus Christ has the power to free people from the enslaving power of pornography.

In *Finally Free*, Dr. Heath Lambert, a leader in the biblical counseling movement, lays out eight gospel-centered strategies for overcoming the deceitful lure of pornography. Each chapter clearly demonstrates how the gospel applies to this particular battle and how Jesus can move readers from a life of struggle to a life of purity.

> *"This book is richly biblical, soundly Christian, and centered in the gospel. Christians should read it and quickly pass it to others. It will be of enormous help to pastors, youth ministers, college ministers, and the Christians of all ages struggling against the tide of our pornographic age."*
> —R. Albert Mohler Jr., president Southern Baptist Theological Seminary

Available in stores and online!

ZONDERVAN®
.com

Theology of Biblical Counseling Video Lectures

The Doctrinal Foundations of Counseling Ministry

Heath Lambert

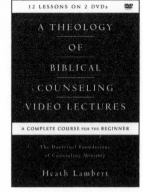

For over four decades, biblical theology has been at the core of the biblical counseling movement. Leaders in biblical counseling have emphasized a commitment to teaching doctrine in their counseling courses out of the conviction that good theology leads to good counseling and bad theology leads to bad counseling.

In *A Theology of Biblical Counseling Video Lectures* Heath Lambert unpacks the core convictions that underlie sound counseling and gives practical wisdom for our counseling practices today. Together with the accompanying book, *A Theology of Biblical Counseling*, these lectures show how biblical counseling is rooted in the Scriptures while illustrating the real challenges counselors face today.

A Theology of Biblical Counseling Video Lectures is accessible for working biblical counselors and for counselors-in-training at colleges and seminaries. In each lesson, doctrine comes to life in real ministry to real people, dramatically demonstrating how theology intersects with the lives of actual counselees.

Available in stores and online!